VENETIAN VILLAS
THE HISTORY AND CULTURE

First published in the United States of America in 1986 by
RIZZOLI INTERNATIONAL PUBLICATIONS, INC.
597 Fifth Avenue, New York, NY 10017

© 1986 - MAGNUS EDIZIONI SpA, Udine, Italy

Library of Congress Cataloging-in-Publication Data

Muraro, Michelangelo.
    Venetian villas.

    Includes index.
    1. Architecture, Domestic–Italy–Venice.
2. Venice (Italy)–Buildings, structures, etc.
I. Marton, Paolo. II. Title.
NA7594.M86 1986 728.8'4'094531 86-42731

ISBN 0-8478-0762-2

English language translation by Peter Lauritzen,
John Harper and Stephen Sartarelli

Designed by Arsenio Scalambrin

Printed and bound in Italy

VENETIAN VILLAS
THE HISTORY AND CULTURE

Text by
MICHELANGELO MURARO

Photographs by
PAOLO MARTON

RIZZOLI
NEW YORK

James S. Ackerman: Introduction

The richness and depth of the research conducted by Michelangelo Muraro on *Venetian Villas* is the fruit of a career devoted entirely to the study of all aspects of Venetian art, to university instruction and to the conservation of monuments, paintings and sculpture, in the roles of director of Department of Monuments of Venice and Venetia and museum director of the Museo della Ca' d'Oro in Venice.

His kind invitation to write these words of introduction gives me an opportunity to extend thanks to him on behalf of scholarly colleagues of all nationalities, for having so generously shared with us his knowledge of Venetian art and culture and the pleasure of his conversation.

In the present volume, embellished with the spectacular photographs of Paolo Marton, Mr. Muraro gives an indication of the studious efforts through which he has, over the last twenty years, helped us come to know what he calls the "Culture of the Venetian Villas."

He was in fact the first to take up this subject, which previously had barely attracted the attention of such scholars as Wittkower, Pane and Zorzi, who limited their studies exclusively to the work of Palladio. Not until the early 1950s was a broader interest awakened, when, with a number of exhibitons devoted to Venetian Villas, Michelangelo Muraro, along with Renato Cevese and Giuseppe Mazzotti, emerged as the central figures of this revival. And it was precisely to Michelangelo Muraro that fell the task of exporting these exhibitions to France and America.

The idea of the "Culture of the Venetian Villas" met with great success; this was due in part to a profound shift of interest in the field of art history. From its initial concentration on questions of stylistic definition – essential in the formative period of our discipline to assigning the attribution and determining the cronology of artworks – which encouraged monographic studies on individual artists, research has subsequently moved towards an interpretation of art in relation to its social, political, economic and cultural context.

The importance of Muraro's contribution toward this end is demonstrated in the text contained herein, which served as a guide to Paolo Marton in his painstaking photographic campaigns across the entire region.

"Culture" [*Civiltà*], as Muraro suggests, is a broad concept, one which embraces all aspects of human endeavor, especially the manner in which man weaves his relations with the natural environment. The art historian is, in this respect, in a position to interpret the various different aspects of the "human sciences." The value of these texts lies above all in their ability to interpret, in a unified manner, the most disparate historical forces as they interact in the formation of a culture: the social structure, the relations to the domestic and foreign political situation, the economic realities, the technologies, the road systems, the topography and use of the terrain, phylosophy, literature and painting.

At the basis of Muraro's interpretation of the Venetian villas in his indigenous familiarity with the territory. He was in fact born and raised in a country town in the Vicenza province. His experience of villas therefore appears to be deeply rooted in these places, whose characteristics he knows very well – roads, rivers, canals, and above all, the way in which the working of the water system and the gradual draining of the marshes contributed to the development of the agricultural economy as a foundation for the rise of the villas.

The term "reclamation" appears repeatedly in these pages; the conquest, through reclamation, of vast stretches of terrain originally unsuitable for cultivation, becomes a key to understanding the extraordinary promptness with which the Venetian nobility of the Renaissance turned their attentions away from maritime commerce and toward the utilization of farming estates on the mainland. This initiative constitutes the main difference between the villas of the Serene Republic and those of Florence or Rome, which were rarely conceived with the purpose of contributing to the economy and only partly served an agricultural purpose.

Muraro shows how this shift in objectives was not solely motivated by the desires of private citizens to obtain personal gain, but was above all dictated by the need for the Republic to ensure its self-sufficiency in times of war and to protect itself from famine.

This phenomenon also has its intellectual side, which was clearly formulated in the writings of Alvise Cornaro, a Paduan humanist of the early

Cinquecento. This passionate promoter of land reclamation tried to raise agriculture to the level of an art which, because of its ethical ends, would appear worthy of being practiced by the nobility itself, according to the guiding principles set forth by a writer of republican Rome, Cato.

Venice, in the meanwhile, saw its own awareness of being heir to ancient Rome grow during the formative period of the villa culture. Venetian villas drew inspiration from those built in the Roman provinces, even though medieval and Renaissance builders could not have had any direct knowledge of the ancient models.

Palladio's villas illustrate the complexity of this "culture," which combined the results of scientific research into Roman texts and monuments with elements of traditional Venetian farms and with forms derived from medieval castles.

One important contribution of Muraro's is his recognition of the import of the persistence of the feudal system in the Venetian countryside and in the orbit of the villas. It has in fact been shown that, starting in the late Middle Ages, feudal rights on the mainland were not only passed on from father to son (through customary succession), but could also be passed on to the eventual buyer of the fief. As a result, Venetian merchants could buy landed property and obtain a noble title in the bargain; the Doge, in accordance with a fourteenth-century agreement, would confirm them as vassals of the Holy Roman Empire.

This opportunity must have increased the demand for landed property on the part of members of the Venetian ruling class, who up to that point, as citizens of the Republic, had been unable to acquire noble titles through services rendered to the state. They were no doubt annoyed by the fact that representatives of the most influential families of Vicenza, Verona and other mainland cities (which had been pro-Empire until Venetian preeminence in the 15th century) possessed fiefs and ancient titles of Imperial nobility.

The question of the self-assertion of the classes comes up often in these pages. Indeed, since ancient Roman times, the ideology of the villa has taken the shape of a myth of the benefits and pleasures of country life, a myth cultivated by the urban bourgeoisie which the farmer, serf or small landowner could not allow himself to indulge in, as Goldoni repeatedly points out.

The reader, confronted with the variety of scholarly disciplines that form the basis of the arguments contained in this book, might get the mistaken impression that they are nothing more than a series of subtle academic exercises. Though they are indeed subtle, they are far from academic in nature.

The text of *Venetian Villas* is structured almost like an impressionistic tapestry around the weft of which many different threads are freely woven; one observation might be drawn from an archival document, another from the author's own imagination or sensibility.

The style is therefore quite different from what one finds in academic journals. In certain "illuminating" passages it is comparable to the sort of approach that Lévi-Strauss, in *Lapensée sauvage,* called *bricolage* – that is, a manner of constructing an argument based on traditional elements and at the same time on myth and sensorial reactions, and constituting a stimulating alternative to scientific analysis.

Comparisons aside, these studies offer a wide range of rich and varied experiences which produce in the reader a deep understanding of the significance of this "Culture" [*Civiltà*] that goes beyond the keen desire to visit, perhaps on foot, all of the places mentioned or illustrated in this book.

JAMES S. ACKERMAN
Professor of Fine Arts
Harvard University
Cambridge, MA.

Michelangelo Muraro: The Venetia of the Villas

The title chosen for this volume, "Venetian Villas, The History and Culture" indicates a desire to explore the phenomenon of the villa in all the variety and richness of its components, as a symbol of the mentality and history of an entire region.

It is not perhaps irrelevant to the conception of this work that I live and work in Venice, while having spent my childhood in the Venetian countryside. These autobiographical considerations might also have contributed to a sense of history that is a personal psychological and cultural reconquest of the past, and has helped to give meaning to the present time.

This project may be ambitious, but it corresponds to the vastness of the publishing endeavor, and takes account of the latest studies with the goal in mind of presenting and testing new modes of research.

Aware of the crisis of the traditional method of historical investigation, which centers on indisputable data and documents, we have tried to base our own research on different foundations, favoring the interpretative aspects, the "poetic reappropriation" of persons and events, and the imagination.

Alongside the ancient testimonies, the words of the writers cited almost as keys to understanding the individual chapters, the loving pages that Giovanni Comisso and Guido Piovene devoted to the landscape and people of Venetia were of equal importance to me. I am indeed convinced that, as Georges Duby has maintained, the faculty of the imagination aids one in rediscovering the context of an epoch and in reorganizing into a unified vision all the uncertain and fragmentary vestiges that the past has left behind for us.

The context of the "Culture of the Venetian villas" itself, which today represents a very precise stage in Venetian history and art, is also the fruit of an acquired awareness of the gradual emergence of a reality that was initially vague and undefined. Historical knowledge, as many maintain nowadays, first arises from feelings or curiosities of various sorts and only secondly looks to scientific support for enrichment.

This long study of villas had, in fact, as its starting point my bond of affection with my native land, the emotion and esthetic pleasure I feel for the cities populating it, and lastly, my curiosity and eagerness to understand the reasons behind certain architectural solutions and certain economic choices. In attempting to find answers to these questions by studying the hydrography, politics, economics, and nature of the society and culture of the Venetian mainland, what emerged and took shape was the concept of a villa culture spread all across the region, a key episode in any understanding of the history of Venice and of its most lively and enduring sensibilities.

This volume is first and foremost an invitation to anyone visiting or studying Venetia who might be hypnotized by the myth of Venice, by its artistic and cultural treasures and by the changeable fascination of the lagoons. It is not enough to see just Venice, isolated there on the sea, if one wants to understand the many-sided variety of its life and history. An "amphibian" city, she is enriched by her double connotation, her maritime and land identities; and while the former aspect is easily perceived, the latter remains someone obscure and hidden. One must penetrate into the mainland to unveil the secrets of a centuries-old history, to uncover the imprint of the Serene Republic, its contribution in the unification of a territory whose individual provinces nevertheless retained their distinct physiognomies.

The beauty of the Venetian countryside arouses strong emotions in the traveller, with its vast, ordered and intensely cultivated spaces, the coursing of abundant waterways and the sudden appearance, amid the verdancy, of stately architectures and elegant patrician residences. We come to understand and see Venice's greatness, her far-sighted politics and refined culture, in every corner of the fertile landscape and in the happy rolling hills. And the villas, though expressions of power and wealth, reflect the cordiality, the fanciful and extroverted nature of the Venetians, and become symbols, *boutonnieres,* episodes embodying an age-old history that saw the peoples of Venetia struggle to make the entire region fertile, beautiful and hospitable.

Thus our appreciation and gratitude, amply expressed in these pages, goes out to the forefathers and founders of the villa culture – the Venetian legislators and noble patrons, the regional inhabitants who, in the face of difficulties and sacrifices, welcomed the new mentality and established with the villas' proprietors an active relationship of trust and collaboration.

A scholar of Venetian things cannot, therefore, ignore the complex reality of the mainland that one finds documented in the villas, even though in the present day it is no longer possible to reconstruct that splendid culture in its entirety. Lost forever, for example, is the former relationship between the villas and the environment; we need only imagine how prominent they must have once looked, with their noble, durable architectures, in contrast with the precarious straw-roofed wooden structures of the nearby rural homes.

But the losses could have been much worse; for many years, indifference and ignorance caused many of the villas to fall into a state of disrepair which at a certain point seemed irremediable. If today it is possible for us to enjoy the beauty of these architectural works, to study their histories, and to understand their functions and purposes, the credit must go to the scholars and enthusiasts who, starting in the 1950s with exhibitions, catalogues and publications, have reawakened an ever-growing interest in the villas, calling for restorations and promoting new initiatives.

It is also to them that I should like to dedicate this volume: to the work of Giuseppe Mazzotti, Renato Cevese, and the honorary Supervisors of Monuments, thanks to whom Venetia has preserved its original physiognomy and the small provincial centers have regained their dignity and prestige. It is owing to them that the pride in our "little country" has been reborn, especially among the young, that the villas have begun to take on new representative functions as community symbols, town halls, cultural centers, and that research and studies of local history have blossomed. All these efforts have made it possible to recuperate past life for the present-day society and to relive our history, rediscovering the ancient bond between Venice and Venetia.

This is a phenomenon that does not seem destined to disappear and that, even today, presents new and important contributions. One need only think of the praiseworthy endeavors of the Andrea Palladio International Center of Architectural Studies of Vicenza, which each year hosts a large number of Italian and foreign scholars.

What induced me to undertake this study was indeed the inexhaustible wealth of our villas and the gradual discovery of the culture of Venetia that they unveiled to me – the history, laws, institutions and religion. It is my hope that this effort will constitute a new contribution toward ensuring that this vast patrimony will never be lost, but become instead the precious possession of everyone.

Acknowledgments

In his volume on Palladio, James S. Ackerman writes that echoes of our discussions appear in every chapter of his book. Now it is my turn to make the same statement, since on every page of this volume I make reference to opinions and judgments drawn from my reading of Jim's works. I thank him for his valuable advice and generous accessibility.

For the chapters on Carlo Goldoni and the villas of Carlo Scarpa, I should like to thank, respectively, Arnaldo Momo and Francesco Dal Co.

For research and verification I availed myself of the work of my friends Gigliola Bianchini, Maria Ida Biggi, Gian Giacomo Cappellaro, Giorgio Emanuele Ferrari, Alberto Lembo, and Domenico Luciani, who contributed in various ways to the realization of this volume.

I also benefited greatly from the constant advice and proximity, each for his area of specialization and expertise, of my collaborators and students Silvia Colla, Renzo Fontana, Benito Ghezzo, Anna Lanaro, Giuseppina Menin Muraro, Daniela Puppulin and Antonio Trevisan.

I am especially grateful to the state agencies and institutions that made our work possible: the State Archives of Venice, the Archives and Libraries of Padua, Vicenza and Treviso, the St. Mark's Library, the Regional Institute for the Villas of Venetia, the Giorgio Cini Foundation, and the Correr Civic Museum.

Paolo Marton: The Photographs

Almost three years have passed since I began my voyage among the villas of Venetia. During this long period I took thousands of photographs, travelling the roads of Venetia through all of its provinces. Now that the volume is finally ready to go to the printer, I find myself re-reading the pages of my work diary with a bit of nostalgia.

Amid all the technical notes I take pleasure in rediscovering the vivid impressions of some of the more exhausting days, or the observations I made on the best way to approach and resolve certain photographic situations.

I always asked myself, each time I set out to photograph a new villa, what angle would be the ideal one in the mind of the architect himself. In many cases, there was no answer to this question; no doubt that vantage point had once existed, but the changes brought about in the landscape over the centuries had vastly altered the environmental situation, creating obstacles and impediments to a perfect view of the subject. Moreover, the architectural work, which is conceived and situated exclusively in three-dimensional space, cannot always be represented in the entirety of its design when one chooses a single point of view to portray it.

Since the photographic image is obviously two-dimensional, the representation of spatial effects remains dependant on the skillful control of planes and perspectives; such control may be achieved by making use of the specific features of an optimal technical device such as the optical bench. I therefore concentrated on a choice of framings and lights that would bring out the best in the architecture and its relation to the landscape.

Some of the most admired Venetian villas, such as the "Rotonda," the Maser Villa or the "Rocca Pisana," are still wonderfully visible in their original environmental context, set like splendid jewels in the green of the surrounding hills, just as they were when first designed and built. I waited through all the seasons to find the ideal light for bringing out the harmony of their architecture.

In the shots of interiors, which are essential in a book of this sort, I often had to create the light in the rooms myself, patiently experimenting by arranging and rearranging my lamps in order to accentuate the spatial rhythms and to bring out the full chromatic range of the frescoes and decorations, which would have been inaccessible in natural light. Finally, I tried to interpret some of the masterworks of the greats who frescoed the rooms of the villas of Venetia, masters such as Veronese, Zelotti, Fasolo, and the two Tiepolos, father and son.

In studying the details, which I chose through a careful cutting of the whole image, I was truly moved as I rediscovered the extraordinary vitality of these pictures, whose fascination remains unchanged after so many centuries.

To realize the images in this volume I used a *Sinar F* camera with optical bench, equipped with *Schneider* and *Rodenstock* lenses, backed up by my trusty *Leica,* which I used for specific situations.

I would like to express my gratitude to all the proprietors of the villas presented in this volume for the courtesy and availability they showed me in allowing me to work freely in spaces often intended for private living. I ask all these people – descendants of ancient Venetian noble families, private citizens, foreigners enamoured of Italian art, finance companies and public institutions – to accept the images in this volume as a heartfelt homage to their kindness and hospitality. Laslty, I must also express a particular word of thanks to my dear friend Luigina Bortolatto who, with her valuable advice, helped me to overcome successfully a rather difficult moment in the planning of this work.

SUMMARY

Scamozzi's Villas and other Sixteenth-Century Villas

Eighteenth-Century Villas with Gardens and Frescoes

From Jappelli to Carlo Scarpa

THE HISTORY AND CULTURE OF THE
VENETIAN VILLAS

HISTORY

The Veneto landscape in the Roman era

Historians, in outlining the development of the Veneto villas, have emphasized the fundamental importance of Andrea Palladio. His art illuminated the sixteenth century and remained a model for succeeding centuries, imitated both within and beyond the boundaries of the Veneto and Italy. The increase in villa construction during the eighteenth century has been at the center of much historical research. The great spread of the Veneto villas and their continuity over time has been explored. We believe, however, that it is necessary to examine both the history of the Veneto villas and their prehistory: that it is useful to look into the immediate as well as the deeper reasons for their success. Only by uncovering the deeper reasons, the links that intertwine around an inexhaustible idea, can we understand why this world of the villas has been reaffirmed and consolidated over the centuries and thereby understand its peculiarities.

The essential program of the villa (distinct from the simple farm in that considerations of pleasure dominate those of utility) has remained unchanged for over two thousand years, since the time when it was defined by the patricians of ancient Rome. As Ackerman says, they were satisfying a need both "psychological and ideological" of the city dweller who conceives of the country not only as an area for possible investment, but also as a place for amusement, relaxation, rest, and study.

But, in an amphibian city like Venice, the need of man to live with nature, to own a piece of land assumes a particular value and importance. The subtle nostalgia for the terra firma, which characterizes the lagoon city through the centuries, is not without profound repercussions. Nor is it insignificant that Venice, while never forgetting her own origins, always cultivated and exalted the myth of antique Rome. Never invaded by the Barbarians, she kept the spirit alive in her laws and claimed to be Rome's heir.

Andrea Palladio wrote that "Venice alone is like a surviving example of the greatness and magnificence of the Romans." Thanks to this continuity one can understand, as Ackerman has demonstrated, how that architectonic form, derived from the primitive Mediterranean house and from Roman and Byzantine villas, found refuge amid the lagoons and contributed to the flowering of the open villa type that enjoyed such success in the Renaissance.

In antiquity, it was Rome that, profiting from its own experience and that of other Mediterranean civilizations, gave the most complex and advanced

form to the idea of the villa. In terms of architecture, this became one of the most important Roman conceptions. "If there is a class of building that one can consider the historic expression of Roman society and civilization," writes Mansuelli, "that class is the villa." The very structure of Roman civilization, based on agriculture, favored the development of the villa and the ideals connected with it. The country, through the settlement of the centurions and land reclamation, crossed by an efficient road network linking the various regions of the empire, enjoyed an organization that permitted the villas to extend themselves everywhere, not only in Latium and Campania, but in all its territories: along the African coasts (see, for example, the evidence furnished by the mosaics of Tabarca), in France, in England, and even along the Adriatic, in Istria and in Dalmatia. Because of its diffusion and its representative qualities, villa architecture as created by the Romans has exercised a greater influence on successive civilizations than the most famous classical monuments.

From the centurions to the forest and the marsh

With the fall of the Roman empire came a progressive weakening of the power of the state and a decentralization of wealth. The decentralization of authority became immediately apparent with the Barbarian invasions. Profound changes in the political order brought about a structural breakdown that led to the collapse of the agrarian systems, to the decay of the great road system and the displacement of traffic along new arteries. There were also other disastrous consequences. A continuous onslaught of famine and epidemic, following the devastating attacks, resulted in a marked population decrease. The countryside was abandoned. Provincial potentates proliferated: new kings created immense *latifondi* on the borders and governed them with a tyrannical authority unfamiliar to the Roman republic and even to the empire.

The villas of these new princes increasingly resembled luxurious and well-protected palaces: there arose great porticos where the produce of the fields was gathered; immense courtyards were overlooked by monumental loggias where the lord, surrounded by princely pomp, attended to ceremonies staged in his honor. These buildings would be the ultimate symbolically significant model for all those who in the future aimed to display, through architecture, that power which we may call feudal in substance. Villas of this type can be found in provinces far from Rome. But the example of Piazza Armerina in Sicily serves for all of them. For the complexity of its architecture, it has been compared to Hadrian's villa. As Mansuelli writes, it became famous because of the mosaic decoration which gave its interior the quality of landscape.

The landscape in this period underwent a profound change. Forest undergrowth and bush invaded the remains of the Roman urban system the road network, the aqueducts, the temples, villas, and the baths while marshes submerged lands once parceled out to the centurions. The population lived miserably on the scarce fruits of the earth and by fishing and hunting. Their dwellings were poor huts of straw thatch, mud, and wattle. Built with local materials, these constructions are the typical functional expression of an economically self-sufficient type of living.

The *casoni da valle,* still found in the Veneto lagoons today, are descendents of one of these ancient structures. They have a central empty space, the *portego,* off which open the rooms and the stable. This simple solution, dictated by practical exigencies, lends itself to infinite variations, not only in rural architecture, but also in that of the villa. This was an evolution remarked upon by early theoreticians and even by Palladio.

Stone plaque found at Pojana Maggiore. (Padua, Archeological Museum).

Towards feudal organization:
the castle

A lady and a knight meet in front of a medieval castle, which had already taken on the function of the villa; a peasant woman spins wool by her cottage; in the background, on the left side, there is a dovecote, and on the right, the pergola of the kitchen garden. (Piero De Crescenzi, De Agricoltura Vulgare, *Venice, 1495).*

The barbarian peoples who invaded the Roman Empire, upsetting the political and social system, brought with them a way of life antithetic to that of the Latin world. Even the changes in architecture demonstrate that. During the Middle Ages in the West and in Italy, the complex Roman agrarian system was replaced by the fief, which was centered around in the castle, a tool of war and an instrument of power. Closed and battlemented, the castle reflected the mentality of nordic peoples who, as nomads and warriors, fell upon a society that was based on an obsession with the power of a landed property economy and then grafted on to it their own ideals of living.

In certain ways, castles seem far removed from the villa and its spirit. The castle is, in fact, an isolated structural complex placed in a defensive position with regard to the outside world, while the villa has an extrovert nature that integrates itself with its surrounding territory, participating in the life of its neighbors where neither landlord nor peasantry fear siege or invasion.

Notwithstanding these fundamental differences, villas often display characteristics belonging to castles. Like them, many villas exist in a realm of economic self-sufficiency (often in antithesis to the city). Most important, in the villa there survive aristocratic ways of life belonging to the feudal tradition. Even in architectural forms this influence is clear. External elements like moats, walls, towers, and battlements, found in several fifteenth- and sixteenth-century villas and then again in the neo-Gothic revival of the nineteenth century (even if only reduced to a purely symbolic value) testify to a certain continuity between the feudal world of castles and that of the villa. As far as the Veneto is concerned, the intimate relationship with the court of France, that cradle of chivalry and the courtly spirit, must always be kept in mind.

The religious reorganization of the land: the abbey

A new force began to work on the ruined structure of the Roman world; along with feudalism this force exercised its benificent influence all over Europe.

Western monastacism, especially the Benedictine variety, permeated by the ideal of prayer and work, "*ora et labora*," and heir to the Roman spirit of organization, was committed to both the spiritual and the material redemption of society. Among other things, it promoted reclamation in marshy areas, rehabilitating them for agricultural use. The center of this activity was the abbey, which architecturally could be derived from that closed Roman rural complex called the "*fundus*," which perhaps even more than the castle, contributed some of the most characteristic qualities to the Veneto villa.

There were the abbeys of Nervesa and Follina in the Treviso area; in the Polesine, the abbey of Vangadizza; that of Sant'Illario near Venice; that of Praglia which, in the Padua region, extended its dominion over 5,000 fields.

The abbatial complex was organized around a series of cloisters: an upper area for the monks' recreation, a rustic cloister for country produce, and finally the botanical cloister, where the monks cultivated medicinal plants and fruit trees, thus perpetuating the taste in gardens so popular in antiquity and also conveying cultural concepts prevalent in the near East to the Veneto villa.

The work of the monastics was flanked by that of another religious organization: the military-political orders like the Templars and the Hospitalers of St. John of Jerusalem. Along the remaining traces of Roman roads, usually traversed by pilgrims and merchants, they constructed hospices and hospitals which were often situated in the same place where ancient "manors" had arisen.

Much later, Venetian nobles and magnates would erect villas on the same sites after acquiring the ownership of these vast holdings.

The importance of the religious authorities, which was not only spiritual but also political and economic, reached its apex when the count-bishops were imperially invested with the administration of vast regions.

The figure of the count-bishop – there are still some examples to be seen in the provinces bordering Austria – appears to incorporate both Latin tradition and feudal authority. But more widespread was the influence exercised in the regional structure, in the life of the individual village, and in mens' minds by the noblest and most brilliant moment in our history: the age of the city-states.

*A monk enters the crenelated walls of this abbey: the plants, flowers and birds show that there was already an interest in nature and in the garden (*Fior di Virtù *Venice, 1493).*

The revaluation of the individual in the age of the city-states

The age of the city-states affirmed other ideals, not those ideals belonging to the prince, but those belonging to an extraordinarily new character: the burgher now emancipated from feudal power. Both crafts and commerce – the prevalent urban activities – favored human social contact: they encouraged the acquisition of new techniques; they permitted the development of a political dialectic and contact with more distant lands. In the period of the "Free City-States" structures were created that would be valid in the future.

Next to the centers of religious (the cathedral) and civic power (the town hall), the rapidly developing city saw the proliferation of workshops, factories, and private houses which were usually handsome and often rich and where the desire for an increasingly comfortable life was always evident. That was clear also in the houses that the rich burghers came to build beyond the town walls: an early expression of the Mediterranean man's instinctual need to live in direct contact with nature, a need that had been institutionalized in the villas of the Romans.

Commonly, in antiquity, it was enough for the prosperous cultured man to have a vineyard in the country. In the first literary evidence of modern villa civilization, we read of a vine trellis or pergola near a fountain; a rose bush or a few fruit trees in the middle of a farm offering a sweet respite in the summer months. Here is the nucleus and heart of our villas. We will search here for that true spirit which the noblest interpreters of villa architecture will renew.

The ideology of the villa, maintaining itself substantially unaltered, developed in such a way that the repetition of phenomena can be verified without having to establish a direct derivation from one to the other.

In that sense the idealogy of Cato and Varro, that working the earth is a purification of the contaminations of the city, are found again in the Veneto, while later on luxury villas became the places of those pleasures that Pliny the Younger described in his letters. This evolution, which was obvious in the provinces of Imperial Rome, was repeated, as Ackerman noted, in the Veneto during the transition from the simple fifteenth-century house to the elegant villas of Palladio.

The first patrons and villa builders did not feel that the villa required forms different from those of the city, adjusted for a new style of living. They repeated in the country the same structures and style of house they had inhabited within the circle of the town walls, making allowances only for the numbers of family and servants, the private and public functions of the head of the household, and the prestige of the clan.

The kind of life led in the country in the fourteenth century, described by Boccaccio in his short stories, cannot be confused with that of the castles, even though the idea of the courtly manner was anything but forgotten. That same aping of aristocratic models was, in fact, the expression of the bourgeois mentality central to the city-states.

The suburban property, the vineyard and house with its pergola and fountain often appear in accounts of the richest city-states, especially where the threat of war had been overcome and there were periods of peace. Because of the precarious security in the country, war suffocated at birth every desire to reside in a villa.

During the sixteenth century, thanks to the "security" Venice guaranteed the territories placed under her domination, the spread of the villa represented the advanced stages and the vital nuclei of a new, unique civilization.

Venice, the city of merchants par excellence, conserved the bourgeois spirit typical of the era of the city-states. The exigencies of a regime that, even if aristocratic, subdivided its power, taking prosperity into account above all other considerations, continued to be evident in its political and social organization, in its customs, and in its arts. This "republican" structure is one of the explanations for the great number of Veneto villas, a trend that culminated in the eighteenth century's "Craze for Holidays," when the possession of a house for vacationing, which elsewhere was the prerogative of a restricted elite, became in Venice and in the Veneto the prize of many, a pale yet significant symbol of a Modern Era teeming with "second houses".

Even when the princes came into power in Italy, Venice retained a municipal organization which was gradually modified by the elasticity of the mercantile mentality that continued to dominate.

The Month of October, a fresco from the fifteenth century (Trento, Castello del Buonconsiglio, Torre Aquila). Around the castle, the various seasonal agricultural tasks are being carried out.

The phenomenon of "neo-feudalism" in the Veneto did not encompass only a single family, like the Medici or the Sforza, but a remarkable number of Venetians: in fact all those who had the right to take part in the Maggiore Consiglio.

The extent and especially the longevity of the phenomenon of the Veneto villas is due to these families, to their example and wealth.

Princes and the culture of the court take over

In replacing the city-states, the principalities did not suppress the most vital forces, but instead improved upon many fundamental aspects. Despite the frequent changes in the princes, the continual warfare and rebellions, it can be said that the character typical of each city and of each territory continued to thrive. Even later, the activities and the traditions that matured in the era of the city-states would always be important.

In this sense each community preserved and perfected attitudes and customs which were reflected in the character of the people and even in the arts. In each region these were rich in specific attributes and are therefore easily recognizable.

Thus we shall see that in Verona, Vicenza, Udine, and other border cities, the principalities encouraged the military arts. Padua, continuing its traditional vocation, increasingly established itself as a capital of culture and science. Treviso cultivated that gay and chivalrous spirit that made it famous. Meanwhile wealth and power tended to concentrate in the hands of a few lords who loved to surround themselves with true and proper courts, set up in splendid royal palaces where an increasingly refined style of life developed, open to the influence of the most advanced European courts.

In the Veneto, a border region as sensitive to northern influences as to those from the Orient, a feudal, courtly culture developed primarily in the areas most open to Germanic influence: at Verona, Udine, Trent, and in particular in Treviso. This capital of "The Gay and Amorous March" was a city of transit for commerce with the German lands, although at the same time bound to the refined troubadour traditions brought by exiles from Provence. The Della Scala, the Camino, and the Da Carrara families, heirs of an originally nordic feudalism, politically bound to a transalpine world, introduced fashions beloved by the feudal aristocracy throughout all Europe. These customs expressed themselves in art forms characterized by their Gothic source which, although variously interpreted, was common to all the European courts. Princely pomp expressed itself primarily in works of architecture: in houses, royal palaces, and in castles where their lordships loved to live luxuriously amidst festivities, banquets, and tournaments. They lived surrounded by artists and men of learning who, while exalting the magnificent deeds of their ancestors and ancient heroes, stimulated their ambitions, not only for warfare, but also for the kind of peace where they would be seen as munificent protagonists and the patrons of true inspiration. In this period great works of reclamation were carried out at Padua,

Pisanello. Detail from the fresco of St. George and the Princess (Verona, Church of Saint Anastasia, Giusti Chapel). Pisanello and Boiardi interpreted the Renaissance as a return to the world of knights and courtliness.

22

Mantua, Ferrara, and above all at Milan providing Venice with an example and a stimulus.

But it was the appreciation of culture in Verona, Padua, Ferrara, Mantua, and elsewhere that the Most Serene Republic used (just as she did with Byzantium) to increase her prestige.

The ideals of this courtly world would have profound echoes in the future, especially in the art of Pisanello and in the poetry of Boiardo and Ariosto, while remaining relevant throughout the sixteenth century and becoming models for the Venetian "gentleman".

The villa will be one of the places chosen to show off this aristocratic culture.

Petrarch
and pre-humanism
at Padua

The principalities appreciated the importance that culture could have as a vehicle for fame and as a guarantee of lasting influence. This was confirmed by the spreading study of the Classics, in which it was possible to understand the secret of immortal glory.

The new priest of this fame became one of the protagonists of the modern world, the humanist, and Petrarch was the prototype of this new "priesthood." All the great of the epoch fought over him, but he chose to conclude his life in the hills of the Veneto, in that atmosphere of meditation which only the country could offer him. "For me each of the year's seasons offers only throngs of people, dust, mud, clamour and rubbish. The country is always amiable and always full of attractions for nobly disposed souls." Crowned poet on the Capitoline, cherished by princes and popes, he found his ideal home at Padua. He had gone there seeking for antique books and desiring to learn Greek, the language that Latin authors held in such high regard.

He realized himself completely in Padua, the city of Titus Livy: ambassador to Venice and counselor to the Da Carrara. He commissioned the painted decoration for the new royal palace. Petrarch created around himself a culture which found a symbolic expression in the three Da Carrara medallions, the first in the modern world to be taken from Roman molds as symbols of a reborn antiquity.

On the hill of Arqua, in territory pacified by the lords of Padua, the principal artery of the ancients, once trod by Dante, and in an area that had been one of the liveliest centers of the cult of chivalry, not far from Abano and Este where Roman remains were continually brought to light and every stone spoke of a venerable antiquity, Francesco Petrarch built himself a house in the country. There, hermit and priest of humanist culture, he could meditate on the lives of illustrious men and learn ancient wisdom from them.

Near his house at Arqua, Petrarch owned a vineyard, not far from one of those wellsprings that should always be considered fundamental to every human settlement. A little further away opened the valley of Baone, which the poet nostalgically called the "New Vaucluse." Petrarch received his friend

Boccaccio at Arqua and, to the end intent on his studies, closed his life there.

Not only his poetry but his very style of life became a source of imitation. His was a new way of seeing and understanding the country, and Petrarch should be considered the true father of the *World of the Veneto Villas.*

Naturally centuries passed before the idea at the center of our research was accepted: the idea that the architecture appropriate to the villa must be different from that of any other building. But even if the forms of that architecture were still to come, it should be said that the formative spirit of the villa, resurrected from Roman models and writings, was already fully present in the mind of Francesco Petrarch.

While elsewhere, artists and men of letters still lived at princely courts intent on the hunts and the festivities held in royal palaces and castles, there would always be one leaving Padua or Verona for Rome in order to measure the columns and monuments with religious care, extracting the secrets of their beauty and then, like Petrarch, loving the "otio," the idle hours of the classics, retiring to a modest villa to dream of the ancients in blessed solitude.

Portrait of Francesco Petrarch, a minature in a capital "C" of the De Remedius Utrisque Fortunae *(Venice, Biblioteca Mariana). Francesco Petrarch was considered the model for men of culture who, like their ancestors, rediscovered the value of villa life.*

Andrea Mantegna
and classical art

An iconographic document from the Paduan artist Andrea Mantegna offers us an extremely important starting point for the history of villas in the Veneto. In the background of the fresco showing the so-called "Encounter" in Mantua's *Camera degli Sposi,* just beyond the depiction of the medieval city surrounded by walls and tall towers, between the steep precipices of a hill amid ancient ruins where once an ancient city rose, we see a white marble edifice standing: a classical villa. Through classical texts or rather through antique medallions, frescoes, and surviving bas reliefs, Mantegna understood that form of building which Andrea Palladio will know how to revive in his splendid villa architecture a century later.

Mantegna depicts a porticoed edifice with six columns organized on two floors and surmounted by a pediment. It cannot be confused, as might seem the case, with the structure of a temple, but should be understood as one of those suburban villas that Roman nobles, especially in the Imperial period, raised in the city's outskirts for ease of access in their free time, while keeping their utilitarian villas at a distance in more fertile places destined for agriculture.

Mantegna depicted villa buildings on other occasions. For example, in the Tours *Agony in the Garden* there is a rare example of a humanist villa built just outside the city walls. Along with the suburbs and convents these buildings were destroyed when the Venetian republic ordered the "Wasting" which razed any edifice that might have served to facilitate a siege of the city or might impede the city's defensive artillery fire in time of war. As recently discovered documents demonstrate, Mantegna himself obtained a concession to build a villa in the countryside outside Mantua.

Whether it be in the *Proemio* of the The Third Day in the *Decameron* or in Pietro de' Crescenzi's *Trattato* or in the detailed descriptions of the *Poliphilo,* we do have some written evidence of what the humanists thought Roman villas were like.

Based on this knowledge and on the few surviving remains of ancient monuments and on the architectural treatises then available, the new architects sought to satisfy the ambitions of their noble patrons, who had been educated like artists in the ideals of a reborn civilization.

Andrea Mantegna. Detail from the meeting between Marquis Ludovico III of Gonzaga and his son, Cardinal Francesco (Mantua, Palazzo Ducale, Camera degli Sposi). Beyond the city walls Mantegna has portrayed an idealized Roman villa that seems to anticipate the style of the Palladian villas.

The survival
of Rome in Venice

The great period of the villas in the Veneto would not have been possible had not Venice first prepared the ground on which such an extraordinary culture and art could flourish. The conquest of the terra firma, the work of reclamation, and a political coordination on the part of the Dominante offered the protagonists of this operation that degree of authority, of wealth and culture that would be interpreted symbolically in the villas erected by Palladio. Only then did the myth of Venice, which claimed to reincarnate that of ancient Rome, find its most significant expression and become disseminated throughout the provinces of the Venetian dominion. Perhaps the way in which Venice kept herself tenaciously bound to the example and the memory of Rome is not clear enough nor universally known. With her instincts entirely turned to hoarding and with her spirit of conservation, she did not limit herself to keeping alive selected laws or forms of government or to merely inheriting a sense of organization and respect for the state or only continuing the universality of the image of Rome. Rather she

made those aspects of Rome's ancient artistic evidence her own as well. It was the villa of the classical world which transmitted its forms to foreign surroundings once the more monumental complexes of ancient Rome had ceased absolutely to be contemporary or relevant. In fact, amid the lagoons, more than in any other place, it seems ancient prototypes survived in the schema of the oldest type of Venetian house.

Thus a city lacking greenery, without agriculture or the support of the countryside, an urban complex completely conceived and constructed by man on the sterile sea, become important, if not determinant, for the continuity and historical development of the villa's cultural and artistic tradition.

This continuity explains how it was that those forms of open architecture, derived from the primitive Mediterranean dwelling and from Roman and Byzantine villas, should find refuge among the lagoons and contribute to the rebirth of the type of villa that would enjoy such a success in the Renaissance.

The Fondaco dei Turchi (Venice, Grand Canal), as it was before its restoration in the nineteenth century. Also here the arcades and loggias are reminiscent of those used in the ancient world.

Venice:
city of merchants

It is typical of the mercantile mentality to extract the best from every experience: to compare, evaluate, select, and acquire. Even before the twelfth century, nothing was done in Venice except importing and hoarding everything that the

*Cesare Vecellio. The Merchant. (*Degli habiti antichi e moderni di diverse parti del mondo. *Venice, 1590). The figure of the merchant has always been fundamental in the history of Venice where profit has always accompanied the philosophy of experience, and the search for pleasure and beauty.*

merchants came across in the course of their voyages that might increase the beauty and prestige of the city's churches and houses. However, the salient aspects of Venetian art can be distinguished in the character of their choices: a great instinct for quality, a taste for refined and precious things, for beauty in the end. But it was above all the spirit of the lagoon and the island which left an impression of unmistakable peculiarities. "The spirit of the waters," wrote H. F. Brown, "free, vigorous and penetrating passed into the intimate essence of the men who lived on these waters. In the link between a people and its place, Venice manifested the nature of its own personality: a personality so infinitely various, so flexible and so free."

The responsibility invested in everyone, insofar as everyone there was the "maker of his own fate," was publicly sanctioned in an inscription that can still be read on the exterior of St. Mark's Basilica, near the Porta della Carta that opens into the Doge's Palace: "L'om po far e / die in pensar / E vega quelo che gli po inchontrar." "A man can do and speak according to his thoughts, and then see what happens to him."

The life of the merchant, with its risks and discomforts, developed individual and collective capabilities and possibilities while creating men capable of quick reactions, of prudent decisions, rich in courage and experience, and also rendering them more sensitive to the joys of life, teaching them to appreciate prosperity, decorum, and security. These are ideals that translate themselves into custom as well as into the arts, in architecture, in painting, in a style of living, and in the character of a city.

The Doge Sebastiano Ziani
and the new Venice:
open architecture is born

If there was never a substantial break between the ancient world and the modern world in Venice, that was not an accident. It was a matter of a deliberate choice and a conscious decision that occurred at an easily recognizable moment in its history, thanks to one of Venice's greatest doges: Sebastiano Ziani.

Although Venice's origins are lost in the shadows of the Middle Ages, by the time of the Doge Sebastiano Ziani (September 29, 1172 – April 13, 1178), the city had reached its height in every field. The Maggior Consiglio had been created and the guilds were reorganized. The Rialto bridge was built and the Campanile di San Marco erected.

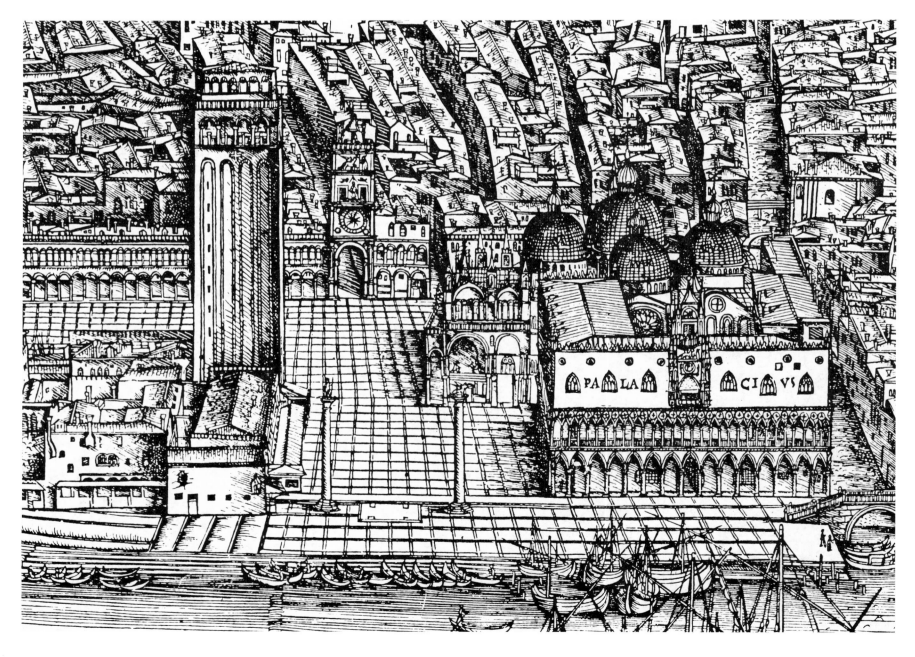

With the Doge's Palace and the squares, the whole of the city's heart was renewed so that it might answer to the republic's new needs and prestige. According to tradition, it was precisely then that Venice was given the right to celebrate its mystical Marriage of the Sea on the Ascension day. The Adriatic was recognized as the true and proper dominion of the Serenissima. The security of this possession had repercussions not only for the Venetians' political conscience. Both town planning and architecture were adjusted to these new circumstances, assuming aspects that remained substantially immutable and constant. The character of this architecture (or rather of this new style, linked to a new idea of Venice) reflected a spiritual and political situation already far removed from that of its origins.

The architecture that rose in the islands of the lagoon before then was one of towers and castles. The local toponymy reveals that (the name Torcello derived from *Turricellum;* one of Venice's districts still keeps the name Castello; the canal or rio delle Torreselle, the small towers between which a chain was hung at night to prevent the enemy from entering the Grand Canal); documents also confirm it, especially those that describe the Doge's Palace with its four-corner towers, its munitions depots, its moats and drawbridge, etc. Venetian architecture was not much different from that seen on the mainland. Buildings were almost without windows or exterior apertures: they were inaccessible and fortified against assault.

But when it was realized that the Venetians' walls and bulwarks were their ships and their fleet's valor and when it seemed impossible that an enemy could tie up at San Marco, just at that moment the open architecture of the Venetians was born: all porticos and loggias, connected courtyards, windows, and liagò.

When Sebastiano Ziani reconstructed the Ducal Palace, he did not give it the forms of an old-fashioned residence. He wished its structures to be open. He surrounded it with porticos and loggias; he opened its façades toward the lagoon and toward the city. From that point onward, Venice would be defended on the high seas, well beyond the Lido sea entrances far from its holy, inhabited places. There is no barrier between the two columns of the Piazzetta: the gateway leading into the heart of Venice is always open.

Demolishing the fortifications was equivalent to transforming the mentality of the inhabitants. It began with Sebastiano Ziani. Customs and fashions may change, but these happy prerogatives would never be surrendered any more than the psychology and security of those living in a city, unique in Europe for never have been invaded or occupied by an enemy, could ever change. The spirit and the laws of Venice were adjusted to these undeclared and perhaps unclear concepts. The arts adjusted themselves to them, too: the open forms of Venetian design; the "empty center" in paintings; the thousand windows in sumptuous palaces; the open villas of the Veneto coutryside. The Venetian experience was also transplanted to the mainland.

Therefore it is logical to think that the type of villa that interests us here – that which tends to fuse interior spaces with the surrounding environment or rooms and loggias with the landscape (virtually to synthesize man's eternal aspiration to live in contact with nature) – justifies itself best, like the Doge's Palace in Ziani's day, when there exists that particular political and social tranquillity such as, when Venice extended her peace over all the Veneto territory, spreading her ideal of justice and prosperity everywhere.

Jacopo de' Barbari. The god Mercury, the protector of merchants, a detail from the plan of the city, 1500 (Venice, Correr Museum).

Ideals of wealth and prestige in the houses and villas of the Venetians

Part of the facade of Ca' D'Oro, a magnificent example of Venetian Gothic architecture of the fifteenth century (Venice, Grand Canal). The ambitions of the Venetian families and their love of beauty were particularly manifested in the very ornate facades of their palaces.

We have seen how, in the time of the Doge Sebastiano Ziani, a new ideal of life took shape in Venice and how this was manifested in an open architecture that became emblematic of the city and the state.

At the base of the two columns, raised around 1175 by the great doge in the Piazzetta, Nicolò Baratteri sculpted in Istrian stone eight groups which portray the arts and crafts, the very foundation of Venetian society. Their form was not taken from Byzantine examples. They reveal clear links with Romanesque art in their realism and with that style which spread all over Europe from France at the time of the Crusades. Up until then Venice had turned its interests to civilizations distant in time and space. Only now did it reinforce links with neighboring areas, especially with Verona, a city from which the Venetians supplied themselves with grain and also with marble for their buildings. The cultural-political ties with Byzantium were not abandoned, but Venice now opened herself more to the Western world. Often reluctant to accept certain novelties (Giotto's later masterpieces were left in Padua in vain) Venice immediately understood that only by calling to the lagoon specialized workers in the metal and leather goods that were increasingly sought, only by welcoming the masters of silk weaving exiled from other cities, only by imitating the best craftsmen of every nation could she furnish the European markets with the best products at the lowest price.

All this happened primarily in the fifteenth century, when the city was contributing to an international artistic culture and had assumed a completely new appearance. The florid Gothic seemed most congenial to Venice because it exploited those characteristics of open architecture best suited to the city ever since the epoch of Ziani.

Beyond this, Gothic art corresponded to the need for magnificence, to the taste for decoration, to the love of festivity and ceremonies that constituted another aspect of the Venetian world.

Marble was treated like easy wood; architectonic structures acquired the transparency of crystal, embellished by color and the use of noble materials already employed by the Byzantines and Arabs. Philippe de Commynes, visiting the city in 1495, remained dazzled by the vision of so many

stupendous palaces. "They conducted me along the principal throughfare, called the Grand Canal, which is very wide and runs through the city for its entire length... I believe it to be the most beautiful street existing in the world, flanked by the most beautiful buildings. The palaces, built of beautiful stones, are very big and extremely tall. The oldest houses have their façades painted while in this century they dress them with a white stone that comes from Istria, a hundred miles across the sea. Scattered over façades are pieces of porphyry and serpentine marble. Venice is the most triumphant city I ever saw..." The palaces admired by the French ambassador are those that we still see today: the Ducal Palace, just then renovated; the Ca d'Oro; Ca Foscari and hundreds of other "houses" large and small scattered along the Grand Canal and along the most hidden Venetian canals. This is the moment when architecture excelled over all the other arts. "Among all the languages of the arts of visibility in fifteenth-century Venice," writes Coletti, "architecture is precisely that one which has the most profoundly original imprint. The architectonic language finds the representative synthesis of practical motives that condition Venetian architecture in its airiness and lightness of structure, a language that the imagination of brilliant artists often succeeds in transfiguring into a noble poetic expression destined to become the small change useful for the most humble utilitarian constructions."

Jacopo de' Barbari
and the portrait of the city

Jacopo de' Barbari. Plan of Venice, 1500 (Venice, Correr Museum). From the thousand palaces of Venice there spread a culture and civilization, of which the villas, too, are a testimony.

In the fifteenth century the city had already assumed a precise appearance. The view engraved by Jacopo de' Barbari in the year 1500 shows us, in fact, a Venice complete in all its parts, a finished and efficient organism. The centers of political and economic power are distinctly recognizable; the various squares are surrounded by the palaces of the principal families and, around these, there are the houses of the "clients." Various activities can be identified, such as those exercised by the guilds in the boatyards, in the arsenal, or even in the warehouses. Various architectural styles are just as recognizable, as is the prevalence of Gothic art.

How precious would a similar map that, executed with the same diligence and precision at the end of the republic, gave us in an overall view of the Veneto provinces with all their towns and all their villas be. We could then observe various stylistic changes as well as the prevalence of the Palladian style. The different functions of the various villas would also be evident: the villas erected as part of a reclamation with their broad surroundings; the pleasure villas; the villas with buildings corresponding to various activities; the villas of the bureaucrats; those of military men, etc.

Once the city had been formed, particularly at the beginning of the sixteenth century, the Venetians devoted increasing attention to the neighboring islands of the Giudecca and Murano. There broad green areas permitted the Venetian merchants to construct buildings and gardens for meeting with discreet friends. On the Giudecca and Murano, humanists and men of letters could attend to their studies in tranquillity far from the gaze of the indiscreet. Jacopo de' Barbari's view is a precious document of this life, where the first Venetian villas in the Gothic or Lombardesque style are clearly visible.

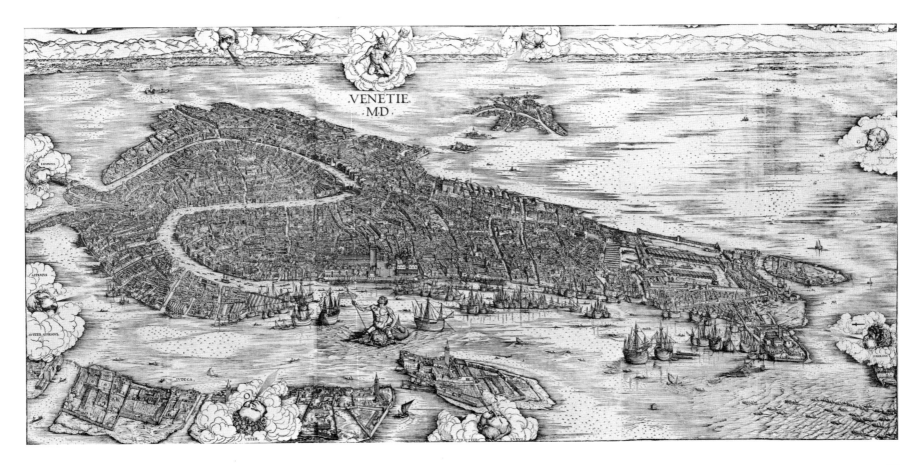

Venice
the amphibious city

Vittore Carpaccio. The Lion of St. Mark. (Venice, Doge's Palace). The Lion of St. Mark, coming out of the water and approaching the luxuriant landscape of the Veneto, symbolises the growing interest of Venice in the terra firma.

Venice, city of islands, "the stone fleet," has a double nature, aquatic and terrestrial.

When speaking of this city, one thinks immediately of its relationship with the sea. But Venice is an amphibious city: it has two squares (that of the land and that of the sea) just as it has two dominions (the seas and the mainland). Vittor Carpaccio represents the *Lion of St. Mark* with his hind legs in the water while the other two stand on lush land. However, he was the last sixteenth-century painter to do seascapes: Giorgione, Titian, and all the others turn their gaze by preference to the conquered mainland.

The Venetians never forgot their origins in Padua, Aquileia, Altino, and Oderzo, which were abandoned when, fleeing from the grip of the Barbarians, they sought refuge among the lagoons. The profound reasons for the city's fortunes can be found by going back to the origins of Venice, right to its ancient relationship with the mainland. The Venetians left memories, tombs, relations, and property on the mainland. Their thoughts turned to the mainland in a nostalgic idyll nourished by exhaustion with dangerous sea voyages and by the longed-for paradises of the Bible and mythology.

The love that the Venetians showed in every period for the villas and their gardens is the symbol of this never satiated yearning for the land.

Gardens
and the revaluation
of the Venetian life

In the Arab world extremely tall walls surround a rectangle of green in the center of which falls the jet of a fountain–enclosed Islamic paradises, an anticipation of celestial joys.

The love of plants and gardens comes from the East. The Venetians learned it from their voyages or else by passing part of their lives in lands of Islamic culture.

Doctor Gualtiero was famous for his garden of medicinal herbs in the fourteenth century. Subsequently botanical treatises and Arab tracts on hydraulics became even more widely known. This was followed by the introduction of exotic plants to embellish and make the house more comfortable. Venice enjoyed a sort of primacy in Europe as far as botany was concerned. One writer even claimed that there were a larger number of gardens in the lagoons then there were in all the rest of Italy.

But beyond the Oriental component, there was another source for the culture of the Venetians and their appreciation of the gifts of life: their links with the courtly customs of France.

The language (Martino Da Canal wrote the first history of the Venetians in French), music, and the dances of France, along with the poems of chivalry with which Italian literary history begins, all enjoyed great success in Venice. The places celebrated in these poems had characteristics that could not but touch the soul of the Venetians: magic trees and fountains; grottos and valleys of dream and fantasy. In the poems of chivalry antique mythology returned under another guise with the predominance of the element of fable and enchantment.

The art of the International Gothic (present above all at Treviso, Verona, Udine, and Trento) brought to Venice the echo of delicious landscapes with which to decorate the walls of the Ca d'Oro, painted by Giovanni of France with "gardens and hunting scenes." Pisanello and other artists of the Flamboyant Gothic transmitted the taste for those paradises and the "barchi" that would play so great a role in the Veneto villas.

The influence of Islam
and the Adriatic villas

The villa typical of the Veneto region, open and free on every side, constitutes a step forward compared to the buildings constructed by the Arabs for their pleasure. For example, the Alhambra is crude and inaccessible from the outside. Once we cross its drawbridge and pass through the entrance gate, a series of open spaces stretch in front of us, one after another, free and infinitely interconnected, like being in the interior of a single great house. And all of these places – the fountains, the patios, and the gardens – are accessible and freely offered up for our pleasure.

"I am no longer alone because from here I contemplate a marvelous garden" is inscribed on one of the arches in the Patio of Lindaraja.

If, as far as the exterior is concerned, the Arab's example has not had any evident influence in the development of the Veneto villas, we should not forget how much Westerners owe the Arab love of the family and the house, how much, Venice especially, learned from their wise and lavish use of waters; from their love for plants and gardens. The taste for nature (and this will be the way that leads Venetian landscape painting to success) flourished when the nightmares of the Middle Ages were forgotten. Wars were fewer, and man's conscience became freer to enjoy the gifts of nature and life. Well-being and optimism spread among families, bringing peace and prosperity.

Venice found herself, more than other countries, in a position to respond to these conditions. She was ready to generate a flowering of villa buildings: and so it was.

It is nevertheless interesting to recall a precedent for the Veneto villas. It did not exist in the lagoon islands or in the mainland territories near Venice, where Gothic and Lombardesque style villas are extremely rare. We must cast a glance over the territory that belonged to the ancient republic of Ragusa on the other shore of the Adriatic. There we encounter a whole series of Lombardesque and even Gothic villas, still retaining their original forms, scattered amid the green of lush gardens with the white of their handsome stones reflected in the sea or in cool fish ponds. These are not civic palaces, castles, abbeys or the small houses of the humanists. Here we can speak of true and proper villas in our sense of the word.

Even if to explain this abundance, we must recall the riches of the Ragusan merchants and their ties with the Muslim world, Onofrio Della Cava must not be forgotten. His aqueduct watered the entire valley. As Praga has shown, there was also lively archeological activity that, among other things, resulted in a study of epigraphy which anticipated Alberti's own discoveries.

So even in this case we see villas flourish at the same time as a new wave of reborn antiquity.

The villas of Ragusa, even in their undeniable primacy, should not, however, be considered simply an isolated episode without any great consequences for the future. Neither can they be placed on the same plane as the Veneto villas. The *World of the Veneto Villas* cannot be the work of a single prince or of a subjugated province as was the case with Vicenza. It needed the Serenissima to realize the vast phenomenon that remained vital, not for a brief period, but until the fall of the republic. In fact, it was Venice, with the unity of its political and economic power, with the solemnity and authority of its principals, and with the prestige of its fame, that succeeded in making a norm of all that elsewhere was sporadic or exceptional. She was always ready to make the most vital experiences her own, no matter where they came from. Venice made over the partial and isolated experiences we have alluded to by using exemplary, organic forms.

The Veneto villa
in the fifteenth century

The stupendous illustrations of the *Poliphilio* give us a clear idea of the gardens where the Venetians liked to retreat to discuss Plato and Petrarch. They were small enclosures with fountains and trellises, embellished with the sàrcophaghi and sculptures of that classical antiquity which humanism was rediscovering. Nature was experienced in a somewhat literary fashion, even if refuge from the city meant seeking restorative comfort amid the nearest green islands, indicating the importance that the custom of villa life had already assumed in Venice by then.

The gentlemen of the fifteenth century knew that grandiose villas emulating the delights of Baie had been built, as Martial records, on the nearby mainland and outside the *municipium* of Roman Altino.

That perfectly aristocratic, completely private pleasure of finding oneself alone with a few friends is the principal characteristic of these first resorts, far removed from sixteenth-century grandeur and the pomp that will distinguish villa life in the last years of the Venetian republic.

From the outset, Venetian architecture was distinguished from that of the mainland by its opening outwards of windows, porticos, and elegant loggias. This style characterizes even the suburban houses which, no longer connected with agricultural activity, frequently sprang up not far from the city walls.

One can see several of these houses on the Giudecca in the view of Jacopo de' Barbari. They are still Gothic or already impressed with the style of the Lombardo family, but they are also faithful to the divisions of traditional Venetian civic architecture. The Da Mula palace on Murano is one of the most significant examples of this.

Indeed the island of Murano seems to have been, from very ancient times, one of the resorts preferred by Venetian noblemen. Among other things they were convinced that the numerous glass furnaces made the air purer.

In the fifteenth century, in the same places where the Venetians had owned mills since the eleventh century, there arose the first suburban villas closed in by orchards and agreeable gardens. The aristocracy "spent blessed hours in the spring and autumn seasons, educating the mind, raising up spirit and body." And here, for more than three centuries, humanists, merchants, navigators, and poets, along with artists and magistrates of the Serenissima, enjoyed the refined pleasures that nature offered.

Benedetto Bordone in 1547 wrote that the island of Murano was "very similar to Venice», but that it offered greater amenities. In 1620 Poracchi also compared it with Venice, while Coronelli extolled it for the stupendous palaces built there by the most important exponents of the Venetian patriciate. Zanetti recalled, among others, the "splendid residence of Catherine Cornaro, Queen of Cyprus." "Of the most splendid residence that once delighted that famous lady who had transferred to her native land the rights of a kingdom, there today remains at San Salvatore on Murano nothing but the vast right wing of a building, reduced to poor housing and the walled up arches of the gardens of San Bernardo. In any case, it will not displease the lovers of our history to hear it described. The resort of the Cornaro family was laid out on Murano, as is well known, for the Queen of Cyprus. There were two magnificent buildings, each one of which was in itself a sumptuous princely palace. These two buildings stood more than a quarter of a mile apart from each other. They were united in the middle by a vast, richly ornamented gallery that was supported by a majestic arcade. The first of these palaces was built on the outer edge of the *contrada* of San Salvatore, just opposite the monastery of San Mattia. It had been reconstructed in handsome Roman style by Vincenzo Scamozzi in 1605. Father Coronelli made a drawing of it which is now in the National Museum. The other building overlooked the canal on the quay at Santa Maria degli Angeli, having just in front of it, to the left, the well-designed Da Mula palace and on the right, the very ancient abbey of San Cipriano. The gallery ran from the Palace of San Salvatore along the wall to the left of the monastery and church of San Bernardo, crossing the square of that name and, with the lagoon washing up against it on the right side, finally reached the other palace. Gardens and orchards were planted beneath both palaces. The space set aside for ball games was flanked by an ornate terrace for the spectators; a colossal fountain

*Palazzo Contarini dal Zappo
(Venice, Grand Canal).
The grace and vivacity of the
Lombard palaces inspired
the first architects of the villas
of the Veneto.*

with 24 jets of fresh water; a grandiose triumphal arch; a larger than lifesize statue of the Queen of Cyprus crowned and holding a scepter; and another statue, standing in front of her, representing Marco, her father. As those who were living there at the fall of the republic recall there were not a few other statues embellishing the palace of San Salvatore, which was the largest and most conspicuous.

What can one say of the rest? What about the grandiose galleries through which one passed from one garden to the next, from one palace to the other? All that could be had of the richest, the most splendid, and the most rare was abundantly

displayed: armories, ballrooms, music rooms, fountains, library sculpture, paintings in every style: indeed every profusion of Oriental luxury. Every treasure of the fine arts seemed to have found its home there."

The particular humanist atmosphere which characterized these fifteenth-century "resorts" found its highest expression in the fine figure of Andrea Navagero, distinguished man of letters and Venetian diplomat who had a villa with orchards and gardens on Murano. "Extolled and described by the finest pens of his time, the gardens that he possessed on this island were the first botanic gardens in Italy," wrote Vincenzo Zanetti in 1866. "He passed happy, relaxed days in them amid friends and literary colleagues. Those gardens were, in fact, rich in greenery, flowers, laurel, cedar trees and exotic plants... even during the most serious times, Andrea never forgot the Muranese gardens, which were more pleasing to him than any high office. When he was in Spain he sent to his dear friend Ramusio warmly recommending him to take jealous care of the gardens."

Notwithstanding the extraordinary abundance of villas which, from the fifteenth to the seventeenth century, made the island into a place of pleasure and amusement, only few traces have come down to us: fleeting clues to a celebrated moment against which the destructive powers of time and men seem aligned. Only Palazzo (it would be better to call it Villa) Da Mula can still offer us tangible evidence of this particular type of villa.

A great number of suburban villas, places for pleasurable and erudite encounters, also rose up on the recently conquered mainland. Despite the centuries of celebration in literature, only slight traces remain of these villas, which were once the setting for refined gatherings and the leisure of the humanists. A common destiny of destruction seems

to have overtaken them, preventing us from gathering up that first flowering of the villa civilization in all it richness.

What were the causes? Several ended by being absorbed in the continual growth of urban centers. Once incorporated in the urban fabric, these villas suffered radical modifications that upset their original style. But the greater number of those villas, as we have already hinted and as we shall see more clearly later, owe their disappearance to a precise event linked to strategic and military exigencies: the "Guasto" or Wasting, which Venice ordered in the early sixteenth century in order to clear vast, easily controlled open plain areas around the walls of the cities. This massive operation, inspired by the need to safeguard the Most Serene Republic, did not spare even the most beautiful fifteenth-century villas in the territory around Padua and Treviso. These had been built in the immediate outskirts of the city, as in Mantegna's fresco where, one sees the white façade of a Renaissance villa of the characteristic Venetian type standing out in the background. It rises on the ruins of an ancient Roman city and at its back one notes the looming presence of the towers and battlemented wall that encircle the city.

If the fifteenth-century villas erected in the open country (and we are thinking, as far as the province of Vicenza is concerned, of the Villa del Verme at Agugliaro and of the so-called Ca' Brusà at Lovolo di Lovertino) are excluded, then very few other such humanist residences managed to survive. We are left with too little evidence of one of the culturally and artistically most refined moments of Venetian civilization.

Villa Dall'Aglio, the ground floor loggia (Lughignano, Treviso). Many of the villas of the terra firma copied the layout of the Venetian houses.

Treviso and the mainland penetration of the Venetians

De' Barbari's view of Venice, with its representation of the Giudecca and Murano, is precious evidence of a change in Venetian custom of fundamental importance. However the villas built in the islands of the lagoon were not as yet characterized by the specific architectonic forms corresponding to the new style of living in contact with nature. Even the *villetta* erected in the territory of Padua by Pietro Bembo was little different from a city house. The gardens of these first villas only have a function of pleasure. Their utilitarian function was minimal: perhaps a little fruit, just enough for the family's use. The relationship between the building and natural space (which will have a great importance in the Palladian villa) did not require any particular solutions that did not already exist. It will be on the mainland that new horizons are opened to the Venetians and that the building – natural space relationship will have a determinant value.

The gardens of the houses and convents of the city, the villas of the Giudecca and Murano, are the first stages in a long story which, almost as if by concentric circles, spreads the Venetians' villa-houses first along the rivers and canals of the neighboring provinces of the mainland (above all in the Treviso province) and then increasingly further away, right up to the borders of the state.

The Veneto villa reaches its definitive physiognomy step by step. Next to the garden, the heart of the villa, is situated everything necessary for agriculture. This is the beginning of a process which will see many of the best energies of the Venetians directed towards investment in landed property, reclamation, and agriculture.

Treviso was the first mainland territory to submit voluntarily to Venice and the only one to remain faithful. Indeed we may add that experiments were made in governmental and administrative systems in this province – previously tried in Crete and other colonial possessions in the East – that were then adopted in all the other mainland provinces.

The greatest Venetian families had already begun to appear in the "Trevigiana" by the thirteenth century because of its proximity to the capital. For example, Giacomo Tiepolo had a villa at Marocco in 1289 "where he spent his

amusement and where he enjoyed residing." Other similar documents refer to Conegliano, to Nervesa, to Montebelluna, and to Asolo.

Recognizing the benefits that could come from agriculture, it was the Venetian nobles who had interests in this region who solicited the government of the Serenissima (they were easy to heed since they frequented the Doges' Palace) to intervene and coordiante the earliest land reclamation. This was not in the sixteenth century, but rather a century before the creation of the *Magistrato dei Beni Inculti* in 1556. In fact, following requests advanced in 1425 from Castelfranco, the Senate published a decree for reclamation in the province of Treviso with a preface that anticipated almost word for word the famous pronouncement of Alvise Cornaro: "All holdings will be improved. Many families will transfer themselves there and there will follow an increase in our tax receipts. The harm that was done in earlier times when men and animals were obliged to drink muddy, swirling waters gathered in the ditches will cease with this operation for the conservation of life."

A branch agency of Venice's *Ufficio delle Acque* or Water Board was formed in Treviso several decades later, in 1469. It coordinated the reorganization of all the Brenta tributaries with "incredible benefit to 59 villas in the area." But that was not all. In the same year a grain warehouse, the *Fontego del grano,* was built in Treviso, a full half century before the famous one built by Andrea Gritti. This was a decision that proved to be one of the Serenissima's most efficacious instruments of propaganda, particularly for the people of the countryside laboring under the nightmare threat of frequent famine.

Reclamation gave new life to the "Trevigiano." It become known as the "garden of Venice," providing a haven for politicians as well as being preferred by Venetian and foreign humanists. Francesco Barbaro, a disciple of Barzizza and Guarini, sent by Venice as Podestà or Governor of Treviso, already had a villa near Montebelluno in 1422 which he called *Vigilianum* and dedicated in Latin "to a philosophic and tranquil mind."

But even more than the beauty of these places and the fertility of the country, still rich in good water, there was the "securitas" that encouraged the humanists to sojourn there. The consequences of this security guaranteed by Venice was immediately evident, not only in the customs and character of the people, but also in the forms assumed in architecture. Castles and fortifications were no longer necessary and, as has been mentioned, villas make their first appearance with the open forms of their structure.

The *Palazzo dei Giustinian* at Roncade seems to straddle two worlds. The moat, the drawbridge, and the medieval bastions of the castle still seem to protect the villa. On the other hand, the windows, the porticos, and the loggias, along with other arcades and more loggias, frescoed on their outer walls, have the function of accentuating the joy of being able to live in a welcoming and "transparent" architecture safe from every threat.

It is not unlikely that the open structures of the villa at Roncade derive stylistically from the *Barco* at Altivole built between 1490 and 1509 by Catherine Cornaro. The farsighted queen had continued to improve her fairy tale realm. She was following the counsels of Fra' Giocondo, whose merits are commemorated by the monument which, in our day, was dedicated to him at Altivole. Both in the *Barco della Regina Cornaro* and at Roncade, colonnades proliferate along with the beautiful style of the palaces of Venice and Treviso, thus anticipating by many decades the Renaissance structures of Palladian villas. Decoration in fresco also increased, following a tradition long beloved in the province and which Paolo Veronese would make triumphant in the villa at Maser.

This is what appears about the new architecture in the *Dream of Poliphilus,* set in the outskirts of Treviso: "The dignity of the construction reconciled a joy and a beautiful grace... What a worthy vestibule, what a regal portico... added to by the dignity of the fenestration... What an admirable order of ornament, and what lastingly fine colors... what well regulated columns and intervals."

The most harmonious and happy open villa of this period and place is probably that built on the banks of the Sile at Lughignano. It is known incorrectly as the *Villa of Fiammetta,* after the maid of Catherine Cornaro mentioned by Bembo. The building certainly reflects the elegance that the

Queen of Cyprus, with her humanists and her Greek and Cypriot courtiers, disseminated in a region which Carrer, perhaps following the *Poliphilo,* described as a second "land native to Venus". The happiness of the Trevigiana is celebrated by an uninterrupted literary tradition. One often reads the word "hilaritate" in the *Poliphilo* but already in the *Entreé d'Espagna* there is mention of courtly Treviso's *joyeyse Marche.* Even Fazio degli Uberti wrote of this land:

Which smiles on all with clear fountains
and with love's pleasure here refined...

Priuli, the historian, reports on the "dolce vita" led by Giorgione's friends, and I believe that it is in Treviso, more than in Venice, that one should seek to better understand the happiness of the Veneto at this time. Cornaro's "Lady Happiness"; the "joy of tranquility" recorded by Paruta; the happiness which, according to Carlo Goldoni, is the primary characteristic of the Venetian people, all find their most celebrated models in the lands of the Trevigiana.

The Trevisans' love of festivity culminates in the famous tournaments and with the Castle of Love in 1214. Their emblem seemed to be a classical bas relief of a Bacchante inserted into the wall of the city's cathedral. The elegant paintings of Tommaso da Modena and the happy coloring of Cima da Conegliano are other signs of the courtly and social character of a province celebrated by many Provençal poets of the troubadour and courtly traditions who preferred to frequent this land of the Venetian domain more than any other. Astrological and hermetic research flourished where there was none of archeology's obstinate persistence, nor the wiles of commerce, nor the cult of warfare, nor the rude manners of mountain folk. The native land of Giorgione, lush and tranquil, refined and "amorous" in its every aspect seemed profoundly different from every other region of the Veneto.

A page of the *Poliphilo* records the legend concerning Morgano (a significant name, both for the cultural rapport with France and for the poetic fantasy of the Trevisans) and the plain where Giorgione was born. The mythical lords of the land, overbearing in their "great handsomeness and

beauty, reputed to be beyond human conception," attempted "improperly to associate themselves with the celestial gods." Their people dared to raise temples to their honor, "the popular cult having decreed that Morgania was Venus herself." But the retribution of the gods was swift. "The royal palace and realm..." were destroyed "by terrifying lightning bolts..."

The legend continues with the metamorphosis of Lelio Silio "changed into a famous river bearing the most purified waters still to be seen circulating smoothly and freshly in that region."

The Sile's "region of circulation," "an area of most graceful atmosphere and of refreshing rivers and springs," with its cultivated visions and legends, was translated into painting by Giorgione.

The new idea of the Veneto landscape matured here and was substituted for the gold ground and the "black ground," which Michiel recalled from antique painting.

Fra' Giocondo:
synthesis of Tuscan culture and Venetian ornamentalism

Venice and the mainland were two distinct entities during the Middle Ages. One gravitated toward Byzantium, the other belonged to the Holy Roman Empire.

Even during the fifteenth century, despite the fact that Venice had conquered all the Veneto, the Friuli, and eastern Lombardy, there were still marked differences between the lagoon city and the territories conquered by her. The creation of the Mainland Dominion and the aggregation of mainland provinces did not alter, at first, either Venice's character as a maritime power nor her cultural horizons. Almost a century and the lessons of a lost war, that of Cambrai, would be needed to convince the Serenissima to adopt a unified and organic policy (one which would have the villa as one of its emblems) toward the Mainland Dominion.

First, and one may say for all the fifteenth century, the relationship with the conquered provinces was of an economic character. It obliged Venice to control the rivers and the principal routes of overland communication in order to protect a flourishing traffic with Europe and northern Italy.

Even though many Venetians had acquired property in the territories of Padua and Treviso from the thirteenth century in order to guarantee food supplies in case of famine and to offset the risks of overseas commerce, they – and especially the conservative faction – regarded the mainland with a certain hostility. The antithesis between Venice and the mainland of the Veneto endured for a long time through various forms of suspicion and distrust.

Even the cult of humanism which flourished in the nearby cities of Padua and Verona was welcomed quite late in Venice. The Venetian spirit was alien to abstract erudition and remained attached to the concrete realities of practical life, being interested primarily in all that was advantageous to the individual and to the state.

Not that Venice was insensitive to culture. But theirs was still that modeled on examples. The "*Humanae litterae*" of Florentine intellectualism and Paduan archeological studies remained secondary. Only when Venice began to compete with the most important states of the peninsula did she realize that humanistic culture, already

accepted at the principal courts, could be considered an instrument of extraordinary prestige. At first timidly, then with increasing decisiveness, Venice welcomed the new forms that art had assumed. Sculptors and architects of the school of the Lombardo family translated the still completely Gothic taste for color, dear to the Venetians, into buildings on a tentatively Renaissance scale. The work of Mauro Coducci was more innovative. He harmonized Florentine architectonic principles – particulary those of Alberti – with the peculiarly Venetian environment, still nostalgic for a Byzantine sense of space. Tuscan artists like Andrea del Castagno, Paolo Uccello, and Donatello were called to work in the lagoons: Venice could not be less than other cities. The first villas, in the sense that later became the classic definition for this type of building, had already appeared in Tuscany some decades earlier. For example, there were already present in the *Villa di Poggio a Caiano* many of the elements that would become characteristic, such as the triangular pediment, the colonnaded loggia, and the decoration depicting agrarian deities. This masterpiece of Giuliano da Sangallo anticipated the passionate "exhumation" of antique models carried out by Mantegna in the fresco at Mantua and the theorizing on architecture illustrated in the *Poliphilo.*

The architect who had the merit to translate erudition and theory into works of an extraordinary cultural importance was Fra' Giocondo from Verona. No one was better able than he to understand and use the archeological learning which had been developed in the Veneto by Tuscan architects.

Coming from a city imbued with classicism like Verona, that in the late fifteenth century had seen personalities like that of Guarino, Matteo de' Pasti, Felice Feliciano, and Fracastoro, Fra' Giocondo was not only in a position to absorb the most vital essence of local culture, but also revealed himself to be open to the most advanced experiences of Italian culture.

"*Architectus prestabilis, nobilis, in architectura omnium facile princeps,*" as Poliziano calls him, Fra' Giocondo is the true protagonist of the relationship between the Veneto and the reborn art of Florence. His primary merit was to have

Fra' Giocondo. Loggia del Consiglio (Verona, Piazza dei Signori). In Fra' Giocondo's architecture, Tuscan dimensions blend with the Venetians' refined taste for decoration.

transmitted to the artists of the Veneto not so much the Albertian lesson, which might have arrived in another way and which already had an original interpreter in Mauro Coducci, but rather what Giuseppe Fiocco called that "Brunelleschian informative conception" which the Veronese friar had learned working alongside some of the most refined of Filippo Brunelleschi's followers.

Fra' Giocondo was already famous outside his native territory when he was called to Naples to work at the *Villa di Poggioreale* after Giuliano da Majano and Giorgio Martini, the distinguished military architect for whose *Trattato di architecttura* the Veronese friar provided illustrations. A document of 1489 records him still in Naples, together with Sannazaro, who was perhaps responsible for bringing him back again to the Venetians.

A "universal man," as Vasari defined him, Fra' Giocondo was second only to Leonardo in the vast extent of his interests.

He ranged from theology to philology from archeology to architecture, and from town planning to painting, distinguishing himself by the clearly scientific character of his researches. His competence in archeology was famous and

profound. He collected inscriptions, studied ruins and antique monuments. It was he who published Vitruvius' *De Architectura* in 1511, taking responsibility for its philological accuracy and enriching it with the woodcuts that bear his name. This edition signaled the beginning of a wave of passionate studies that involved the historians of antiquity as well as artists, and the creation in the Veneto of one of the liveliest centers of architectonic research boasting the names of Cornaro, Falconetto, Trissino, and Palladio.

But Fra' Giocondo was not the apostle of "holy Antiquity" alone, nor did his merits limit themselves to architectonic theory and the editing of Vitruvius. He was a true architect, much appreciated for his technical skill, honored and sought after as a military engineer and as an expert in hydraulics.

Architecture and reclamation: these two disciplines are the basis for the *World of the Villas* and are the two disciplines Fra' Giocondo was the first, great master.

Alvise Cornaro has a description of Fra' Giovondo in his *Trattato delle acque* that alone would establish a man's glory. He asserts that we should "reserve an eternal sense of obligation to the memory of Fra' Giocondo who could rightly call himself the second builder of Venice." This testimonial on the part of a devotee of land reclamation like Cornaro is sufficient to guarantee the recognition of the Veronese hydraulic engineer's merits even if (as is often the case for a theoretician and humanist like him) documents often neglect his name in favor of that of Aleardi, the official responsible for the expenditure for the operation. Giorgio Vasari, directly informed of Fra' Giocondo's merits by Alvise Cornaro, continued a eulogy of unconditional praise that is often inexplicably passed over by many students of Venetian matters. If discredit or at least neglect had not befallen Fra' Giocondo, then when the study of Alvise Cornaro as protagonist of the *World of the Villas* was revived, a substantial affinity linking these two fathers of our Renaissance would have been noted: that of their villa life, their living in contact with nature.

In the preface to his *De Re Rustica,* a significant publication which collected the writings on agriculture of Cato, Varro, and Columella as early as 1497, Fra' Giocondo wrote to Pope Leo X: "I long to dedicate myself to rustic labors and remove myself far from the clamor of the courts and secular affairs. I think about entertaining myself with the pleasant observation of nature for my repose and amusement." Evidently he is using a commonplace that even Petrarch had taken from antiquity but which Alvise Cornaro will render famous in modern times.

Fra' Giocondo was particularly esteemed as a military architect. For this reason the Serenissima recalled him from France, where the king had named him "deviseur de batiments," in order to bestow on him the high office of official architect of the state. On June 5, 1506 Friuli refers to him as *Fracter Jocundus Veronensis Consiljii X maximus architectus,* Fra' Giocondo of Verona, Chief Architect to the Council of Ten. How then can we explain the general lack of interest in Fra' Giocondo? Why is there so much controversy over the works attributed to him? It is strange that even the conception of documented architecture, like the *Fondaco dei Tedeschi,* is not attributed to him.

When Pietro Contarini, celebrating the return of the Procurator of San Marco, Andrea Gritti, speaks of the recently reconstructed *Fondaco dei Tedeschi,* he has no doubts as to its conception: "*Teutonicum mirare forum, spectabile fama, nuper Iucundi nobile fratis opus.*"

But even in this case critics neglect the name of the inventor in order to give credit for the work solely to those officials responsible for the construction. If we look at the Fondaco's façade and compare it with the central section of the villa erected at Altivole near Asolo for the Queen Catherine Cornaro, we see affinities that confirm Fra' Giocondo's presence in the area around 1507, when he was employed there on the systemization of the Brentella canal and the reclamation of all the territory surrounding the *Barco della Regina di Cipro.*

Unfortunately the great villa, known to us from old drawings, was destroyed, and we can but examine the *barchessa* outbuilding that survives. The great loggia at Altivole introduces us to that most characteristic world of the Veneto villa with its open structure and the presence of elegant columns (both real and *tromp l'oeil*) and with the character of its decoration, where sacred and profane subjects mingle (on one side Apollo and Daphne and on the other Saint Jerome in the Desert) as evidence of the profound relationship between man and nature.

Not only in hydraulic engineering, where the Veronese friar was Alvise Cornaro's master, nor only in military architecture, where he was the master of Sanmichele and Falconetto, but also in villa architecture, Fra' Giocondo had the opportunity at Altivole, even in calamitous times, to reveal some of the most surprising aspects of his genius.

It is known that Andrea Palladio erected his first colonnaded façade for a villa only in the mid-sixteenth century. Yet we shall see how, especially on the plain of Treviso, villa buildings were erected with grand ground floor loggias and colonnades long before other provinces. The *Loggia di Fra' Giocondo* in Verona is the prototype and symbol of this new chapter in the architecture of the Veneto evident both in the cities as well as in the country. Up to this time, no one has been able to prove that it was the work of Fra' Giocondo (even in this case the documents seem to contradict the attribution). Certainly the loggia reflects the characteristics of a style that recalls Florentine experiences but which, at the same time, seems to correspond to the culture and sensitivity of Fra' Giocondo: that is to that love of ornamentalism that is the halfway between archeology and the picturesque of the Gothic and the Lombardo family. It is a chapter of history that still awaits an adequate interpretation. The incredibly early date of 1476-91 for such a building in the lands of the Veneto must be taken into consideration.

Giorgione
and the discovery of landscape

Giorgione. The Tempest (Venice, The Gallery of the Academy). The pleasantness of the secluded position, the presence of water and ancient ruins, seem to suggest the perfect place for the villa of a humanist.

It was not an easy undertaking to distract the Venetians from the vision of sea ports and cities (think of Carpaccio's canvases) that they had always encountered in their voyages. When they thought of the neighboring mainland, they had in mind inaccessible, marshy places, scarcely inhadited by hermits. Reading classical texts or Petrarch's writings was not enough to make them understand and love the country. It was only after Cambrai, when wealth and stability had been reconquered, that we see how the Venetians discovered a nostalgia for the provinces from whence their progenitors had come. The love of gardens, which up to that point Venice reserved for the orchards in the city, partly in association with Eastern countries, and for the villas built on the Giudecca and Murano, gradually extended itself to ever more distant territories of the mainland. Writers and humanists were the first interpretors of this movement, which began with nearby Treviso and had its emblem, even more than in the pages of Bembo's *Asolani,* in the painting of Giorgione.

Considering its treatment of space, the *Tempesta* presents an evolved and complex situation. Michiel's brief description of the painting uses the word "*paesetto,*" or small landscape, then notes the meteorological characteristics of a storm and then mentions the characters present. This scale of interests is not without significance. In the foreground we see depicted a *locus amoenus,* fertile and inviting, outside of time and we would say immersed in natures's eternal breathing. The people who live in the "fabulous" and fortified city which one sees in the background evidently stay away, fearing the ruins of the antique world, not yet overtaken by the wilderness. In fact the two young people, almost symbols of all humanity (and for this reason liable to limitless cultural interpretation), do not take part in the life of the society which belongs to the walled town. They meet in this landscape, selected by the ancients for the construction of a classical villa near a fresh spring. A villa brought to destruction by time and events.

The nature that surrounds the "gypsy" and the "soldier" is interpreted as friendly although neither tidied up nor humanistically ordered as in the gardens of Murano or Asolo or in those of the *Poliphilo.*

The times were not yet ripe to raise up villa buildings corresponding to the beauties of the place and to the requirements of humanist leisure. But the ideals expressed by Giorgione in the *Tempesta* would not be forgotten by the Venetians when the highest and most complete moment of their villa civilization was reached.

We search to see if among Giorgione's works there is a thread connecting the gradual acceptance on the Venetians' part of that new interpretation

of the country that will culminate in a cultural moment still distant, the moment of the *World of the Villas of Palladio.* The *Fête Champêtre* in the Louvre is one of the most significant and indicative moments in that confidence and harmony between man and nature. It takes place in a land of soft hills, welcoming yet inhabited at last, where a group of young people, in full "securitas," comes out of the city visible in the background, happily and humanistically enjoying the consolations of the countryside. In the *Fête Champêtre* we can see the poetic climate fixed emblematically a climate that, from Bembo and Sannazaro, goes back to Petrarch and the ancients. But here, as in the *Tempesta,* the presence of the ancient world still has a certain literary taste, and nature is still seen as outside of history in the generic way intended by Bembo's friends: "An earthly paradise for the charm of the airs and the site... Place of nymphs and demigods...," as Calmo will write with his usual artifice.

Only with the *Donna Nuda* of Dresden does the "classic fertilization" take place that leads to the rising of a new day. It is neither a portrait nor the representation of a divinity reconstructed piece by piece by a learned archeologist. Rather it is the portrayal of a great emotion that awakens and takes consciousness in an extensive country which has been "humiliated" as a mere backdrop and complement to the human figure.

Titian, working on the painting that Giorgio left incomplete, respected the master's idea. Evidently he intended to suppress the values of the landscape in order to exalt the luminosity of the figure.

But throughout his active and extremely short life, Giorgione continued to change, and in the last works he presented himself yet again with a new face.

I see the last work of Giorgione in the drawing that depicts "A wanderer contemplating the flowers in the walls of Castelfranco." Neither a literary nor ideal landscape, nor yet a symbolic event, but the painter's very homeland: the walls and towers of his city.

This is the most advanced point reached by Giorgione's art in respect to the interpretation of space as it interests those studying the acceptance of the ideal of the villa. We have finally reached the interpretation of a known and loved reality: one of the foundations (even if not the only one) of the success enjoyed by the Veneto landscape and its villas.

The other great interpretative moment in the history of landscape will occur several decades later and corresponds to the more mature phase of the *World of the Veneto Villas.* It is a moment that will not be the work of men of letters or artists or patrons, but of an entire nation of government officials and workers on the land. An admirable moment that neither Giorgione, Sannazaro, nor Bembo could have either understood or appreciated.

"It cannot be both beautiful and useful," wrote Leonardo da Vinci, but this was the thinking of those humanists who lived far from politics and reality.

Venice, after Cambrai, will know how to accomplish the miracle. It is true that she will never forget the beautiful (Fra' Giocondo and Alvise Cornaro say so explicitly), but beauty will no longer suffice for the "gentlemen" and in Palladio's villas we shall see the "beautiful" and the "useful" happily united in an admirable whole.

The new attitude of Venice toward the mainland after Cambrai

Between the end of the fifteenth and the beginnings of the sixteenth centuries events of exceptional importance, such as geographical discoveries, the invention and spread of printing, and the use of firearms, all radically changed European civilization. Venice, a city open to international influence, was ready to welcome novelties and adopt them to increase her prosperity and prestige.

For example, Venice immediately understood the importance of printing to be not only economic, but also cultural and propagandistic, thus giving impetus to the most flourishing publishing industry of the time.

The Serenissima, the most powerful state in the peninsula, favored by economic prosperity, brought a broader political vision to maturity while cherishing he dream of an empire that extended not only over the seas, but also onto the continent.

The expansionist tendency of Venice that in the fourteenth century had conquered the Friuli and Eastern Lombardy, in addition to the Veneto, acquired a renewed vigor at the beginning of the new century, menacing the papal dominions in the Romagna.

Fearful of Venice's increased power and ambitions, many Italian states and with them, Spain, France, and the empire inspired by Pope Julius II joined together in league at Cambrai (1508) against the republic. They accused Venice of wishing to create a "monarchy similar to that of Rome." The Venetian army was defeated at Agnadello (1509), and the allies penetrated into the territory of the Serenissima reaching the edge of the lagoon. As distinct from other wars fought outside the Venetian state, the war of Cambrai involved the Veneto provinces. Venice, suddenly deprived of financial, military, and food supplies, recognized the impossibility of further recruiting mercenary captains and trops.

The damage that the invading armies inflicted on virtually all the lands of the dominion constituted a fearful ruin for the civilian population and for the very economy of those territories.

Venice, exhausted and bled dry by military expenditure, was in the midst of a commercial crisis at the time of the defeat of Agnadello. "From haughty they became most humble," wrote Friuli.

The Venetians, remaining "as if dead" in their "tried and starving cities," began to examine their consciences and to consider the reasons that had led to their undoing. Notwithstanding the grave danger, Venice knew how to raise herself up again, thanks to her proverbial diplomatic ability and to a series of lucky circumstances. After alternating military and political episodes, protracted until 1517, the republic was again able to enter into possession of the greater part of her ancient dominion as confirmed by the Treaty of Bruxelles in that same year.

The defeat of Cambrai did not then signify the end of Venice. Indeed it can be said that hard experience was pregnant with positive consequences. "The Serenissima," wrote Nani, "turned its thoughts to the arts of preservation and peace" which from that moment on were at the top of everyone's thinking, citizens and state alike.

The decisions that the Venetians were obliged to make after these events remained fundamental for three centuries, until the end of the republic. They also favored one of the most splendid moments of Venetian history: that represented by the *heroic ideal of the Renaissance* and by the birth of the *World of the Villas.*

Indeed, this latter was rendered possible precisely by that renewed thrust of initiatives that characterized Venetian policy in relationship to the mainland after the crisis of Cambrai. Never again did Venice concentrate so on the organization of her bureaucracy and the appreciation of her territories, including the embellishment of their cities, as she did then. The defeat had represented the end of the imperialist dream as such but had also revealed the importance of the Mainland Dominion. Venice was persuaded of the necessity of fortifying it and organizing it, of profiting from its energies and exploiting its resources. To this end the hundred years of experience that had matured in the governing of the Treviso province provided a precious lesson.

There, where Venice had intervened early and directly, the Serenissima found the support and loyalty of the population during the recent crisis. While Padua, Verona, and Vicenza submitted to the emperor, Treviso alone among them all remained faithful, resisting the armies of the coalition.

Thus, after the Cambrai experience, Venice committed herself to a policy of direct and extended intervention in her provinces. The decadence of levantine commerce, thrown into crisis by the Atlantic routes, by the competition with new fleets, and by the growing Turkish power, convinced many Venetians to invest in landed property on the nearby mainland.

48

Sanmicheli: fortified cities and secure lands

Venice was able to establish more organic investment on the mainland only when her actual possession of it was guaranteed. Prudence counseled that it was not enought to have reconquered the ancient dominion. One had to avoid the repetition of tragic episodes like Cambrai. And since the Veneto nobility still felt profoundly obligated to the emperor, with whom they were allied during the war, the Serenissima made a substantial contribution to Maximilian Hapsburg in order to release his subjects from every feudal obligation within the empire.

Finally, by reviving the ancient right, granted by the emperor, to hold noble investitures within her own territories, the republic could control the mainland aristocracy on whose property the state continued to recruit the "*cernide*" or peasant militia which went to swell the Veneto armies.

At the same time they reorganized the army, Venice committed herself to the fortification of the cities so that they could resist any enemy attack. The old defense systems had been inadequate against a barrage of artillery, the revolutionary weapon that revealed its decisive importance during the war of Cambrai.

At the height of the crisis in 1510, Fra' Giocondo, inventor of "projecting walls for greater safety," was invited by the Republic to equip Treviso with new walls. It was he who, as Vasari again wrote, "first introduced a new manner of making war." Before Sanmicheli's invention, he deserves the credit for having restructured the defense of the Veneto territory. Even the fortress of Legnago was constructed "entirely according to Fra' Giocondo," Operating in the various provinces as architect, hydraulic engineer, and land reclamation official, Fra' Giocondo spread his teaching and his style, furnishing a primary basis for that artistic unification which, taken up again by Sanmicheli, would culminate with the presence of Palladio everywhere in the region.

Paruta, the state's official historian, gave evidence of the Serenissima's quickness in realizing the vast plan for fortifying her mainland dominion. "She urged the souls to see to the provisions for two most noble cities, Padua and Verona, the strongest foundations of the Mainland Empire. Not sparing any expense, the Senate turned to transforming them into well-defended fortresses so that in the future... the enemy would think twice before coming to besiege them. Therefore many things were rebuilt which had been destroyed in the war. Many other things were added anew: buildings in various parts of the great walls, and strong bastions suited to the use of modern artillery batteries. Several places were remade at great expense and with the noblest art not only for security, but also for adornment. Thus those cities acquired a greater security against the enemy and, at the same time, a reputation for splendid workmanship." The first cities to be fortified were those nearest at hand: Padua and the faithful Treviso.

Treviso's gates of the *Santi Quaranta* and *San Tommaso* were of 1517 and 1518 respectively. The *Santacroce* and *Pontecorvo* gates at Padua are of 1517. The *Portello* and *Ognisanto* gates were of 1519.

However, the most important interventions were those of Michele Sanmicheli at Verona. He was a follower of Fra' Giocondo, yet rather than follow the Brunelleschan elegance advocated by the Veronese friar, Sanmicheli was attentive to Roman models present in Verona and in Rome (where he worked with Antonio da Sangallo) in order to bring a robust and fervid classicism to the maturity which he would translate in his palaces. Sanmicheli's military architecture was distinguished by the modernness of his solutions. It was he who surrounded Verona with a powerfully bastioned precinct adorned with monumental gates like the Porta San Giorgio (1525), Porta Nuova (1535), and the Porta Palio begun in 1542. He also erected the Cornaro and Santa Croce bulwarks at Padua.

These grandiose projects assumed an extraordinary importance to the development of techniques and architectonic styles common to all the Veneto provinces.

For the construction of these imposing defenseworks, conceived and carried out by Sanmicheli, great masses of peasants bricklayers and stonecutters were mobilized. Returning to their respective homelands, they retained the master's lessons and helped more or less faithfully to spread his style.

As is evident from the predilection for severe rustication and for the massive appearance of its structures, it was a style born for warfare. It is characteristic of some villas like the Villa Soranza at Treville, built by Sanmicheli himself, and many other of the oldest villas built by anonymous collaborators and scattered throughout the region. Even Palladio's masters, as well as the Vicentine architect himself, would reflect Sanmicheli's taste.

Sanmicheli's lesson seems to us translated by Andrea Palladio's peculiar brilliance at Bagnolo, at Santa Sofia di Pedemonte, and at Caldogno. It was also often enriched by Giulio Romano. In 1525 he was at Mantova attending to the construction of the *Palazzo del Te,* which had been conceived in monumental forms, foreshadowing the new Mannerist sensitivity.

The fortification works of the mainland corresponded to the region's political, bureaucratic, and military unification while favoring the acceptance of a common architectural language.

A similar assertion can be made if we examine the urban reorganization of the cities. In the same years as the fortresses were being constructed, Venice provided for the renovation of squares and public buildings in order to confirm its reestablished domination through architecture.

Jacopo de' Barbari's view demonstrated that Venice was already a completely formed city in all its aspects in 1500. A few years later the Venetians were dedicating themselves with the same industry to the organic systemization of the Mainland Dominion. A centrifical force emanating from the Giudecca, Murano, and Treviso now spread over all the region. Taking the capital as a model, the federated cities reproduced its most significant characteristics on a small scale. The symbol of the two columns, the public palace, the loggia, and the clock tower contributed to make them all so many "little Venices."

The Column with the Lion of St. Mark was placed in Verona's Piazza delle Erbe in 1533. The *Palazzo dei Tribunali* and that of the government were erected in the same city in 1530-32. Udine's Piazza Contarena was rebuilt in 1530 and during the same years the *Palazzo del Capitano* was built in Padua.

The situation created by the fortification of the Veneto cities was alluded to by Paolo Veronese in his *Allegory of Venice,* painted for the Hall of the

Maggiore Consiglio in the Doges' Palace. Venice is depicted seated amid the Olympian gods, protected at her back by a long, imposing fortress intended as an emblem of the fortified and secure mainland.

The *World of the Villas* as a unified and definite phenomenon finds its most characteristic expression only at the outset of the fourth decade of the sixteenth century. However, the year 1517, when the war of Cambrai was concluded and Venice was recognized as lord of all the mainland provinces, had a fundamental and definitive importance for the new direction taken by Venetian civilization. After that, the cities themselves become responsible for security in the country: controlling and coordinating the territory through the military, the administration, the economy and culture. A new aristocracy emerged from those cities and from their organization of power, giving birth to a greater flowering of feudalism in a country which was, in turn, controlled with an apposite magistracy by Venice. Thus all the lands of the mainland assume a their role and significance within the pacified and reorganized region.

Only keeping this in mind can one explain why the open architecture of the Veneto villas, instead of the fortification of castles, proliferated in the plains, on the hillsides, and along the rivers.

On the other hand from, every part of the region lively cultural forces flowed into Venice: men of letters and poets like Ruzante, and, in even greater numbers, artists like Fra' Giocondo, Giorgione, Titian, Sanmicheli, Pordenone, Palladio, Veronese, Bassano and Alessandro Vittoria, who contributed to the character and glory of the capital and of the entire region. Only after 1517 did the Veneto province begin to acquire its own distinct physiognomy or appearance, reflecting that of the Serenissima, but also recalling a world apart from Venice: neither commercial nor bourgeois, but essentially of the peasantry. The happiest results from this osmosis come when local cultures embrace a Venetian traditions, absorbing and appreciating its best energies. Then Venice would gradually impress on local culture throughout the entire region its own unmistakable character. Religion, politics, economy, culture, and art were no longer the sole expression of single

Portrait of Michele Sanmicheli (Giorgio Vasari, Le vite de' più eccellenti Pittori, Scultori ed Architettari, *Florence, 1568).*

municipal entities, but of a more complex organism that had its heart in the Palazzo Ducale. The history of Venice was no longer only that of a city; it now began to be that of a nation.

Michele Sanmicheli.

A Veronese architect, renowned especially for his military fortifications, Michele Sanmicheli (1484-1559) contributed to the spread of Roman classicism throughout the Veneto. The son of an architect originally from Lombardy, he worked mostly in Verona. Unfortunately, his Villa Soranza, which was the sole example of his work in the Venetian countryside, no longer stands, but his influence on villa architecture is still very evident in the province of Verona.

The Doge Gritti and the heroic ideal of the Renaissance.

Titian. A portrait of Doge Andrea Gritti (Washington, National Gallery, Kress Collection).

The vast program of reevaluation of the cities and the mainland carried out by the Serenissima after the Treaty of Bruxelles and especially after the Peace of Bologna made the organic restructuring of the Veneto provinces possible. It was a program that had as its true political protagonist Andrea Gritti. Doge from 1523 to 1538, he made these years one of the most splendid periods of Venetian history, renewing the triumphs of Doge Sebastiano Ziani, the true founder of Venice. At his coronation in 1523, Andrea Gritti officially undertook to see that the grain stores would be sufficient to overcome any famine. The Florentine historian Giannotti recalls how the Doge boasted that he had personally mastered all the states' receipts and expenditures in order to act in time to prevent any crisis.

In the same year, 1523, Ambassador Gerolamo Contarini disclosed Venice's precise policy. It was decided to give up expansionist politics, "predominance in Italy," in order to concentrate on the organization and improvement of the resources of her own territory.

In 1553 the Serenissima established, among other things, the obligation on the part of the governing officials in the provinces to send regular reports or "*relazioni*" to the Venetian government concerning the precise economic and political situation of those areas assigned to them. This was an indication of the detailed organization that permeated the entire region, notwithstanding certain contradictions in the laws and the ruses adopted by the nobility.

Thanks to Gritti, the primary creator of the state's bureaucratic reorganization, the Ducal Palace assumed an increased role as pulsing heart of the republic, the guiding organism of all its forces. Never before had the "Myth of Venice" reached such splendor. It was fed by the riches of a city which, in the hour of peril, knew how to bring together from every corner of the lagoon supplies accumulated by generations and generations of Venetians. The alacrity of its decisions confirms this, along with the proverbial expertise of its diplomacy, and above all, the efficiency of its administration and bureaucracy in the guidance of all the territories subject to the Serenissima.

Venice's vitality remained an irrefutable fact especially since, with the fall of Rome (1527) and Florence (1530), she remained (as the Florentine historian Donato Giannotti has recognized) the only Italian state to conserve her ancient liberty. This was the moment of full affirmation when men of letters and culture took refuge in Venice, seeing in the lagoon city their natural refuge when the rest of Italy was almost completely subjected to foreigners.

Two Tuscans of genius, Pietro Aretino and Jacopo Sansovino, would assume, above all others, a prominent role in the culture of the time.

These, together with Titian and the publisher Marcolini, and under Gritti's aegis, would give life to a virtual "tetrarchy" destined to dominate the political, cultural, and artistic life of the city with the complete realization of that heroic ideal of the Renaissance that in this period permeated and exalted Venetian civilization.

More than ever before, Venice was now conscious of being the legitimate heir of the recently defeated Rome and Florence. She had to represent then, not only herself, but all of Italian Renaissance civilization.

Gritti, more than anyone else, favored the inundation of triumphant Romanism that would dominate the culture of the humanists and artist of the period.

The "heroic ideal" was dressed in classic guise directly inspired by Imperial Rome whereas, before Cambrai, there had been an appeal to the Hellenistic graces or to the philological rigor of Paduan archeology.

A similar classical exaltation had a profound influence on the villa movement which, draping itself in Roman culture, took advantage of every surviving souvenir of the classical world. It ennobled itself in comparisons with the world of antiquity. It gave life to a natural philosophy of pagan inspiration. But above all it had faith in its own mission in the history of mankind.

The rivers:
arteries of the Venetian penetration onto the mainland

Beyond the defensive and urbanistic restructuring of the cities after Cambrai, the Serenissima committed itself to the administrative reorganization of the commercial routes that crossed its entire territory. As a city of merchants, Venice was always preoccupied with the control of the highways and rivers along which her merchandise passed. Such a policy often brought her into conflict with countries on her borders, like Ferrara (and hence with the Pope), with whom she contended for control of the Po river. In fact, the rivers had been, since ancient times, the principal route for the extension of the Serenissima's commercial traffic.

Expert as they were in every sort of navigation, the Venetians found that the waterways provided more rapid and economical ways of communication. They had a constant commitment to supervise their efficiency and to construct a system of bases and markets along the rivers.

In the preceding centuries the expansion into the Po area had prevalently commercial ends, but after Cambrai the waterways became the arteries which kept alive every sort of communication between the pulsing heart of Venice and the rest of the dominion, right down to the most distant villages.

The Venetian expansion was now animated by a new spirit, a "Roman" spirit which coordinated and rationalized everything, gradually giving the mainland a new appearance. New ports, larger or smaller according to necessity, were constructed and developed in ever increasing numbers along the rivers. Together with arriving or departing merchandise, Venetian officials disembarked in the river ports, bringing a sense of organization along with orders from the capital.

Villas began to appear along the riverbanks as outposts of a new territorial structure long before they were built on the roads. No villa stands more than a few hundred meters from a waterway sufficiently deep, at least in flood, for the transport of necessities.

Many of these villas turned their façades to the river. There were famous villas like those of Palladio at Bagnolo and Malcontenta, where from the loggia one could greet the arrival of an illustrious guest by water. Mills and factories multiplied along the rivers; settlements became denser, and villages were formed. The river became a necessary appendage and a continuation of the city.

The villa did not benefit solely from the river's utilitarian aspect, but also derived a certain decorum and "pleasantness," embellishing itself with attractive landing stages, fish ponds, fountains, and grottos. Water was always understood as a symbol of wealth and abundance, and if a villa were erected a long way from a river (in which case both villa and lands lost a part of their value), the owner took care to divert a stream for ornament and pleasure and then to make a canal and cistern for utility's sake. But rivers and canals were not only means of communication or aspects of a villa's ornament, they were also essential for the waters draining away in reclamation projects and to bring water for the irrigation of agriculture. The Veneto plain was in a miserable condition in the first decades of the sixteenth century because of the frequent flooding that submerged vast areas, reducing them to unproductive and unhealthy swamps. The need for reclamation had already been urgent in the past. Dante recalled the enormous works carried out by the Paduans "to defend their villas and their castles..." For the same reason Francesco Petrarch praised the Da Carrara for having liberated the valleys in the Euganean hills from stagnant waters. The Della Scala, the Este, and the Gonzaga also rendered themselves praiseworthy with similar undertakings. Even in central Italy, many villas rose on reclaimed land such as La Petraia, where Palla Strozzi had carried out the reclamation. But it was primarily in Lombardy and through Lombard workmen that the most advanced systems of hydraulic science (one of the greater Arab accomplishments) were spread among us.

Once the mainland had been reconquered after Cambrai, even Venice interested itself in the regulation of its territory's waters. She was able to profit from the experience gained over centuries in the lagoons where the conservation of the extremely delicate equilibrium between water and land had always been a primary preoccupation.

Every intervention in Venetian hydraulics depended directly on specific magistracies bearing

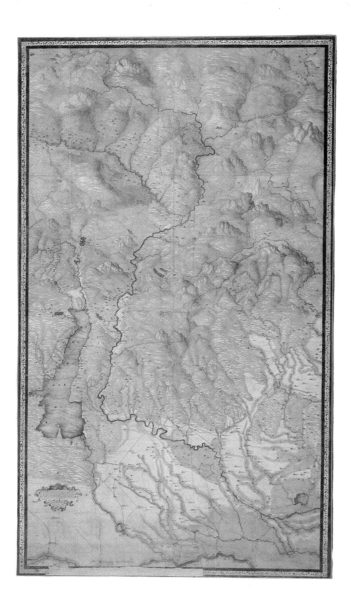

already recorded in 1505. There were studies and
reports on individual "*retratti*" or hydraulic
regulations and on the ordering of the rivers. The
first report by Alvise Cornaro appeared in 1541
and is fundamentally important for understanding
the *World of the Villas.*

The establishment of the *Magistrato sopra i
beni inculti* in 1556 was a consequence of all these
initiatives. There were precedents for it which went
back to 1545 with the institution of the *Tre
provveditori sopra lochi inculti del Dominio e sopra
l'adacquazioni dei terreni.*

All that had been done in Brescian territory,
(also part of the Serenissima's dominion) was
of fundamental and exemplary importance in the
history of reclamation and the improvement of
agriculture, and without it the *World of the Villas*
could never have been born. Experience derived
from contact with modern reclamation projects in
Lombardy was spread over all the Veneto by
Brescian technicians, especially after the sacking
of their city by the armies of the League of Cambrai
in 1511. At first the lessons of Brescian reclamation
influenced bordering regions like that of Verona.
Fra' Giocondo, who came from Verona, had been
invited by the Venetian Senate to prepare a project
for regulating the waters of the Bacchiglione near
Limena, a crucial point in Venetian hydrography
where later Sabbadino and Sansovino worked.
Another Veronese, Sanmicheli, was occupied with
similar problems, writing to the Senate about the
regulation of the waters of the Musole river, which
was silting up near Treville, creating marsh land
conditions. And it was precisely at Treville that
Sanmicheli erected the Villa Soranza, one of the
first modern villas in the region. In the Veneto,
however, the problem of reclamation was
particularly complex. On the one hand, there was
need to free the mainland countryside from
marshes by channeling the waters into "*retratti*" in
order to make them flow smoothly to the sea, while
on the other hand, it was important not to
compromise the equilibrium of the lagoon, which
might be threatened by the increased discharge
of silt and waste brought to the sea by the rivers
and canals. The lagoon was sacred and inviolable
for Venice because it was the primary source
of the city's existence and history.

different names (*del Piovego, delle Acque,* etc.) but
always equipped with immense authority and
financial means superior to those of any other
magistracy. The first references go back to remote
times. There were provisions in 1231, in 1328, etc.,
without speaking of the many decisions taken in
the course of the fifteenth century.

The most ancient magistrates took the name
Officiales supra canales and *Officiales paludum.*
The institution of the first *Collegio delle Acque* was

Alvise Cornaro
and the generation
of the "founding fathers"

These problems were at the center of the thinking of Alvise Cornaro. His teaching emphasized land reclamation and "holy agriculture" as the way to stimulate Venice. This was accepted with enthusiasm by the many rich "provincials" who constituted the base of a way of life, no longer tied to the sea and trade, but rather to the land and to agriculture.

The capital regarded the mainland with increasing interest because of the mainland's own original contributions. Alvise Cornaro became the most important spokesman of this new interest. At first his solutions met with indifference, incomprehension, and even with opposition from the most conservative Venetians yet it was thanks to Cornaro that the "Venetian capital was invested in the acquisition of landed property and sundry reclamation projects," becoming the foundation for future stability.

Cornaro's example and urgings finally led the Serenissima to establish that *Magistrato sopra i beni inculti,* which was the basis of the Venetians' new political economy. It also represented the decisive and most representative period for understanding the true significance, the basis and the timeless success of the Veneto villas.

Cornaro had learned from his family's experience with commercial failure that, despite his own claims to the most illustrious Venetian noble descent, it was not at sea, but in agriculture that prosperity and the future of the state should be sought. Once he had made himself rich, Cornaro sought and found the support and, in a manner of speaking, the ideal justification for the excellent results of his own personal experience in the classical culture that had always had one of its principal bastions in Padua. "The accepted practice that recognized agriculture as the sole legitimate and honorable activity for a free man" seemed valid to Cornaro as well.

"Whoever is wise should leave the ship
And settle on the land to live in peace,"
wrote Andrea Calmo. Cornaro recounts, "The fact that my ancestors were Senators and Princes availed me nothing. I had to acquire the advantages of nobility in my own country. Even though my family had been extremely wealthy I acquired all that I was born without. And I acquired it all in the best and most laudible way, that of "holy agriculture" and not by recourse to arms and harm to others, nor by means of sailing the sea with its infinite dangers to life and limb, nor by other dangerous ways. I acquired all in the only honorable way."

Moving from the lagoon to Padua, Alvise Cornaro was following the example of his maternal uncle Angelieri, a canon of the church who dabbled in architecture and who advanced himself along with Barozzi, the Bishop of Padua. But Alvise distinguished himself from his uncle by his sense of social responsibility and his much more profound interest in culture.

The solidity and extent of his interests were a part of the nature of his Paduan surroundings where an open and pragmatic spirit viewed the University as the center of the most advanced studies. There, where Copernicus had studied and where the unprejudiced teaching of Pietro Pomponazzi was welcomed, scientific research developed freely (freedom of investigation was guaranteed by the laws of the Serenissima), culminating in the new scientific anatomy studies of Andrea Vesalio.

But Fra' Giocondo could also be Cornaro's true master. Like him, Cornaro combined the competence of an hydraulic engineer and reclamation expert with a talent for the arts, which made him one of the principal protagonists of the history of architecture in the Veneto. Cornaro had derived from Verona (particularly through Fra' Giocondo's teaching) the sense of a serene and balanced architecture, otherwise quite exceptional in the Veneto. And from Verona he wished to take the architect Gian Maria Falconetto to Padua as a collaborator in the building projects that he was planning for his properties. As a writer and patron, Cornaro loved to surround himself with "men of fine intellect", forming that which could be considered a true "Academy."

"I take pleasure," Cornaro wrote "in visiting friends, being with them and discussing with them and with those whom I find with them: architects, painters, sculptors, musicians and agriculturalists; men of fine intellect who abound in this age. I see their works newly finished: palaces, gardens and collections of antiques..." Agriculturalists were also included in this "ideal academy of men of fine intellect."

"Even humanism," Cian wrote "eminently practical and positive in a Roman sense, becomes a vital action, a coefficient of life in a people born to act... The new studies, which in other regions awakened phantoms and ruinous fetishes, were here understood only in the measure of the benefits that they could bring to the nation. Whereas elsewhere there was upset and fatal dissension, the Venetians found an accord between life and the culture reborn from antiquity; between study and the contemplative life; between the *otium* or leisure and the active life, the *negotium*." These words describe the environment of Cornaro and his friends particularly well. In one or another of the villas, they held convivial literary reunions with performances of comedies and music, but also with reports and discussions of a practical order: the latest novelties in cultivation methods, architectural styles, or the iconography of frescoes. These were the themes that appeared most often in their poetry and prose, reflecting that happy moment when so many of those who could be considered the "patres" or founding fathers of the *World of the Villas* were united.

The meetings directed by Cornaro certainly gave primary importance to the best and most worthy means for solving problems connected with agriculture, building, and decoration. Arcadia, with its choruses of satyrs and nymphs, was somewhat out of place in such a passionate and vital atmosphere. Trissino and Serlio, with all their utopias and culture, seem anemic in comparison with Alvise's concrete vision. However, such was not the case with Palladio who in his "Books" on architecture seems to have given substance to Cornaro's ideals.

It was precisely Cornaro's friends who favored Palladio's work. They were the contemporaries of the great architect and fathers of those noble patrons who intended to interpret with the creation of their villas the ideals of their parents as founder of the family. We read in the *Four Books of Architecture* that many of the villas, such as those at Montagnana, Campiglia, and Quinto Vicentino, for example, were made not for the present owner, but after the explicit desire of his father, one of

those noble friends of whom Alvise Cornaro spoke: agriculturalists, men of letters, and even architects, splendid "dilettantes."

The fortunate moment of this "civilization" did not find its only expression in architecture. Even the "Petrarchism" of Cornaro's circle assumed a serious and committed tone and in Ruzzante's *Epistole* Petrarch recalled his experiences of rural life, struggling against the marshes to create a new plantation.

And this is what the venerated Petrarch said: "And he said to me: these are the Euganean hills which are so loved by your noble lords because they have freed them of marshland, bringing them under cultivation."

Alvise Cornaro's social conscience – as self-interested as it may have been – was always of decisive importances clothing his works with ethical and religious significance. Speaking of his lands at Codevigo, he explained what he and his uncle Angelieri achieved after so many years: "And thanks to God one finds it now well inhabited. Before it was not so because it was all marshy and stagnant. Snakes were better off there than men. But having taken away the waters, the air improved and men came to settle and began to multiply so as to bring the place to the perfection in which you see it today. I can truly say that thus I gave to God an altar and a place here for a temple with souls for His adoration."

Even though Alvise Cornaro took inspiration from Rome in external appearances and in the spirit of organization and in the nobility of his enterprises, it was through a Christian spirit that he conveyed a concept of communal life quite different from that of antiquity. The Veneto "gentleman" considered his peasants in a familiar way as distinct from the Roman of the *latifonda*, participating with them in the principal events that marked life in the villa during the year. When Cornaro presented himself as a ancient priest or as a biblical prophet renewing with his people the sacredness of an ancient festivity, elements derived from the Roman legacy are joined with the Christian tradition. He himself described the ceremony in which he, vested in a Roman military cloak, recited the mythical fable of the Golden Age with his peasants.

Compared with the villas of other regions, the humanizing process evident in every phase of Venetian history is characteristic of the Veneto villa. And this is not so simply for humanitarian reasons, but rather because the peasants who, at the time of Cambrai proved their loyalty to St. Mark, were now equally valuable and indispensible for improving the economic situation in the entire region.

Angelo Beolco, called Ruzzante, was a valuable witness to many aspects of this situation. "A man who perpetrates a villainy is not someone who lives in a villa, but rather a villain," said one of his characters, paraphrasing Cornaro in *Reduce.*

The old antagonism between the city and the country seemed to enjoy a truce at this time. Indeed the most interesting aspect of Ruzzante's great innovation was that the country was not presented to us from the landlord's point of view by the extraordinary Paduan writer as is the case in almost all the other historical and literary sources that we know, but from below, specifically from the point of view of the peasants who lived in the same environment where the villas are born. Naturally Beolco speaks of Alvise Cornaro, his friends, and their ideals of villa life with great respect. "I shall tell you. Those are called good men who, according to their rank and talents, know how to dispense their goodness honorably; who have increased rather than diminished their talents; and who take pleasure in building and bringing valleys and woods under cultivation. They have enough friends to give them aid when they are in need. They favor the virtuous of every class and condition. Above all they are happy men and *not melancholic."*
However, the enthusiasms of Cornaro and his friends were also reflected in the peasants' way of thinking and in their concept of life. Ruzzante confirmed this for us. Bertevello, a character in the *Piovana,* founds a treasure and in a dream, seeing himself rich, spoke thus: "I'd like to be a gentleman. I'd go happily throughout the Po valley buying land and properties. I'd make a house with solid walls. I'd get married, make children, and bring along my relations so that the Bertiviegi would be the first farming family in the Po valley. I'd buy enough land. Instead of a house I'd build a villa which everyone would describe as the *villa de Bertevello."*

A moral conscience developed from the political and economic movement that produced the villas as soon as the first fruits were gathered in, filling all those who had participated in it with

pride and satisfaction. There was an ambition, widespread among many, to do good for the state. There was the just satisfaction of having brought dignity and power to the family, always considered the highest of all aims, and to have accumulated, thanks to fortune and providence, an impressive patrimony. There was the great joy of giving life and beauty to a squalid and ruined landscape through reclamation.

But socio-economic programs and ethical committment were not the only forces to guide and sustain Cornaro and his partners. An outspoken aesthetic criteria directed their every move, be it in their lives as gentlemen who intended to live in a dignified fashion, or in the works conceived and promoted by them as a reflection of, testimony to their very ideals.

The reclamation projects carried out by Cornaro, at least as far as he himself specified, had the merit of making areas of marshland "once ugly, beautiful." Always guided by aesthetic considerations inherited from Fra' Giocondo and Valla, he declared in a another passage from the *Vita Sobria,* "I enjoy traveling above all, going and returning to where I can observe the beauty of places and countries which I visit in passing. Some on the plain, some in the hills, near rivers or springs, often with many beautiful buildings and gardens around them." Vasari described him as "a gentleman of an excellent judgment." Alvise Cornaro delighted in architecture, proving himself as the builder of Falconetto's work. It is still not clear where the participation of Falconetto ended in the works commissioned by Cornaro. It is certain that in his paintings, now displayed in Verona at the Castelvecchio, and in some of his isolated works like the Padua gates, there are disproportions and an architectonic insensitivity that cannot be found in the elegant Cornaro Loggia and Odeon. In the *Four Books of Architecture* Palladio claimed that Cornaro himself was the architect. The publisher Marclini said even more explicitly in the preface to Scamozzi's *Treatise,* "And if a gentleman or other private person wants to know how buildings are built in the cities, let him come to the Cornaro house in Padua. Should he wish to build a villa, let him go to Codevigo and to Campagna. Who seeks to make a princely palace, should go to Luvigliano."

Like the most worthy men of antiquity, Cornaro asked of life all the joys that it could offer. For this reason, he enjoyed his "suburban villa" located near the Basilica del Santo at Padua, his utilitarian one built in the middle of his farmland at Codevigo, and that one reserved for "relaxation" and for hunting situated amid Este's pleasant hills.

While today we can still admire the Paduan buildings, the Loggia and the Odeon, as conspicuous examples of the most balanced teaching of contemporary Roman architectonic culture, there remains of the Este villa only a harmonious and refined triumphal arch known as the *Arco Benvenuti.* But among all the buildings erected by Cornaro, it is the complex at Codevigo that more than any other merits the term "villa" in the sense that we recognize today as applicable to the Veneto villas. With the landlord's house as its centre composition were appropriate to agriculture.

Today it seems that the mediocre and insignificant village church is the only remnant of Cornaro's presence at Codevigo. His uncle Alvise Angelieri was buried in the church of Codevigo. It was he whom Cornaro considered the renovator of his clan, having had the symbolic role of confirming to his family the possession of recently reclaimed land.

In this he evidently wished to follow Venetian practice when they buried their early doges at San Nicolò del Lido, at Sant'Ilario, and at San Benedetto, in order to encourge the defense of those border areas sanctified by the tombs of their loved ones.

The tradition and the cult of tombs are often fundamentally important for understanding the continuity of villa buildings, situated in what otherwise might seem the least suitable areas. However, these areas assumed a precise significance because they were linked to the survival of the ancestral spirit. Cornaro's example became emblematic as far as the world of life in the villas was concerned.

"I pass my time," he wrote, "in the greatest delight and pleasure at all hours because I find I frequently have the opportunity to converse with honored gentlemen, with men of great intellect, men of fine manners and of letters: excelling in every virtue. And when I do not have their conversation, I set myself to reading some good book. And when I have read enough, I write. In all this I seek to please others to the limits of my abilities.

All these things I do in their own good time and in greatest comfort in my rooms, which are located in the best neighborhood of this noble and learned city of Padua. I built them on the principles of architecture which teach us how it should be done. Beyond this I take pleasure in my various gardens and with the running waters that flow nearby. I always find something there to delight me.

I have yet another means of relaxation to which I resort in April and May and also in September and October. For several days at a time I enjoy a hill of mine situated in the most beautiful part of the Euganean hills. There are springs and gardens and above all a fine and comfortable room where I relax after the easy and pleasant hunting I permit myself at my age. I delight in my villa on the plain for just as many days. It is beautified by the number of handsome streets which meet in a fine square with a church in the middle. Given the possibilities of the place, it is a well-maintained building. The beauty of the location is also enhanced by a broad and fast-flowing stretch of the Brenta river which divides the property. The large areas of land on either side are fertile with well-cultivated fields."

Beyond his merits as an hydraulic engineer, as a writer, as a patron and architect, that which best defines Alvise Cornaro's character and his social and historic importance was his idea for a *Magistrato ai beni inculti.* It is for this that he may be considered the founder of the *World of the Veneto Villas.* He did not limit his experience to the private sector, but through his political activities he made himself the link between the state and individual proprietors, between the capital and the mainland. According to the typically Venetian spirit which Alvise Cornaro personified, individual initiative should be accompanied by a collective, integral commitment, leading to a central coordination and working to help rationalize the structure of the region.

It was Alvise Cornaro, acting as a private individual, who urged the Serenissima to pledge a commitment to land reclamation and the agricultural improvement of the whole Veneto territory. "Of 800,000 *campi* in the districts of Treviso, Padua, Verona and the Polesine," he wrote bitterly, "200,000 are marshland." And he concludes: "The *Signoria* has the obligation to transform its lands from the ugly into the beautiful, from a melancholy aspect to a good and healthy, and from fallow to cultivated."

It was primarily thanks to him that in 1556 the republic created that magistracy that undertook all the reclamation work, giving the region an appearance that distinguished it from all others.

Reclamation and the
Magistrato ai beni inculti

Following the *Terminazione del Magistrato dei beni inculti* or the "Termination of the Magistracy of Uncultivated Properties" of June 30, 1563 and the publication of the *Piano generale per la sistemazione e regolarizzazione di tutte le acque scorrenti fra i Colli Berici e gli Euganei* or the "General plan for the ordering and regulation of all the waters flowing between the Berican Hills and the Euganean Hills," provision was made for as many consortia as there were rivers to control. An overall integral plan, based on the altimetry of the territory, coordinated the flow of the rivers, the drainage of ditches, and the irrigation of land endangered by drought. With a complicated system of sluice gates, dykes, and raised beds, the waters began to follow a course determined by man. The marshes were dried while dry lands were furnished with the water necessary to guarantee constant harvests. "It is with great pleasure and

Hydraulic machine (Fra' Giocondo, M. Vitruvius, per locandum solito castigator factus cum figuris et tabula ut iam legi et intellegi possit, Venice 1511).

contentment," Cornaro wrote in the first discourse of the *Vita Sobria,* «that I see the success of an undertaking so important to this state as bringing so much uncultivated land under cultivation. And this begun because of my reminders. Knowing that great undertakings are usually begun late by republics, I never thought I would see it carried out in my life. Yet I have seen it and I personally have

been here in the marshy area with those elected to take charge during the summer's greatest heat."

To have an idea of the spirit in which the Venetians set about the great works of reclamation, we read in the *Parti prese dall'eccellentissimo Senato in materie de' beni inculti,* the "Senate debates on the subject of uncultivated lands," report number 21: "That in the Moncelese network the procedure should be of three orders in imitation of our Lord God who, in the making of the world, first divided the skies from chaos; then separated the land from the water; and finally had the earth give birth to specific things: animals, trees, and grain. Thus each network can be completed in three stages. The first, bringing the waters up out of the earth..."

There was an ever increasing amount of the land available for agriculture thanks to reclamation. This was constantly improved through the introduction and increased production of new crops, such as corn and mulberry trees, and the adoption of systems of crop rotation that provided for a more rational exploitation of the soil.

Industrial activities were strengthened (thanks to the large amounts of money coming to Venice, during the war, from all the Venetian trading posts), favoring the manufacturing specialities of each territory–arms at Brescia, textile working and silver at Vicenza, silk in the Friuli, hemp in the Verona area and wool at Padua, as can be seen in the allegories of each province which artists painted for the public palaces of the capital and the state.

Political functions, craft workmanship, and industry are reflected in the types and the location of buildings, each of which reveals its significance through the choice and application of structural and decorative elements.

Thus what had happened many centuries earlier with the birth of Venice herself materialized on the mainland. A new city was born, the *City of the Villas.* Just as the deserted beaches of the lagoon were populated with ever grander and prouder buildings, so the desert land of the mainland reclaimed and brought under cultivation was peppered with villas. In a short time the whole of the Veneto assumed the aspect of a marvelous organism, with stupendous buildings like royal palaces, placed in the center of vast farmlands.

Palladio

"He was especially pleasant and entertaining in conversation and greatly delighted the lords with whom he dealt as well as the laborers he employed, who always were kept happy and working contentedly by his many pleasantries. He took great joy in teaching them with much charity, all the proper terms of the Art, in such a way that there was no bricklayer, stone dresser or joiner who did not know all the movements, parts, and all the true terms of Architecture" (Paolo Gualdo, Vita di Andrea Palladio, 1617)

Many of the characteristics typical of the villa world were already defined by Cornaro's day, but only with Palladio did these reach full maturity. Despite representing the noble forms of classicism, the villas of Cornaro, Sanmicheli, and Sansovino were singular, isolated episodes. Palladio's villas, on the other hand, summarized and spiritually elevated all the multiple and complex components considered up to now, translating ancient and modern aspirations and ideals into urbaned and architectonic terms.

They interpreted the peculiarities of the site and the patron's requirements with an absolute equilibrium without diminishing their fundamental and unmistakeable stylistic and poetic unity. Because these villas taken together were the expression of a great and complex movement, they seemed to share uniform characteristics throughout the vast territory. They were no longer "exceptions," but models that could be realized and exported outside the Veneto and even outside Italy.

The work of Palladio, the definitive consummation of all the preceding periods, was built on a substratum of political and economic factors as well as social and cultural considerations. But whoever judges Palladio's lesson solely in terms of his architectural proportions and forms – the erudite abstractions of a brilliant architect – and sees them solely as models of absolute beauty has not taken into account that these buildings, removed from the natural context for which they were created, would seem dried up and deprived of the roots that tie them deeply and inextricably to the climate, the landscape, and the history of the place. As Ackerman observed, only those who have never visited the Veneto can reduce Palladio in the formulas of the classicists to the role of theorist in the *Four Books.* Palladio was also "a magician of light and color, the Veronese of architecture." It was precisely "this synthesis of sensual and intellectual elements" that explains the success of his genius in different countries and epochs, even though the eighteenth-century purist reaction attempted to fix him within their rigid scheme of eternal law.

In addition one can not underestimate the fact that Palladio's villas rendered concretely the ideals of an epoch important for the West. In one of the most significant aspects of Palladio's vision of the world, the villa seems to be the complete expression of the Renaissance. The Veneto villa represented the arrival of a revolution that had put an end to a medieval concept of the significance of man's life. Christianity had preached scorn for the gifts of life for centuries. It had taught men to value each thing with regard for its moral value and to consider the entire universe exclusively in relation to religion, thus minimizing the works and aspirations of man. The permissible artistic creations were collective works (cathedrals, municipal palaces) more than the work of single artists. Their function was that of exalting God or else the social structure considered as a divine emination.

In the people's imagination the forests, the springs, and the country were all populated with malignant spirits who haunted classical ruins, the surviving testimony of pagan antiquity. Even though they loved antiquity passsionately during the humanist movement, men regarded it as an inimitable, remote Golden Age. Even in the erudite poem *Poliphilo,* the ancient world appeared fantastic. The author did not consider himself worthy of reviving it except as a dream, a fable or a fantasy. But when the "new man" regains full faith in himself, when he recognizes the value of history and honors those who in the past have behaved in a memorable way, then he will learn to have reputation, fame, and secular glory as his ideal goal. To give continuity to his passage on earth beyond the limits of mortal life, man will then begin to appreciate his ancestors. He will commit himself to increasing the prestige of his ancestry, convinced that he will survive through his sons and the sons of his sons who will safeguard and continue his works. And he will assign to poets and artists – now emerging from the anonymity of the religious orders and the craftsman's workshop – the job of immortalizing his ideals. Finally he will see that architecture constructs the *monumentum* as a witness to itself and through which he will continue to communicate spiritually with men. Buildings are not, therefore, destined to glorify God as in the past but are intended to magnify the virtues of one's own family and to give form and expression to one's own genius. The place where this new man is

61

born or rather which he, as a true demiurge, has redeemed and ennobled, is identified through him. It becomes his ideal native land: a land that often assumes his and his family's name, thus contributing to and perpetuating their fame.

Without wishing to follow a rigid scheme inapplicable to Palladio's work, one can describe a division of architectonic types which takes the patrons into consideration. Thus "the villas in the first, unadorned style, lacking columned porticos," such as the Villa Godi at Lonedo, were constructed for Vicentine noblemen, while the villas formed of a two-story block, like the Malcontenta, and that with a single floor with long wings, like the Villa Badoer at Fratta Polesine, were ordered by Venetian nobles.

In the same way, the Rotonda was repeated at Meledo for the Trissino, who were also Vicentine patrons, while the Villa Serego, which remains unique in Palladio's oeuvre, is evidently linked to the culture of the Veronese noblemen who commissioned it.

The love of the "new man" for his lands expressed itself in a problematic way with regard to the care he dedicated to the villa, the seat of his pleasure and the heart of his world.

With respect to the first villas that the humanists erected among the gardens of the Giudecca and Murano or along the rivers of the Treviso province, the Venetian "gentleman" did not think solely of the beauty of these "terrestrial paradises" idealized by the Petrarchan tradition. Fantasy and fortune, consciousness of history and the virtues all converged to create a new interpretation of the world. The "total vision" that existed in Palladio's villas combined "beauty" and "utility" in harmonic symbiosis, thus superseding Leonardo's memorable judgment. In a passage of his *Italian Journey,* Wolfgang Goethe noticed the presence of two components in Palladio: that of a solidity based on history and that of idealism. According to Goethe, the poetic essence, the real fascination of Palladian art, was born from the coexistence and equilibrium of these two components. It is precisely this solidity that freed Palladio from rigid classicism. The first years of his life were particularly important in this regard. The origins of Andrea di Pietro della Gondola were

rather humble. Even his artistic training was of a modest and essentially practical character, taking place in stonecutters' workshops, first in Padua and then in Vicenza.

The essence of his poetic spirit already had its roots in the youth he spent in Padua, the city of Cornaro, where classical culture was based simultaneously on "*experientia*" and on "*scientia*" – theory and practice.

Literature, agriculture, military technique, and archeology all found expression in treatises that allowed men to participate in a climate of fervid experimentation, creating the desire to communicate knowledge through concrete example. It was the period when a new ethic was born and spread abroad, no longer the medieval sort, but one that considered men capable of marvelous things, capable of understanding the supreme rational order that permeates creation. Religion was humanized in this way, with man feeling the need for a continual uplifting. This process of "humanization," which always characterized civilization in the Veneto, can be said to have found its best realized examples in the Palladian villas. The role which Palladio reserved for his patrons demonstrated this. He felt the villa must offer the patron a virtually complete portrait of the wealth, nobility, culture, and prestige of those who had ordered it. In *The Four Books of Architecture* he illustrated his architectonic undertakings while at the same time extolling his patrons. Conscious of their dignity, he offered them a way to glorify themselves. "And why it is convenient that one should say something about that which will be consonant with the quality of him who will inherit. Its parts should correspond to the whole and to each other. But above all the architect should take warning (as Vitruvius says in his first and sixth book) that grand gentlemen, the greatest of the republic, will require houses with loggias and spacious and ornate rooms so that they can entertain those who await the master to greet him or beg some help or favor. For lesser gentlemen, lesser buildings are seemly, costing less

*Andrea Palladio, Fontispiece
of* I Quattro Libri
dell'Architettura *(Venice,
1570).*

and with fewer adornments. For lawyers and advocates one should build in such a way that their houses have pleasant, decorated places to walk in so that clients may remain there without tedium. The houses of merchants should have places facing the north where merchandise can be stored in such a way that the landlord need not fear burglars."

We can already see, in these phrases of Palladio, the distinctions drawn between various types of patrons, distinctions that correspond to various types of villa to be built.

Andrea della Gondola, Gian Giorgio Trissino's favorite and protege, found the perfect atmosphere for his training in Vicenza. It was there that, ennobled even in name as Palladio, he made his official entry into the most refined society. The explanation for this lies in his earliest experiences. If Palladio had not formed his "spirit" in the archeological and classicizing atmosphere of Padua, then neither Trissino nor the ambitious Vicentine nobility would have considered him one of them. "I will be held to have been very fortunate having found such noble, generously spirited gentlemen of excellent judgment to believe in my arguments and willing to depart from the old way of building without grace and without any beauty whatsoever."

Vicenza, for its part, contributed the chivalrous and humanistic atmosphere of its perisistent feudalism to Palladio's development. Reading only one of the Vicentine tales, that of Marzari, one finds constant mention of warriors and soldiers. From the Pojana to the Trissino, from the Repeta to the Da Porto, from the Thiene to the Trento and the Valmarana, there was a military atmosphere that contributed to the spread through the province of heroic and courtly attitudes rather unusual in the republic's other territories.

The proud warlike spirit of the Vicentine nobles expressed itself particularly in the ambitious architecture with which they liked to surround themselves. As Marzari recalls, Ottavio Thiene "captain in the armies of Henry II displayed his brilliance in battle... Returned home, he had proud and marvelous buildings made both in and outside Vicenza. They could be compared with those of any great prince" These continual comparisons with the deeds of "great princes" and emperors which the literature of panegyric continually

offered was not without significance for Vicenza.

To satisfy the requirements of the Vicentine families, Andrea Palladio constructed palaces in the city and villas scattered in a countryside that, not long before, had been rich in towers and castles. The souvenirs of these were revived in the prestige of Palladio's art forms. The artist did not remain entrapped in Trissino's narrow circle but, increasing the number of his patrons, gave a vast scope and new possibilities of expression to his art in a series of directions that extend from the Villa Cricoli to the Rotonda.

He also made himself into the spokesman of that Roman spirit that pervaded the "myth of Venice" as well as the heroic ideal of the Renaissance. Just like his compatriot Mantegna, Palladio, a miller's son, rose through all the levels of the social scale to become not only the architect and consultant to the most noble families, but also the heir of Sansovino as the principal architect of the Venetian state.

The artist was formed first as a "modern" man and he approached architecture, associating himself with the ancient world, not in order to reflect it like a mirror, but to capture spirit and apply it in a "modern" way. Palladio traced that vaguely anthropomorphic hierarchy of parts that inspired his architecture back to antiquity. Thus the central part "corresponds to the head and to the torso of the human body while the axis of symmetry corresponds to the spine." In the villas this hierarchy established the predominance of the residential building over the wings of the *barchesse* or outbuildings. A more elegant Ionic order was chosen for the principal architecture while the Tuscan order usually characterized the other. But organic nature was not discernable in Roman houses and villas. The Romans used free plans for private dwellings. In fact Palladio was able to find the inspiration for his dream of classicism only in public buildings and especially in the Imperial baths. Palladio sketched Roman ruins with great fidelity on the spot, while in his studio he "reconstituted them into a rigorously Palladian scheme" following the three rules recorded by Ackerman: hierarchy; integration of the parts through proportion; and the coordination of the interiors with the exterior through the projection of the internal form onto the façade.

The antique world was not, for Palladio, a model from which to take various architectural motifs, but rather an ideal in which the new "religion" of his era could be recognized. His architecture was permeated with this ideal, which he brought into existence with the spirit of a true "demiurge".

It was only natural that his gifts revealed themselves particularly in villa architecture, where spaces were more ample and freer. Palladio designed like an urban planner. "The city is nothing more than a particular enormous house, while a house is a small city." Thus, in contrast to the architects of the early Renaissance who designed for aggregation rather than integration, he conceived of the entire villa building with its various functions of the useful and the beautiful as an organic entity, closely linked with nature, seen both as a landscape setting and as agricultural land.

All of this was supported by laws of harmony,

The Roman Theater at Berga.

Even before Palladio's all-important visits to Rome, he had had the opportunity to study the ancient arts, developing that taste for the classical which would be such an essential component in his work. He was able to study the ruins of the Roman theater at Berga, one of the most important archeological monuments in the Veneto, whose last remains were completely obliterated at the beginning of the Settecento. Mentioned in various parts of the Quattro Libri, *the theater at Berga provided Palladio with invaluable information and inspiration, allowing him to reconstruct the typology and important characteristics of the theatrical buildings of ancient Rome. Furthermore, an intimate acquaintance with extremely refined statuary, which can still be seen at the Vicenza Civil Museum, undoubtedly influenced the architect a great deal, encouraging him to break free from the closed world of the province, and helping create in him a nature which was extremely sensitive and receptive to the spirit of classical culture.*

according to the proportional relationship that extended into the third dimension and that can be considered "harmonic" in a narrow sense, associated with musical theory. Palladio's naturalism was rationalism, a research carried out in the laws that regulate life, as distinct from Michelangelo's naturalism, which was rigorously biomorphic and alien to mathematical abstractions and, as Ackerman observed, where architecture was understood virtually as a living body. It was precisely this rational and abstract aspect of his

work that was the source of his success in nordic countries.

On the other hand, the fact of his having been trained in the "stonecutter's craft," and having tasted and experienced every sort of material, never hurt his art, but rather prevented him from becoming excessively abstract. His working methods and the healthy relationship that he enjoyed with his collaborators and with his best foremen also benefited.

Thus, if on the one hand Palladio's architecture was the expression of pure relationships, in another way it was concrete work that can be appreciated almost like sculpture.

Palladio derived his linearism from remote and subtle Byzantine and Gothic influences, typical of the Veneto traditions, the same influences that Mauro Coducci knew how to transform into harmonious spaces and Renaissance forms. Palladio did not align himself with the Flamboyant Gothic and its festive decoratism or polychromy: his was the line that cut through pure space.

Palladio neglected no stimulus, no suggestion, no historic psychological or literary factor needed to bring his vision to maturity. He welcomed points of departure like castles or "casoni," huts or other agrarian structures. He learned from Vitruvius, Serlio, Alberti, Sansovino, Cornaro, and from Roman ruins – especially those in Vicenza like the Berga theater.

On his travels to Rome he was continually stimulated by the antique monuments that he measured endlessly, as he did those buildings designed by Bramante, Raphael, and Michelangelo. Nonetheless his personality remained independent and autonomous. Thus in his works, he offered a new and concrete point of reference to the architecture of the time with forms that would be recapitulated and would have a vast distribution because they had been humanized in the Veneto fashion. They were neither removed from reality, nor were they archeological exhumations of the sort that could have been created by Mantegna, but rather they were forms that flowed with culture's living streams passing under the aegis of the "myth of Venice" in whose wake the artist placed himself. He was the ideal citizen of Venice during the magical and exultant moment which followed the

65

Peace of Bologna (1529-30) when, Florence and Rome having collapsed, the city reached the peak of its splendor. Palladio belonged to this moment and exalted it with his work.

Although always republican in its institutions, the city was, in reality, set on becoming and acquiring the appearance of a principality. Just as sumptuous palaces were rising up along the canals, for the same reasons, splendid villas belonging to the capitalistic Venetian aristocracy flowered in the "new" countryside. To these were added those belonging to the proud mainland nobility: *Condottieri* or mercenary captains, experts in the military arts, humanists, prelates, rich land owners and nobles from Vicenza, Verona, Treviso, and Padova who little by little became bound together by a common language and by the golden thread of Venetian culture. Their habit of residing for long periods in the provinces in order to administer their properties accustomed them to needs and ideals which they all shared and of which Palladio would be the interpreter.

No one has known how to offer man more dignified dwellings better than he. These men were not just invested with political power but were like demigods at the acme of the heroic ideal, rulers of their world and of life. Palladio made their myth concrete and became the intermediary for an ideal which has stimulated men for centuries.

These ambitious dwellings were not, however, interpreted by the artist in a disproportionate fashion. His villas are never too "aulic." They adapted themselves almost naturally to their environment and to their functions. Even though they were magnificent, they belonged to a wholly Venetian scale. This is because Palladio intended the villa to be a beauty that gave pleasure, like health and the respect for mankind, like profit and work for all, or like nature and art: art as the symbol of man's domination of nature.

The teachings of Venice and its exemplary history were often used as a models by other nations that hoped to achieve the immortality to which the Republic of St. Mark seemed destined. And the Venice that seemed easiest to comprehend was that which identified itself with ancient Rome. Perhaps this explains why Palladian architecture, especially that of the villas, had such a success in England and America. It represented that particularly Venetian humanization and adaptability that succeeds in presenting a utility and convenience available to everyone.

The rediscovery and appreciation of the Veneto landscape, begun at the beginning of the sixteenth century in Giorgione's painting, also found affirmation in another mainland artist, Andrea Palladio. In the one as in the other, we witness the realization of a miracle of harmony that is born of the most varied experiences but that has that unmistakable fascination of an extraordinary freshness.

"Along with truth and fiction, Palladio molds a third element that carries us off," we repeat with Goethe: something divine that in Palladio corresponds to poetry itself.

Kitzinger wrote that in all periods the art of the Veneto and that of Venice in particular seems to be animated by a constant yearning, a yearning for Hellenism that probably goes back to the Byzantine and Ravennate origins of the city: to that fascination with light and space, with precious techniques and beautiful materials, and with that noble refinement that seemed, from Master Paul to Giorgione and Veronese, congenial to the souls of the highest Venetian traditions.

I believe we must consider the most exalted message, the most fascinating idealism of Andrea Palladio's art, in the light of this perennial Hellenism. The most significant example of this art, partly due to Veronese's presence in the decoration, is probably the Villa Barbaro at Maser, where beauty and utility meld together in a perfect expression of harmony. In order to verify that Palladio's abilities adapted themselves to the settings and the patron's requirements, we can linger in the Basso Vicentino, where I was born and which I know in all its aspects. There we shall find evidence of the profound ties that link the Palladian architectonic plan to the ideals of his noble patrons.

The villa of harmony at Maser

The concepts that guided the brilliant Palladian intuition in the realization of the villa at Maser were an ideal of superior harmony, a refined humanistic culture, and a profound link with the natural environment.

The selection of the site was significant above all. The bond between the edifice and its surroundings surpassed the choreography outside of trees and lawns and took root deep in the land from which the "Maser spring" emerged, ceding its name to the villa. This spring, rich in symbolic interpretation, acted as the go-between in an ideal marriage between the human, earthy element and the sky. It became the protagonist of the humanist dream which the Barbaro brothers, refined cultivators of antiquity, transmitted to Palladio.

In a letter written before 1559, Giulia Da Ponte lamented the delayed return to Aquileia of Monsignore Barbaro, who had been kept at Maser by "sweet and delectable pleasures, by his charming gardens and by that divinely beautiful fountain built by him with such marvelous ingenuity and art." Palladio was a profound student of classical architecture, partly thanks to his collaboration with Daniele Barbaro on the illustration and publication of Vitruvius and he undoubtedly sought to interpret the models of antiquity in a modern key. The villa at Maser lent itself wonderfully to his project. The Palladian building extended horizontally half way down the slope, opening onto the green Treviso countryside, almost repeating the gentle rolling of the hills. From the decisively projecting central block, crowned with a classical pediment, stretched two long arcaded wings culminating in picturesque

Andrea Palladio. Villa Barbaro at Maser.

Paolo Veronese. Portrait of a cellist, symbol of Harmony, (Maser, Villa Barbaro).

dovecotes. Ackerman suggested comparing the villa at Maser with a typical Roman villa of the period, such as that which Pirro Ligorio constructed for Cardinal Ippolito d'Este, in order to immediately understand the originality of the Palladian solution. In the Villa d'Este "nature remains confined behind tall retaining walls," almost as if the great official for whom it had been built wished to remain ignorant of country labors. For his noble Venetian patrons Palladio and architecture in which the residential buildings and those destined for agriculture fuse while the entire villa "inserted truly into the country, cordially opens toward its surroundings." The Barbaro were certainly not country folk, but were distinct from Roman nobles closed up in their palaces. Venice's aristocratic families had made their fortune in maritime commerce, and this had given their culture a sense of the practical that was maintained even in their humanistic studies.

This is perhaps one of the keys for understanding the "poverty" of Palladian material. While the patron's residence bestowed nobility on the outbuildings which, even though hierarchicly inferior, were an integral part of the villa, at the same time these rustic additions seemed to transmit their essential simplicity to the main building.

Palladio thus became the greatest interpreter of Veneto culture in the classical mode. And in this sense, it is opportune to recall what Ackerman observed: that Palladio was the first to discover "the unadorned style of the ancients," the buildings that had been built by engineers like the exterior of the Pantheon or like the Baths, which were bare of any decoration.

The central square hall of the villa was the fundamental nucleus of the building, an almost sacred place that provided, in perfect harmony with the patron's ideals, the setting for Paolo Veronese's fresco of *Olympus.* From this room there was direct access to a raised level outside where the Nyphaeum appeared, emerging from the thick vegetation that surrounds the villa. The atmosphere of this area, where the sacred fount of Maser was celebrated, was a profound one. From here burst the jet of perpetual waters that fed and enlivened the place. Palladio himself wrote "the fountain makes a pool that serves as a fish pond. From this, the water flows into the kitchens, and then waters the gardens that are situated to the right and left of the main drive up to the villa. It continues down the gentle slope to form two more fish ponds and watering troughs near the public road and then serves to irrigate the extensive orchard full of excellent fruit trees and other growing things."

The Barbaro's residence is universally famous for the vast cycle of frescoes carried out by Paolo Veronese. Critics have frequently put forward the hypothesis that there had been a disagreement between the painter, whose name is never mentioned in the *Quattro Libri,* and the architect. Yet no other artist could have animated these rooms with figures, decorations, and perspectives so perfectly in harmony with the purity and nobility of the Palladian architecture. Climate, landscape, nature, and human activity all seem wonderfully intertwined and fused together in this villa, one of the highest poetical peaks of Palladian art.

Andrea Palladio and noble patronage in the Basso Vicentino

An effective understanding of Palladian buildings cannot ignore a direct, firsthand experience of the sites or an analysis of the territory's historic and geographic characteristics. My continuous research undertaken in the Basso Vicentino, bordering on the provinces of Verona and Padua, permits me to stand decidedly apart from those that consider Palladian architecture as abstract creations, torn from any contingent reality. I have sought to apply to each of these buildings the phrase that Faccioli found on the walls of the Villa di Ca' Impenta on the outskirts of Vicenza: *Si Cupis Animum Domini Cognoscere Aspice Et Respice Domum,* that is, "if you wish to understand the personality of the patron, observe and consider carefully every aspect of his house." This simple sentence, which seems to paraphrase Saint Jerome writing to a prelate "*Domus tua... quasi in speculum constitua,*" could be considered one of the keys for interpreting Palladian villas. The multiplicity of their aspects leads to the variety of interests and tastes of patrons who, as far as the territory under consideration was concerned, came primarily from a noble class of feudal and military origins. The importance of the role of these nobles,

who turned to Andrea Palladio to build their country residences, has been demonstrated in a significant episode. In his conception of the Villa Trissino at Meledo, the architect, strongly influenced by the boundless ambition of that noble Vicentine family, ended by proposing an absolutely impossible project that did not even take the topography of the site into account. Inspired by the Acropolis-like complexes of the Roman world, disposed on various levels linked by majestic staircases like the Temple of the *Dea Fortuna* at Preneste, the Villa dei Trissino could never have been adapted to the site at Meledo, which was situated on a tiny hill a few meters tall.

However, for Palladio, this was rather an isolated case. Generally the Vicentine architect gave great attention to the characteristics of the site in order to exploit what nature offereed him. At this point it is opportune to observe how the villas that interest us almost all grew up in the area included in a map drawn up in 1567 to show the enormous reclamation project known as the *Retratto di Lozzo.* The Basso Vicentino constituted a point of confluence for various water courses (coming from the territories of Verona and Padua) which created marshland and made thousands of acres unsuitable for cultivation. This unfortunate situation in the three Basso areas obliged them to fight constantly against the waters. The intervention of the Venetians resolved this in the first half of the sixteenth century when the marshes were drained and the rivers that had flowed free and uncontrolled were redirected back into their beds.

We have already seen that the reclamation of the mainland constituted one of the fundamental points of the Venetian political economy in the fifteenth and sixteenth centuries. The principal promotor of this was that same Alvise Cornaro whom we find frequently present in the zone included in the *Retratto di Lozzo.* Naturally all this activity, which required a notable expenditure of funds and great organizational capacity, could only have been brought about by a strong dominating class, the nobility which was considered, as Botero recalls, "the backbone which held the structure of the states upright." Without this solid scaffolding, without this tried and tested structure, it would have been virtually impossible to reorganize the

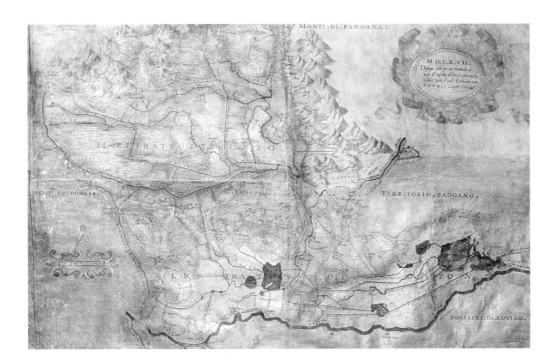

It is said that Thomas Jefferson, the President of the United States, who was a great admirer and imitator of Palladio, took back cuttings of grass and plants from the Colli Berici to Monticello in Vermont, in order to recreate there surroundings similar to those of the Palladian villas. Obviously Thomas Jefferson had understood that in order to revive the art of the great architect it was first of all necessary to try and reconstruct the inseparable unity between monument and Nature.

mainland territories. Even in the territory of Vicenza the country would not have the appearance that it has today without the presence of the nobility. An agricultural vocation and specialized production in certain sectors led to the presence of these patricians in the sixteenth century. The peaceful coexistence of the noble with the peasant was an interesting and very special phenomenon in the Vicentino. The relations between the Repeta family and the community of Campiglia dei Berici document this reality.

The Repeta as feudal lords presided over the sittings of the local council and when it came to putting highways in order, draining marshes, defending the village in difficult legal quarrels, or providing doctors and medicines during epidemics, these local lords undertook to meet all the needs of the population. There can still be seen a tablet in the old town hall at Campiglia inscribed *Venustate Genio et Comodo Comunitatis Camiliae Comites Repeta P/AD/P/ MDCLXXIII.*

The same was true for the church and for other public buildings. *The World of the Veneto Villas* was characterized by a particular modus vivendi: by an osmosis between the noble patrons and the local population. The townsman mentality of the villa builders conditioned the life and mentality of the country folk.

The map of 1567 is quite interesting for understanding the particular geographic situation of the zone and its hydrography. First of all the course of the Canal Bisatto can be seen: its systemization benefited the entire Riviera Berica. Rivers and canals like the Liona, derived from reclamation, the Ronego, L'Alonte, and others were important for the zone.

Andrea Palladio appeared in the Basso Vicentino and in the adjacent "Basse" or lowlands of Padua and Verona with villas which, despite certain characteristics and a common denominator, were clearly different in character.

Our itinerary could begin with the Rotonda situated in the immediate outskirts of Vicenza a short distance from the Bacchiglione, a navigable river famous for having been used by the Vicentines for flooding the city of Padua. Only after the systemization of the Bisatto Canal did the Riviera Berica, no longer menaced by flood waters, acquire

many inhabited settlements and villas. The patron of the Rotonda, Paolo Almerico, a "man of the Church" as Palladio described him, had been nominated "Apostolic Referendary" during the papacies of Pius IV and Pius V and by virtue of his merits had become a Roman citizen. Having enriched himself, he returned to his homeland, where he increased his prestige by having Palladio build his suburban villa. Almerico collected rents from different parts of the Vicentine territory including the church at Lumignano. With Almerico Palladio found a type of aristocratic and ecclesiastical patronage somewhat different from other examples under consideration. He was to design a building in which the utilitarian functions were assigned a role of secondary importance. The purpose of all this was to express Almerico's ambition and cultural attainments, crowned by his sojourn in Rome. The location chosen for the villa was already known by the name "Rotonda." It was famous for its amenities and the rare beauty of the panorama, celebrated by Palladio himself: "Above a small mount of easy access, washed on one side by the Bacchiglione, a navigable river, and on the other, surrounded by other delightful hills that give it the aspect of a grand theater".

Even Giovan Battista Maganza was not insensitive to the fascination of the situation: indeed he was one of the first to speak of the villa, "That Rotonda, dear monsignore, which in such a short time has been built here is the envy, the marvel, and the astonishment of the wealthiest."

Even though the Rotonda seems a monument to itself, it still reveals a genius distinct from that of the Villa di Meledo in that it was perfectly proportioned yet also well rooted in the province and in the landscape by a deeply harmonious relationship. The interior decoration, rich in stuccowork and painting, constitutes an ideal portrait, bringing together the patron's classical reminiscences and his ecclesiastical activities.

The descendents of Almerico's Rotonda, lacking a precise bond with agriculture or with landed property, made only brief appearances among the protagonists of the villa world. The Rotonda itself soon passed to the Capra family, who gave it utilitarian equipment designed by Scamozzi, making it suitable for country management, as is clear from the following inscription: *Marius Capra Gabrielis Filius Que Aedes Has Arctissimo Promogeniturae Gradui Subiecit Una Cum Omnibus Censibus Agris Vallibus Et Collibus Citra Viam Memoriae Perpetuae Mandans Heac Dum Sustinet Ac Abstinet.*

We find in this region marvelous examples of villas in which the humanistic impulse dictated, such as the *Villa Eolia* or the "Prison of the Winds" at Costozzo, built, as Palladio writes, by the most excellent gentleman Francesco Trento.

Hot or cold air was brought to the villa from the caves and galleries of the nearby Berican Hills by a network of air ducts, rendering even more pleasant the "symposia" held there by famous personalities of the day.

The underground pavilion, frescoed by Giovanni Antonio Fasolo, seemed to express a new and different relationship, almost an osmosis with the subterranean cosmos. The Eolia seemed to collect and dominate nature's most hidden and mysterious forces, suggesting an inverted parallel with Palladio's Rotonda, where the architecture fused so harmoniously with the surrounding landscape.

The Guà, which had also been variously named the Agno, the New River, the Furious, and the Frassine, was one of the rivers that finally found peace with the works carried out in the *Retratto di Lozzo.*

Just outside Lonigo, at the point where the Roman road meets the river at Bagnolo, rises the Villa dei Pisani. This Venetian family had bought at auction the properties (and hence also the ancient feudal rights) belonging to the noble Nogarola family from Verona, who had fallen into disgrace at the time of Cambrai.

Having acquired these vast holdings, the Pisani directed their energies into agriculture, increasing the cultivation of rice and hemp, products that were easily shipped to the Dominante along the Guà river. These nobles could make use not only of cheap labor but, as Dalla Pozza has recalled, they also enjoyed the feudal right to "oppress" or impose obligatory labor that was not paid. The great Doric colonnade that was built along three sides of a threshing ground as big as the Piazza San Marco evokes the scale of the Pisani's activities. The type of noble patronage represented by the Pisani at Bagnolo, which we call "feudal", appears frequently in the Veneto. It is characterized by a city family establishing itself and bringing to the province the Venetian's practical and commercial mentality while adjusting to the customs and ambitions of the mainland's feudal, military, and chivalrous nobility.

Palladio was charged with giving this concept a form while conferring on the villa the aura of prestige and authority which was characteristic of its builders.

In an area already known for its ancient settlements, the building conserved some of the details of the castle that preceded it. There are the two small lateral towers, while the heavy rustication of the river façade was clearly inspired by Sanmicheli.

The interior of the villa is characterized by a vast hall inspired, as Palladio said, by "the houses of the Romans." The lords of the land, representing the Serenissima, held their public functions in this hall. The villa at Bagnolo is distinguished stylistically by the presence of rather distinct elements. The monumental and robust riverfront façade stood in contrast with that which, with a classical pediment, should have opened onto the courtyard. The frescoes of the vaults and walls celebrate the river for the benefits it brings in agriculture and commerce and for the delights that it bestows on life in the villa.

Following the course of the Guà, one reaches the area of Cologna, called "of the Venetians" after May 18, 1406 when the Maggior Consiglio added it to the Dorsoduro quarter of Venice in order to end the dispute between Vicenza and Verona. There appeared in the territory of Cologna an original type of patronage linked primarily to the principalities of central Italy (the Medici for example) rather than to Venice. All the villas of this fertile and well, cultivated land belonged to a single family, that of the Counts Serego.

As administrators the Serego were always ready to use the most highly developed discoveries in hydraulic engineering, in agriculture, and in gardening. A letter illustrating this speaks of a shipment of special plants from Constantinople, where a member of the family had been sent as Venetian ambassador.

It is not possible to document Palladio's activity at Veronella, at Cucca, at Miega, or Beccacivetta – all place names that appear frequently in Palladian literature – because few of these projects were ever realized. The Serego had insisted absurdly that the architect himself be present and oversee all the building operations since "without Andrea Palladio our booty cannot be put to work." In every likelihood there never developed that understanding, that spiritual affinity or communion of ideas between the Serego and the architect which generally had such importance in Palladio's projects.

The Villa Pisani at Montagnana is the expression of another type of commission. It stood right on a stream that, besides cooling the inhabitants, also drove the millstones of an immense mill that was first built by the Da Carrara for the needs of the territory.

Given its urban character, the villa may have been linked with this industrial activity, from which enriched the Pisani. The direct contact with marketing and distribution centers might have suggested the construction of a port facility, now impossible to envision. Puppi's observation on this is interesting. He compared the posterior loggia of the Pisani house to the façade of the Palazzo Chiericati which I have defined as a "maritime villa" because of certain of its characteristics.

Palazzo Chiericati, built in Vicenza near the Porto dell'Isola, reflects some of the elements of a port in antiquity, with its columns and loggias, so much so as to be placed by Canaletto in an imaginary setting on the Grand Canal as a palace-warehouse next to the Rialto bridge.

The posterior façade of the villa at Montagnana could have been conceived of as a function of its waterway in a period when the greater part of traffic used river ways.

The example offered by the Villa Pojana, which lies four kilometers from Montagnana, is different and subject to analysis in two senses. One is characterized by the military component and the other by agriculture. The name of the Pojana family is related to the castle which was one of the few spared by the Venetians, perhaps as a token of

gratitude for the loyalty of the family demonstrated at the time of Cambrai. In 1514 the Serenissima ordered that, along with many others, the castle of Brendola be dismantled so that it could not become a fortress for Venice's enemies. These provisions demonstrated Venice's evident suspicion of the Vicentines. Marin Sanudo, in 1483 already, spoke of these castles with suspicion: "All situated on top of mountains. Pleasant places with gentle pleasures... hidden from observation and far from prying eyes; but none may inhabit them save at the Dominante's request."

The Pojana instead were enfeoffed of the territory by the Venetians "*cum omnibus juribus et justisdictionibus ad castellarium spectantibus.*" This commission had patently military origins, linked to the arts of war, as is evident from the austere character of the villa's architecture and the frescoes that decorate it, illustrating scenes of battle, Roman emperors, and military triumphs.

Another element, however, helps to define the attitudes of the noble family. In the Hall of the Emperors a fresco represents a procession of people in Roman dress, preceded by an elder who moves toward the Temple of Peace to extinguish the torch of war on its altar, a subject obviously symbolic of the change in the times. A climate of peace spread abroad once warfare was uprooted. Even the Pojana decided to abandon military undertakings and dedicate themselves to agriculture, in the manner of the Roman soldier who left behind a trace of himself in the inscription found at Pojana: *Marcus Billienus Marci Filius/ Romanae Actiacus/ Legione XI Proelio/ Navale Facto In/ Coloniam Deductus/ Ab Ordinae Decuriorum Electus.* This is a particularly interesting inscription that confirms a hypothesis of mine already formulated in 1964. In studying the Veneto villas, it became apparent that they frequently were laid out to correspond with pre-existing Roman buildings. In many localities of the Basso Vicentino and particularly at Pojana, it is easy to see this link between the Roman "*statio*" or outpost, the medieval tower and Gothic house, and the sixteenth-century villa. The so-called *Ca Quinta* at Meledo, whose Roman origins were revealed by numerous fragments scattered in the neighborhood, provides an interesting confirmation.

The climate of "peace in the Veneto" seemed

to have inspired Palladio's conclusion to his
description of the villa of the Pojana. "On one side
of the courtyard are places for the use of the villa;
on the other, a garden that corresponds to that
courtyard. Behind that the fish pond and the
orchard are behind in such a place that these nobly
inspired gentlemen have not neglected to provide
all the ornaments and comforts possible to render
the place beautiful, enjoyable, and comfortable."

Another rather complex and interesting
example of patronage is offered by the villa erected
by the Saraceno at Finale di Agugliaro. It is not far
from another sixteenth-century villa, the one called
delle Trombe, attributed, not without good reason,
to Michele Sanmicheli. Palladio's description
of the Villa di Finale introduces the chapter in the
Four Books of Architecture concerning the villas
constructed for the mainland nobility.

The territory of Finale had been the property
of the family since the fourteenth century when
Pietro Saraceno, nominated Bishop of Vicenza
(ecclesiastical office was always a source of wealth),
moved from Rome with his entourage and his
relations. Thanks to the reclamation and to the
control of the waters of the Liona river, the villa
rose on a site which had become rich and fertile.
These factors encouraged agricultural activity.
That wealth was part of the ideals of the family is
documented in a fresco in the center of one of the
halls, where there is an allegorical figure of riches.
The Venetian mercantile mentality had been
acquired even by the mainland nobility.
Notwithstanding the great achievements of his
artistic production, Palladio seemed to extol a
perennial Hellenism, an idealism that transforms
every component through beauty. Yet in the
Four Books of Architecture there are extremely
few references to the poetic or aesthetic qualities of
the buildings described. On the contrary, it is their
functionalism and utility, their practicality, and the
attention to the most concrete needs of everyday
life that are exalted.

The Villa Emo at Fanzolo is a significant
example. Only those parts associated with the
working of the land and the storage of agricultural
products are described. The presentation of the
Villa at Finale is in the same vein, where "beneath
there are the cellars and above, the granary which

occupies the entire floor of the house. The kitchens are outside, but linked in such a way as is convenient. Those places necessary for the villa's functioning are found on either side."

It is natural at this point to ask which were the motives that led Palladio to this concrete realism. Perhaps it was to avoid the criticisms that would have inevitably been aimed at works that were too luxurious or at excessive expenditure, especially in a period when Venice was passing severe sumptuary laws. For an architect like Palladio, who sought the office of Proto or chief architect of the Serenissima, the celebration of the ambitions and pomp of the mainland nobility would have been counterproductive. But we believe that the peculiar social ethic that inspired his patrons and found its complete expression in the villa suggested this attitude to him. Even if embellished with learned and precious attractions, the building should correspond to the criteria of utility and functionalism. In this treatise, therefore, Palladio insisted on the aspect which had inspired his most limpid and poetic creations. The simpler and more functional his villas were, the more their specific qualities appeared. The greatest achievements of his art are not the latest grandiose works with colonnades and pediments. The ethical and aesthetic vision of the great architect seemed to find its most sincere and efficacious expression in the villas impressed by sobriety, simple elegance, and a suggestive harmony of proportions.

And this is the full realization of the fascinating tale begun with Petrarch and the humanists, who had rediscovered a new "earthly paradise" in the *locus amoenus* of the ancients, exalting the peace and beauty of "rustic life." Now to the concepts of beauty and virtue, utility, "convenience" and art, interpreting and idealizing nature, must be added the creation of an "artificial paradise" for the noble lords whose cultural ambitions were wed with a farsighted financial instinct. One should not forget that, particularly in the early period, Palladio worked primarily for particular patrons who came from the mainland nobility and saw in agriculture the sure way to accumulate in a brief time that impressive wealth that was necessary in order for these particularly ambitious minor nobles, otherwise deprived of every power in the organization of the state, to reach a position of prestige occupying public office and even acquire Venetian ennoblement.

This propensity for agriculture appears clearly documented in the presence, next to the residential block, of the *barchesse,* the outbuildings with dove-cotes and services of every sort designed for the storage of the farm implements and the fruits of the harvest, buildings through which Palladio kept alive the Veneto's popular culture alongside the traditions of the classics.

As is evident at Finales the granaries came to assume a fundamental importance. While the peasantry living in thatched roof huts could not conserve grain for long, the nobles could store and protect it in the villas, waiting for the periods of scarcity when they could sell it at inflated prices. The advantages accrued thus every year more than justified the immense expense of erecting a great villa.

The lands redeemed thanks to the regulation of the waters of the Liona belonged to the Parish of Orgiano, an area which, in the preceding centuries, had been distinguished by buildings important enough to be considered an anticipation of the sixteenth-century villas. In the sixteenth century the river Liona gave cause for concern, and the decrees and provisions regarding it were numerous.

For example the decree of January 8, 1505 affirmed "It having always been the principal concern of the city of Vicenza that its rivers be dredged so that they could not flood the fields and in order to keep them navigable, it is decreed the following provision for the Liona river..."
The Liona-Frassenella consortium was established on March 24, 1533, subject to the continual supervision of the superior magistracy.

On February 1, 1555 the municipality of Vicenza "seeing what an advantage there would be for the country around Orgian, Barbaran and other localities described here, takes in hand the dredging of the Liona to drain away the waters."

Beyond the reclamation of land, the magistrature constantly undertook to keep the rivers navigable as principal routes for the traffic that linked the capital with every point of the region.

In a document of January 19, 1584, conserved

Giovanni Antonio Fasolo. Portrait of a gentleman, detail from the "Partita di tric-trac" (Albettone, Villa Campiglia).

was located in one of the key positions of the medieval fortification line which touched Cologna and Montagnana and stretched from the territory of Verona all the way to the Euganean hills. Even in this case, the Repeta's sixteenth-century residence was none other than the expression of the need to create, even in terms of form, a sense of continuity with the arts of the past. The Repeta had taken possession of Campiglia as early as the thirteenth century, purchasing their fief from the Bishop of Vicenza. From this moment on their feudal investiture would be sustained through to the fall of the Serenissima and even beyond.

Even if during the transition from the era of the city-states through that of the principalities, the system of feudal jurisdiction was reduced, the line of continuity into which the present Baroque villa, like the Palladian villa, inserted is still evident. A *domus dominicali* or nobleman's residence was built on the ruins of the castle and then replaced by the Palladian villa. After a fire destroyed this, a seventeenth-century building was built to coincide significantly in type. Important documentary evidence exists of the survival of the ancient organization, of the feudal system, and of the patronage that the lord exercised, not only over the villa or over the lands subject to him, but also over the tenants and even over the municipality.

As was shown in the Pojana, Repeta family was characterized by two fundamental attitudes, one of a military character and the other of an agricultural and cultural nature. The former aspect can be seen in the seventeenth-century reconstruction ordered by Enea Repeta, the military commander of the fortress of Verona, among other duties. Turning his back on humanistic precedents, he made for himself a closed and austere residence of a soldier, flanked by an enclosure for military exercises.

Much more interesting for us is the case of the Palladian villa whose true patron was not Mario Repeta, as Vasari claims, but rather his father Francesco, a cultured man, far removed from the military interests that in the past characterized his family and were now sublimated and turned toward creating an ideal world. In fact it was the generation of the fathers linked to Cornaro's circle, a generation older than Palladio, that primarily inspired the Vicentine architect. Even his early

in the Bertolina Library of Vicenza, we read the request advanced by members of the noble Dolfin family and other landholders to render the river Liona navigable up to Campolongo, where the seventeenth-century Villa Dolfin still stands.

The Palladian construction at Finale reflects better than any other an agrarian reality suggesting the fusion between architecture and country. In its sobriety and its essential qualities, it constitutes a characteristic example of the villa-farm that, in order to display its utilitarian function, neglects its decorative or representational qualities.

Our research into the Palladio's presence in the Basso Vicentino concludes at *Campiglia dei Berici.* The Villa conceived there for the Repeta family villas should be dated after the century's fourth decade. More than once in the *Four Books* the architect declares that these buildings were not built on the initiative of the actual owner, but of his father.

Although belonging to a younger generation, Palladio considered himself the interpreter of an earlier progeny. The Villa at Campiglia, an extremely original construction among Palladio's projects was published in the *Four Books* as lacking any central elements: there was no central block flanked, as in other cases, by the *barchessas*. The villa stretched along a vast, arcaded courtyard, like an "agora." And with its open forms it led back to the model of the "Greek house" that opened out toward the country.

Puppi observed, "Look how the small pediment, crowned with statues, seems remote from a celebration of the lord's presence. It looms, in an almost argumentative way, over an empty threshold which leads from the gardens marked off by an exedra of classical design to the fields."

Palladio wrote, "This building has the convenience of being able to go everywhere under cover because that part reserved for the owners, residence and that for the farm are of the same height. That which the one loses in grandeur means that it is not more prominent than the other so the dignity and ornament of the farm building is increased, making it the equal of that of the owners for the beauty of the whole work."

The open, hospitable character of this architecture finds its counterpart in the decoration of the rooms, executed by Maganza in such a way that the room where friends were lodged would be decorated with the virtues most like them.

These egalitarian ideals stemmed from two fundamental concepts. The first, of a cultural nature, was the influence exercised by Trissino and his circle which gave a new impetus to the rediscovery of the Greeks and the study of Petrarch's poetry. The other idea resulted from the rather massive presence of the Anabaptists in this territory. This was the religious sect that preached equality, fraternity, and the withdrawal from all public office.

Without adhering to these new doctrines, Francesco Repeta was probably influenced by them, finding in them ideas that could be reconciled with his cultural world.

The villa at Campiglia, like many of the other buildings constructed in the country for nobles of Venice and the Veneto, served as the nucleus of the human settlement and built-up area that later surrounded it. The villages grew up in relation to the villa, from which they gradually could detach themselves. However, they continued to utilize those structures (ports, canals, roads, reclaimed lands, methods of cultivation) that had been developed at the behest and on the initiative of the noble landholders.

It remains to be seen why Palladio, in the early years of his activity, operated primarily in this region.

This area was among the first to profit from the reclamation work carried out by the Venetian magistrates who guaranteed noteworthy economic and commercial progress following the regulation of the waters and the intensification of agricultural activity. Vast stretches of land, formerly belonging to the religious orders, was gradually acquired by the nobility. Already in the fifteenth century they had begun to transform it into fertile land.

These new activities contributed to inspire an extraordinary enthusiasm in those carrying out the reclamation: a renewed faith in their own capacities that made them feel almost like "demiurges", committed to a sacred task such as that of redeeming the land from the waters.

The climate of expectancy and hope that accompanied the operations of reclamation in the region extended over centuries and was expressed in a letter written by Francesco Pojana where he stated his intention "to increase his earnings as soon as the *Ritratto di Lozzo* was brought to an end."

But alone these interests of a prevalently economic character would not have led to any artistic result. It must be remembered that we find ourselves in an area strongly influenced by the lively ferment of humanism.

We know, for example, that "the celebrated Ermalao Barbaro retired to this villa (Sossano) where other illustrious men had gathered and there stayed for some time to save himself from the plague that afflicted Padua." Here he entered into

Andrea Palladio. The Teatro Olimpico of Vicenza.

a relationship with Pietro Miani, the learned Bishop
of Vicenza; with Pietro da Monte, a young man of
refined artistic tastes; with Barnaba of Sossano and
with Leoniceno. On the slopes of the Berici Hills at
Moticello stood the villa of another humanist,

Bartolomeo Pagello, who dedicated a poetic work
to the beauties of this residence.

The amenities and the fertility of this locality
contributed to the fortune of this territory as
Pigafetta rightly observed: "It seems as if the spirit
of an ennobled Nature designated all the excellent

The patrons of the villas.

*In 1555 a group of "virtuous
and kind spirits" from the
city of Vicenza "gave life"
to the Accademia Olimpica.
From 1580 on the erudite
meetings of the Accademia
were held at the Odeon and
the adjacent Palladian
theater, where one can see the
effigies of those aristocrats
who had been so important
in the history and culture
of Vicenza.
Names such as Caldogno,
Trissini, and Valmarana are
to be found at the feet of these
statues, "dressed in the
antique style," men who
dominated the political events
at the time and also gave
their names to the prestigious
country residences which still
today ennoble every corner
of the province.
Aristocrats of refined
learning, Palladio's patrons
transformed their own villas
into direct emanations of the
Vicenza Academy.*

qualities of that sky and soil for the ease and
pleasure of human life."

But one particularly interesting consideration
for us concerns the very origins of Palladio's art.
From many documents, we know that he began as
a stonecutter in Padua in the workshop of
Bartolomeo Cavazza, "stonemason." He was called
"da Sossano," from his hometown which was
famous for the quarries of that soft stone which
Palladio preferred for his villas.

The architect's predilection for this land where
he had his first experiences as a stonecutter can be
recalled in order to find a justification for the
continual presence of Palladio in the Basso
Vicentino. This was also where he came to know
those building materials that would constitute one
of the most determinant characteristics of his art.

The Veneto villas
to the endurance of feudalism

With the Villa of the Repeta at Campiglia one can begin a discussion on a theme that I introduced in a talk given in Vicenza in 1978 entitled "Feudalism and the Veneto Villas."

Students of history often uncover facts and laws which prove particularly useful for the interpretation of artistic phenomena. Thus, the research of historians like Ruggero Roman and even more recently Giuseppe Gulino into the persistence of feudal custom in the Veneto can be applied to the architecture of the villa in order to illustrate a cultural turning point that should not be neglected.

Lorenzo Celsi had been sent in the year 1360 as ambassador from the Veneto government to obtain from the Emperor Charles IV of Luxembourg the investiture of the mainland possession feudally dependent on the empire. The investiture was conceded at Prague a century later on August 16, 1437, and the Doge Francesco Foscari and his successors were nominated Dukes of all the Veneto-Lombardy mainland with the exception of Verona and Vicenza. The empire insisted on the reconfirmation of each newly elected Doge's fidelity.

After many diplomatic skirmishes Venice obtained in 1516 from Maximilian the freedom from every dependence on the empire, even for the provinces of Verona and Vicenza. Venice thus inherited the feudal rights that the empire had exercised over the mainland territories. When in the sixteenth and seventeenth centuries noble land owners turned increasing attention to the country, they tended to revive ancient rights that, in other parts, had not fallen into disuse.

Thus there was a "neo-feudal" mentality which fused the public and private aspects of the *more nobilium* positing as its scope the maintenance of a sure income from the land and at the same time the respect for the republic which these lords felt they represented.

The Venetian patriciate, practiced in trade and governing, turned their capital from investments in commerce, which was no longer secure or remunerative. Utilizing the juridical instruments offered by custom, after having acquired landed property near waterways and possibly in zones free from duties, they provided for the economic organization of the territory, resurrecting ancient benefits or establishing new ones.

Thus Venice in 1587 found the need to institute an appropriate *Magistrature dei Provveditori sopra i Feudi,* legalizing a practice that, up to now, had existed through tradition. Thus an extremely binding system was created, and the subject peoples

were not spared abuses and misuse of office.

In the list of the nobles who requested feudal investiture of the Magistrature, we encounter the names of many families who built some of the most celebrated villas and who believed that feudal rights represented a title to prestige or else simply a source of income.

Anton Francesco Doni.

A Tuscan writer, bizarre and anti-conformist, Anton Francesco Doni (1513-1574) had a restless and wandering life. After a long pilgrimage to the most important centers in Northern Italy he at last settled down in the Euganean hills, not far from Monselice. Entranced by the gentleness of the landscape, he decided to build himself a villa surrounded by a garden adorned with statues, and here he lived, alone and eccentric, until his death in 1574. A brillant and versatile writer, he argued polemically with Aretino, amongst others. Doni dedicated one of his most famous works to the delights of villa life. It is from this treatise, entitled, appropriately, The villas *that we have taken a selection of particulary meaningful extracts to illustrate some of the villas dealt with in this text.*

The families listed by Gullino were not the only ones. In fact, there is no record of the Repeta who obtained an investiture at Campiglia as appeared in a document of 1703 concerning the properties of the Villa Repeta at Campiglia dei Berici.

This document, released by Doge Alvise Mocenigo, began with the recognition of the Manfredi-Repeta to the feudal rights that one of their ancestors had acquired on April 14, 1217. Among other thing the document says "To be embraced with pleasure by Our Senate, their devout demonstration, made for the Noble Enfeoffment in the male line of a considerable independent and ancient patrimony acquired in the year 1217 on April 14 by an ancestor of their House, located in the Villa of Campiglia, Vicenza district, and ornamented with the splendid titles of a Marquisate and a County the right to earnings, to grazing, to a pension, to fishing and to the tithing tax among others and consisting of a notable Palace rebuilt from the remains of the Castle of Campiglia with other rural buildings and peasant dwellings in proportion to the approximately 1,200 *campi* or fields with the purpose of earning the *decima* or tithe from individuals using again as many properties situated in the same territory and near to the villa at Sossano."

This confirmation of an investiture was granted to Enea and Scipione, brothers of the Manfredi-Repeta family, "nobles of our city of Vicenza."

As is apparent in the same document, the investiture involved a "fraternity" or family partnership by Venetian disposition. It established the indivisibility of the patrimony "to the end that such a noble capital and patrimony be conserved undivided."

Among other things, it may be observed that the names of the two brothers were Roman names. That they constructed a palace out of the ancient relic of the castle of Campiglia represented a continuity with the past.

The inscription on the façade of the villa of Campiglia represented other evidence of this remaking of the past: "Remade by us in a nobler form."

We have already mentioned the military tradition of the Repeta family. Before becoming nobles, they were qualified in the document as "extremely loyal Sargents-General in Battle" and further on "these characterized with the decorous name of vassals and suzerain, shall be ready in time of war for military service, not only to the value of twenty ducats a year but also to spill both their substance and their blood for the advantage of Our Republic and to leave a living example to posterity of the quality of their faith which shall be sworn, constant and never decaying on the altar of the Public's Greatness."

The documented military character of these nobles had already been surmised by examining some of the architecture that surrounded their villa. It was architecture that clearly proclaims its military purpose. There was an enormous enclosure with a section of grandiose arcades standing before it. Beyond this opened the so-called Serraglio. This was a place destined for military exercises and the celebration of festivities.

The cult of military traditions also appeared on the vaster horizon of the cult of Antiquity. The same Palladio, such a profound cultivator of the antique, revealed his interest in martial arts.

He spoke of military exercises in the book and the way in which they followed a ritual, taken from the writings of Caesar and how, in the end, the art of war ought to be considered the most excellent among the arts. Palladio took time in his writings to illustrate the military usage in vogue then: nor did Trissino show any less consideration for matters of war. The Repeta's importance lay in their having been men of arms. The Basso Vicentino, an area bordering on Cologna Veneta and Verona's territory, was also traditionally a land of soldiers whose vocation –"*vocatio militaris*"– was evident on more than one occasion during the war of Cambrai. During the Middle Ages the Castle of Campiglia and nearby Mottolo were the key points of a vast defensive system demolished by the Venetians in order to construct the walls of the faithful Cologna with the leftover material.

Another important aspect was the continuity of investiture that should pass to the masculine descendents of the Ripeta "ad infinitum," an indication that everything was done to last throughout time. Building was done not for today, but for eternity. This document of 1703 probably

had precedents that went back to the fifteenth century when the Repeta entered into Venetian service. It is also likely that it had been confirmed during the days of Cambrai. Perhaps this feudalization was exclusively a phenomenon of the sixteenth and seventeenth centuries, but there are good reasons for believing that it goes back further in time.

In the document, moreover, there are references to earlier petitions, one in 1700 and the other in 1701, that sought the confirmation of the investiture, finally bestowed in 1703. The urgency of these requests indicates the importance given to such an investiture.

The document says, in fact: "The abovementioned request being just and reasonable, we have, in keeping with the present documents and in every correct sense, created and confirmed the Title of Noble Feoff, of Marquisate and County to the Palace and all the buildings at Campiglia."

Through this investiture Venice recognized the feudal rights of the Repeta, admitting the feoff even though not conferring the civil and criminal jurisdiction recognized for the Feudatories of Meledo and Alonte.

Campiglia had been a Roman center. In the Middle Ages there existed a castle surrendered to the Repeta by the Bishop of Vicenza. The Repeta's maps and documents are helpful in reconstructing the historical and geographical relationship of their possessions to the entire territory under the Venetian dominion. From the maps it seems that the Repeta had the right to use the water of the Liona and the Frassinella rivers to irrigate the immense rice fields that belonged to them. Another document says that another navigable canal, the "*fosso burchierador*" (a boatman's ditch) ran off the Liona reaching the villa. Rice, loaded from the landing stage, reached either the markets or else Venice itself by water. The relationship with Venice was a close one, as can be deduced from the fact that, for the most part, the Repeta's neighbors have Venetian names.

As far as the description of the property is concerned, the old village square was located immediately in front of and on the sides of the villa. There is an interesting , small religious shrine of fifteenth-century style with terra cotta decorations

CONTA- DINO.

CONTA- DINA.

Contadino al mercato (sec. XVI).

Contadina al mercato (sec. XVI).

*Cesare Vecellio. The Peasants (*Degli Habiti antichi e moderni di diverse parti del mondo, *Venice, 1590). Also the peasants in their Sunday clothes were considered worthy of being portrayed.*

and columns with the Repeta coat of arms. In a tablet on the church façade appears the name of Pope Leo X and the date 1519, a very significant date because it corresponds to the period after Cambrai when Venice was organizing its territory and assigning new responsibilities to the nobles who had showed themselves loyal during the war.

From the eighteenth-century maps it can be seen that the small church was then the center of the village. But up until the nineteenth century, it was the village church. Today it is only the mausoleum of the villa's owners: their family tomb. The present church goes back less than a century.

By examining the map it can be noted that next to the church there existed an ancient building half equipped with a loggia, the other half serving as the town hall.

The municipal offices were organized near the villa. That the church of the villa was also that of the village meant that the landlords attended mass

with the people. This brought them into contact with those reformatory upheavals that were particularly lively in the Vicenza area.

Villa Repeta was, in fact, the meeting place of those nobles who, contrary to the Church of Rome, had adhered to the Anabaptist doctrine we mentioned in connection with the singular typology of the Palladian villa.

However, these religious movements did not attack the fundamental feudal structure that endured well beyond the end of the republic of Venice.

In 1820 the Austrian Government confirmed the ancient nobility of the Repeta. In 1854 the Imperial and Royal Fiscal Office obtained the devolution to the state of the feudal possessions of Campiglia after the death of the last legitimate heir. In 1868, following a trial for the illegal ownership of the fief of Campiglia, Alvise Mocenigo obtained, with the payment of the sum of 95,000 lire, according to a law of the Kingdom of Italy, dated January 24, 1864 the right to state that his possessions at Campiglia and at Sossano remained "free and immune from any feudal bond or any feudal tax."

The feudal tradition was deeply rooted and should be kept in mind in the study of the *World of the Veneto Villas.* Notwithstanding its negative aspects, this feudalism, even if of a particular type in terms of its relationship with the republican state of Venice, did determine the character and the fortune of entire areas of the Veneto.

The villa
in the seventeenth century

The seventeenth century in the Veneto was distinguished by the assertion of a new patriciate who assumed the duty of keeping the ancient republic alive in the face of a new vision of the world that was becoming more evident in Europe. Thus the ideals of the republic were constantly being adjusted to the mentality of an ambitious and assertive oligarchy. At the beginning of the century Paolo Sarpi and his congregation of political friends had vainly attempted to furnish the state with new and more adequate structures. He even tried to bring the Porto Vior canal to compeletion, an enormous undertaking which prevented the Po river's outlets from silting up the lagoon. It was a project which should have led Venice back to its traditional seafaring ways. And Baldassare Longhena, the heir of this hopeful vision, gave an artistic expression to Sarpi's martime ideal by erecting the Temple of the Salute on St. Mark's Basin that piazza of water that was almost an antithesis to the glorious "piazza" on land that faces the Basilica of San Marco.

All this fermentation of rebirth was shattered by the reaction of the Counter Reformation that first punished rebellious Venice with the Interdict (1606) and fifty years later led it to render homage to the Church definitively with the return of the Jesuit Order to the city in 1657.

The deep disturbances of the period can be seen in the abandonment of the principal way that, notwithstanding the Venetians' multiform experiences, had given a kind of unity to their arts and thought. The weakening of the prestige of the central power and its unifying force was reflected in painting. Aside from the committed research that drew inspiration from the art of Bassano and Caravaggio, everything else was a flowering of artifice inspired by the "theater of cruelty" or the hermetic fantasies of Pietro Liberi's followers or else in the miracle working and theatrical inventions preferred by the Spaniards who dominated Italy in that period. Andrea Palladio remained the great master in architecture. There were moments of extravagance with the introduction to the Veneto lands of those grandiose architectonic structures that enjoyed such great success with the courts of central Europe. Despite the lack of really brilliant architects, the better part

of the Veneto villas assumed their actual appearance precisely in this century. The causes for this were numerous. In general it can be said that in the course of the seventeenth century, a propitious historical moment was coming to maturity which corresponded to this art. For example, after the terrible plague of 1630 the great number of victims made for an even greater concentration of landed property in the hands of a few landholding magnates. In addition, between 1645 and 1649 the War of Candia reduced the reserves of the Venetian state, which was obliged from 1646 onward to sell a large number of public holdings which had been expropriated – in the period of the requisitions – from the Della Scala and the Da Carrara.

The proceeds were not sufficient to meet the needs of the war and on payment of enormous sums of money they were obliged to welcome to the ranks of the Venetian nobility, 77 mainland

Francesco Bozza.
Frontispiece of I diporti della vita in villa di ogni stagione spiegati in quattro canzoni *(Venice, 1601). Music was important in villa life, as shown in many of the frescoes illustrated in this book.*

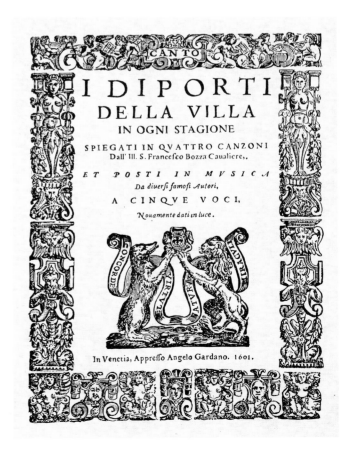

*A remarkable example of the
seventeenth century's taste for
the grandiose, Villa Contarini
itself could be described as a
large theater.
Marco Contarini was,
without doubt, the main
inspiration, if not director, of
the numerous performances
which took place at Piazzola
from 1662 onwards. There
were at least two theaters in
the villa at that time. The
larger one, capable of holding
up to 1,000 spectators, richly
decorated with elegant
furnishings carvings, mirrors,
and gilded stucco, was
famous throughout all
Europe; the smaller one,
reserved for minor works, was
known as the "Loco delle
Vergini" (Place of the
Maidens), because here one
could see the young girls
whom Contarini had
instructed in music, dance,
and song.
In the villa there was also
a printing press which took
care of the publication of the
opera libretti and theatrical
texts. The hall reserved for
auditions was blessed with
perfect acoustics; here the
guests who attended the
concerts would sit, but they
could not see the musicians,
who were situated in an
upper room called the
Chitarra. The outdoor spaces
were also especially and
accurately arranged for
performances and
amusements:* L'Orologio del
Piacere, *a volume which was
printed in 1685, documented
the magnificent celebrations
that took place in honor of
Ernest Brunswick; the naval
battles fought on the fish
ponds; the banquets, that took
place in the vast square in
front of the villa.*

families, and then in 1684, during the War in the
Peloponese, another 47 families were similarly
admitted to noble rank.

The ambitions and economic possibilities of
these new patricians found adequate interpretation
in architecture and in the all the artistic expression
of the Venetian seventeenth century.

Palladio's architecture, which had spread
abroad and was by now imitated even outside the
Veneto and Italy, seemed the best suited to
illustrate the glories of these new patricians just as
it had done for the most famous families of the
Veneto provinces in the second half of the sixteenth
century.

Palladian works that were left incomplete
because of the financial crisis and the plague were
taken up again and brought to completion. If so
many buildings were requested from the Vicentine
master's followers or from the foremen who had
faithfully worked by his side, this was due to the
existence of this new, ambitious patriciate. Thus,
for example, that which Palladio had merely
suggested in the incompleted project for the Villa
Tissino at Meledo was now completely carried out.

The restoration and restructuring of ancient
agrarian residences was very frequent, although
these were often little more than the rustic huts that
had populated the countryside in the course of the
sixteenth century. Consolidated economic power,
secure earnings guaranteed by landed investment,
rising ambitions, and the anxiety to display visibly
one's own proper political function pushed these
patricians to a detailed ennobling of rural villas
whose rather rough and simple architecture was
now covered over in sculpture and decorative
elements. A new sort of management which might
be defined as feudal appeared in this context in the
country and justified itself. This has been illustrated
in the case of Campiglia. Later on we shall examine
other similar evidence.

This was the period in which the Manin, having
acquired an incalculable number of properties,
made themselves into a feudal power on which
Venice could depend to control the entire region –
rendered even safer thanks to the construction of
the fortress at Palmanova – to organize festive
official receptions, and above all to coordinate
productivity by concentrating at Passariano the

provisions necessary for the Venetian armies in the
Levant. This explains the creation, in front of the
Villa Manin, an immense circular market,
reflecting an old tradition and repeated at Badoera
in 1635.

The function of the market and the sense of
urban planning were evidence of widening horizons
and the new economic policy followed by the great
aristocratic families. It can also be found at
Piazzola on the Brenta in the Villa
Contarini-Camerini, one of the largest buildings in
the Veneto country, enlarged and covered with
baroque decoration around the mid-century.
Preceded by a semicircular portico enclosing a vast
area fitted out as a market which today constitutes
the principal village square, the villa offered its
guests every sort of amusement: fish ponds, race
tracks, parks, gardens, and concert halls, all
according the taste and fashion of the times.

In many cases the village organized itself
in urbanistic terms as a function of these villas.
The economic development of Noventa Vicentina
received a stimulus from the agricultural activity
that the Barbarigo promoted in the area.

Their villa at Noventa, built at the end of the
sixteenth century, determined in the end even the
position of the parish church. Abandoning the
traditional east-west orientation, it was rebuilt
perfectly parallel to the Barbarigo's palace in the
middle of the seventeenth century. A clearly
seventeenth-century mentality seems to have
guided both the execution of the frescoes that
celebrate the glories and triumphs of the family as
well as the rearrangement of the gardens, personally
carried out by Senator Giovanni Barbarigo.

The long *barchesse* or outbuilding wings that
enclose the vast square are evidence of the original
agricultural function of this complex from which
the Barbarigo could control the management of
their lands.

If, in these examples, the close relationship
between the villa's function of display and the
agricultural economy is still evident, in other cases
"the mania for growing bigger" takes the upper
hand. It was inspired by the European courts, by
the Austrian castles and by the royal palaces of the
French monarchy.

Thus the Pisani sought to emulate the

lavishness of the Sun King with the creation of the monumental villa at Stra built in the eighteenth century, but in full synchrony with the spirit of the seventeenth century, in order to celebrate the election of Alvise Pisani as Doge. Pisani had already been Venetian ambassador to the courts of France and England and enjoyed the close friendship of Louis XIV. It is this cosmopolitan spirit and these contacts with countries beyond the Alps that offered a completely new stimulus and inspiration for the Veneto provinces.

Despite the flowering of grandiose, theatrical villas, one can say that the seventeenth century in the Veneto was substantially poor in true architects capable of brilliant solutions. Frequently we find ourselves in front of pretentious, inorganic buildings, of added-on architecture that overwhelms the previous structures or else bizzare and hardly functional solutions characterized by the lack of a unifying spirit. In general one notes a change in the typology despite the fact that the lessons of Palladio persisted in some areas. Often the broad colonnades and the classicizing pediments were abandoned in favor of less well articulated architecture, of the heavy unsymmetrical palaces illustrated in Coronelli's and Volkamer's famous engravings.

The Veneto villas of the seventeenth century repeat previous types more or less, often weighing them down and adding more movement to both decorations and structures. The central hall was given maximum importance, evident from the outside because of the raised elevation crowned with a pediment or dome. This hall, two stories tall, would be interrupted halfway up by a hanging gallery into which the doors and windows of the upper rooms opened. The most famous painters of the period were often called to decorate the walls and ceilings of these villas. Walls were transformed into fantastic mythological and historical scenes which anticipated the grandiosity of Tiepolo's decoration.

The taste for the spectacular predominated. Both pictoral and sculptural decoration received a great impulse to the extent that patrons were obliged to turn to foreign artists. There was also an increase in the love of gardens, which now replaced the villa's adjacent fields. Everywhere was found the desire to astonish, to dazzle with water works, bizzare sculptural groups, fountains, fish ponds, towers, and labyrinths. Scamozzi himself, completing the Rotonda, separated the *barchesse* or outbuildings from the owner's residence. He almost hid it, achieving an anti-Palladian separation between the life of the country and the villa that corresponded fully to the renewed psychology of

A performance at a banquet at Villa Contarini, Piazzola sul Brenta (L'orologio del piacere, *Piazzola, 1685).*

the seventeenth century, to its exhibitionist, theatrical spirit.

If one excludes Baldassore Longhena, with his various works – not always rooted in the real nature of the site – at the Villa Widmann of Bagnoli, Villa Rezzonico at Bassano and Villa Lippomano at Vittorio Veneto, the only architect that one could consider a valid interpreter of the spirit of the century was Vincenzo Scamozzi.

He seemed to realize that particular taste that

now guided the world of the villas. He completed numerous Palladian buildings and on the furthest slopes of the Berici hills he erected the Rocca Pisana, that most widely admired homage to Palladio's art. He miraculously paraphrased the forms of the Rotonda, with which the same range of hills can be said to begin.

In the Rocca Pisana Scamozzi seemed to crown the Palladian ideal of a perfect fusion between the villa and the surrounding landscape. He did not limit himself to planning the patrician residence, but personally undertook to modify the shape of the hill, making it assume the appearance of a great snail's shell crowned by the purest architecture that completely reveals the ideals of the artist. He put the "dignity" or worthiness, clearly visible in a "high place," in the first place of his hierarchy of values. "The high place in comparison with the lower is like a comparison between form and material. As is known the form precedes the other in dignity." Scamozzi's poetics also seemed to have been in full accord with the new orientation of the Pisani, who sought pure air and aristocratic isolation in these hills, far from the cares of town life (in the center of Lonigo, they owned a great town palace) and from the duties connected with the management of the immense properties at Bagnolo. The spirit of the architect – outlined in his classification of the various types of villa – seems to find a complete realization in this building, whose relationship with its surroundings is substantially based on the hedonistic complacency of admiring a nature organized by man. This same Scamozzi revealed himself to be an excellent town planner (a quality, as Milizia says, he inherited from his father) not only in his ability to harmonize his buildings with the landscape but also in his restructuring of an entire urban center, as he did in Salzburg. One can say that all of the principal tendencies of the century are summarized in Scamozzi: the scientific, the attention to the natural environment, international culture, the taste for the theatrical (recalling the Theatre at Sabbioneta or his contributions to the Olimpico), and the curiosity for European novelties.

Temanza wrote at his genius was "extremely curious to know how various nations thought differently about buildings."

The art of Scamozzi has a place of great importance that surpasses even the limits of his time. Inspired in his severe rationalism by the architects of the sixteenth century, he contributed to limiting the spread of the bizzare and jagged shapes of Baroque taste in the Veneto provinces, constituting moreover a valid premise for the re-emergence of neoclassical tendencies in the eighteenth century.

The reawakening of the love for the country coincided, in the eighteenth century, with a repetition of Palladian models carried out by a range of Veneto architects. Among the Vicentines there was Francesco Muttoni. Some attribute to him the house of the Fracanzan at Orgiano. The semicircular theater ornamented with statuary and accessible by an underground passage is still evidence of cultural amusements and refined festivities. Arcadia seems revived as if by magic in the inscriptions placed in the grounds of the villa: "Hill sacred to sweetest Lieo" one reads on the gate posts that open into the vineyard. The stone that is still to be found on the orchard wall says *Arvalibus Deis Pomonae Cereri Libero Pro Palilis Et Orgis Pro Venatione Et Piscatu Camoene Charicatesque Posuere* and again in the neighborhood of the fruit trees *Pomarium Hoc / Latifudio, Fructibus, Muro / Ampliavit, Ornavit, Coronavit. Jo. Bapt. Fracanzanus A. 1700,* almost as if to demonstrate the direct intervention of the noble landowner.

But the pomp of the Baroque and the graces of Arcadia should not allow us to forget that the presence of the noble family in the Veneto country had a profound influence also on renewed religious devotion. With deserted convents or parish churches often too far away, the community of the faithful came to gather in those small churches where all could freely attend. The noble patron provided for their furnishing, calling famous artists for their decoration. He turned to qualified and prepared priests for the liturgy. And he reserved for himself and his family an appropriate section, a place set aside for his attendence at religious ceremonies. The seventeenth-century villa was defining itself with structures increasingly like those of a medieval castle. Their architecture was evidence of ambition and the thirst for power. The farms which they controlled provided for the sustenance and the well-being of the inhabitants. The chapel, finally guaranteed a certain autonomy and independence from the religious point of view. It is not an accident that just now the so-called neo-feudalism came into its own: a rebirth of the feudal world, closed and self sufficient, which enjoyed privileges and rights over the rural population, but which at the same time defended it in the quarrels with neighboring centers while offering it valid spiritual guidance.

The frescoes
of the Veneto villas

The admiration which the villas of the Veneto have always inspired is due to an architectonic typology; to the materials of which they are constructed; to the accurate choice of the setting (such as Palladio himself always used for each complex conceived by him), and to the beauty of the gardens and the parks. But their form was also linked to their peculiar function in the Venetian dominion, to the historical significance assumed in the organization of the mainland and differently experienced according to the cultural epoch. Although modes of life and models of architecture can change, the gentleman's sojourn in the country was always experienced or dreamed of as taking place in a place of delight, alleviated by landscape visions, inspired by spaces opening onto a dominant nature.

Although architecture expressed the ideas and the practical needs that have given birth to the villa, the discussion becomes more explicit if we stop to consider the painting and the plastic decoration that ornamented the interiors. This represented a language which, from the sixteenth century, would contribute to making the source of the villa, its culture, and the fantasies of its inhabitants even more explicit.

It is enough to recall the names of some artists in order to understand the importance of this chapter in history: Paolo Veronese at Maser; Alessandro Vittoria at Montagnana; Zelotto at Fanzolo; Giallo Fiorentino at Fratta Polesine; Sustris at Luvigliano; Marinali at Trissino; Dorigny at Grezzana; Zais at Stra; the Tiepolo at Vicenza and at Zianigo; Demin at Conegliano.

Normally Venetian houses were decorated on their exteriors. According to Michelangelo the entire city was a "beautiful painting." Transplanting painting to the interior meant creating it for the sole pleasure of the inhabitants and their guests. Thus it was, for example, for the Ca' d'Oro, painted with scenes of hunting and gardens. Little by little, as the ideal of modern man acquired a clearer aspect, there was evidence, along with developments in architecture, of the internal decoration of the villas.

One of the first and most interesting examples of fresco in a villa was that desired by Alvise Cornaro to decorate the niches of the Odeon in the music room: landscapes and views were designed with a certain illusionism as if they were windows through which one regarded the country.

This motif would find masterly expression in the sixteenth century, for example, in Veronese's frescoes at the Villa Barbaro at Maser. False arches introduced the spectator to realistic country landscapes where ruins of antique Rome perpetuated the dream of an ideal continuity between modern patrons and the ancients associated with those magnificent buildings.

The frescoes underlined or narrated, more or less clearly, the functions fulfilled by the villa. The conception of the villa was always in perfect harmony with the dimensions and the importance of the building (for example there were no representations of Olympus in rooms not sufficiently spacious).

Thus, often enough, we find ourselves before narrative episodes which allude to the spiritual values which inspired the patrons of sixteenth-century decorations.

The villa in this century, as Rupprecht has brought to light, is the proper temple to the agrarian goddess Ceres, often depicted over the entrance as at Fanzolo. There Zelotti represented the Emo's program of life in a villa based on the arts and on virtues. Personages from Roman history were assigned the task of alluding to prudence and to generosity, protected by the peace that guaranteed agriculture.

Elsewhere allegories of the months and the seasons were added to the gods Ceres and Bacchus. As the statuary in the Villa Cornaro at Piombino Dese served to emphasize these were important factors in the rhythm of villa life linked to the country.

Zelotti was asked to speak of peace and justice in the Villa Godi and at Caldogno, while Giovanni Antonio Fasolo told how villa life predisposes us to honest pleasures: card games, balls, concerts, and banquets; and more the hunt and music at the Villa Campiglia at Albettone. The decorations of the Villa Pojana extolled peace, under whose aegis a new course of history began.

The studies and theories that concern "grotesques" – always considered representative of a universal language of pagan iconology – always

end by involving artists of the Veneto. The
grotesque genre, happily exemplified at the Villa
Badoer at Fratta Polesine and executed by Giallo
Fiorentino, often recurred in the decoration of villa
interiors.

But painting was also a means self-exaltation for
patrons who, in a structure designed to survive –
according to Palladio's rules of good architecture –
intended to keep the memory of the gesture and the
glory of the family alive.

In the Villa dei Vescovi at Luvigliano, Sustris
inserted figures alluding to the prestige of the Duke
among the landscapes and the grotesques; at Maser
Veronese portrayed his patrons, capturing them in
the most homely attitudes, next to decorative jokes
designed to amuse and puzzle the spectator – the
little girl opening a door to spy on the guest;
the dog asleep; the broom left behind, etc. Zelotti's
scenes in the Castle of Catajo illustrated the
military prowess of the Obizzi, and the Doge
Mocenigo was portrayed with the insignia of his
office. The frescoes of Antonio Vassilacchi in the
Villa Barbarigo-Rezzonico at Noventa Vicentina
were a self-exaltation with a series of allegories on
the prowess of Marco and Agostino Barbarigo.

There can also be a certain complacency about
wealth and possessions as at the Villa Capodilista
at Selvazzano where, amid grotesques, floral,
mythological, and military motifs, there were
the villas that belonged to the family.

There often appeared decorations that
illustrated myths, legends, literary works, and
fantasies of the sort that enjoyed great success in
central Italy and Rome. Decorators with experience
in the theater spread illusionist motifs, breaking
through architecture with their perspective
inventions.

In eighteenth-century frescoes the most often
recurring themes were taken from poetry. Scenes
of the *Pastor Fido* were painted by Carpioni in the
Villa Caldogno and also by Celesti in the Villa
Rinaldi at Caselle d'Asolo. Or again historical
themes like the foundation of Padua taken from
a literary source at the Villa Selvatico at Battaglia
Terme. With the function of the villa no longer
exclusively agricultural, the hunt became
a common subject as at the Villa Contarini
at Piazzola. Gardens also acquired increasing

importance. And according to the custom begun
by Alessandro Vittoria, they were embellished with
statues, fountains, and water displays. Marinali
appeared at the Villa Trissino with his expressive
sculpture in stone from the Berici hills and also
at the Villa Garzadori at Costozza, while Rubini
sculpted statuary for the Rotonda.

In many cases the *barchessa* outbuilding wings
were transformed into guest wings, where an
important role was given to decoration that should
welcome and amuse the guests.

The concept of amusement and hospitality on
holiday became a primary motif in the eighteenth
century as, little by little, the proprietor's personal
interest in the cultivation of the land diminshed.

The need to renew the villa rooms in terms
of this new concept of holiday use became the
occasion for the displays of the proprietor's wealth
and generosity, with a renewed profusion of interior
decoration now quite independent of the external
architecture.

Historical subjects appeared in fresco where the
theme of the banquet predominated as at the Villa
Marcello at Levada and in the Villa Giovanelli at
Noventa. These were often placed in settings
influenced by Algarotti's neo-Palladianism.

The taste for simulation in both landscape and
architectural subjects was still alive at the Villa
Garzadori, where the paintings with ruins were
designed to suit the "Grotto" built into the
complex. These frescoes, which had lost the
sixteenth century's moralizing key, now bespoke
pleasure and Arcadian leisure: games and hunts at
the Villa Albrizzi at Preganziol. Fantasies and
architectural views in the Villa Mocenigo at Canda.
Astrology with the signs of the Zodiac, or battles
between Centaurs and Giants as recounted by
Dorigny in the Villa Arvedi at Grezzana.

Views of distant places were introduced to
reflect the nobleman's love of travel. Rigid in their
conservatism the nobles assigned the representation
of their cultural environment to Gian Battista
Tiepolo. Thus we can see in the Villa Cordellina
how this artist with theatrical sensitivity bestowed
praise on the patron with the historical subject
of Alexander and Scipio, alluding to the virtues of
magnanimity and clemency. Episodes taken from
literature in the Villa Valmarana ai Nani (the
Gerusalemme Liberata, Orlando Furioso, and the
Aeneid) probably served to mask with epic and
chivalrous costumes the spiritual uncertainty which
characterized the aristocratic class in that era.

Even the bourgeoisie in this period took up the
"villa holiday craze" of going to the country
immortalized in the pages of Goldoni. Gian
Domenico Tiepolo, one of the finest decorators
interpreting the bourgeois taste increasingly moved
away from the assurance and the easy
triumphalism of his father. Instead of praising his
patrons as Gian Battista did in the Villa at Stra
by proposing the apotheosis of the Pisani family,
Gian Domenico, in the guest wing of the Villa
Valmarana ai Nani at Vicenza, offered an
alternative to his father's evasions by painting
images of life in the nobleman's villa next to that
of the peasants in the field, caught in moments of
repose. The call to the theater of Goldoni is heard
not far off with the irony of the "Mondo Nuovo,"
the "Carefree Minuet," the meditative landscape
and the already disillusioned "Pulcinella." This
society is being "photographed" in "detail" and by
placing it next to the "grotesque" of the masks,

Giambattista Zelotti and Antonio Fasolo. A detail from "The Clemency of Scipio," (Thiene, Villa Da Porto Colleoni).

hand, a distinctly utilitarian frame of mind could also reduce the villa to a simple place of agriculturel or craft.

In the context of the proprietor's budgets the demolition of "passive" parts of the villa complex was frequent. The new bourgeoisie, enriched through industry (textile and mining), preferred to display their prestige by building a new building worthy of the "status" they had acheived. They called in artists that continued the tradition of interesting fresco work.

At the Villa Revedin Bolasco at Castelfranco, built after the demolition of the preceding structure in the style of Scamozzi, Giacomo Casa presented the theme of festivities and masked balls with originality. The protagonists were dressed in eighteenth-century costumes, reviving the carefree atmosphere and the happiness of a particular page in the history of the Veneto.

Elsewhere historical themes were taken up according to a precise programe tha guided painting around the mid-century. Thus frescoes in the Villa Gera at Conegliano Giovanni Demin treated episodes of Roman history, with particular attention to the encounters between the Romans and the Helvetians.

Even illusionist painting founds a way to flourish again with particularly pleasing effects, as at the Villa Bolasco, where false loggias frame, the scene. Thus a centuries long tale of painting in the Veneto that reached its maximum splendor in the sixteenth century was concluded with a sort of dignified inventory of the various genres of decoration.

Gian Domenico induces an ironic and detached understanding in the observer.

At the same time, the echo of the Orient is increasingly heard. The chinoiserie which Gian Domenico attempted in the Villa Valmarana went with Rococò taste, contributing, along with stuccowork, to break up the decoration of the rooms, once frescoed with mythologies and histories. In the nineteenth century this taste for orientalizing and exotic motifs, such as that at the Villa Foscarini at Stra, continued to spread.

The conception of the villa as a place of escape was maintained in this century, yet, on the other

The gardens
of the Veneto villas

Whoever visits the Veneto villas today can imagine the splendor of the world of these villas only with difficulty because, even where their architecture remains more or less intact, their gardens, the true stars of the villa holiday, have almost all disappeared. Only by leafing through old documents can one gain an idea of the increasing importance that they assumed, so much so that the villa could be reduced to a scenic backdrop destined to be seen as a background to the garden.

The plan that evolved with the Veneto gardens remained constant until the eighteenth century when, alongside the central axis of stairs or of avenue, more importance was given to the natural element and optical effects of perspective, of arches, columns, porticoes, steps, and gates, sought a more harmonious relationship with a vast and free natural landscape.

Topiary art, the art of the garden, was remade from an ancient tradition. The examples of the Roman classical world were alive in the organization and in the symbolic function of the garden as well as in the villa house. The classical world proposed a structure borrowed from the model of the "paradise" of Persia (the Orient

always inspired admiration and the desire to emulate) where a network of canals, the central presence of a small lake, the distribution of the fruit trees and flowers with space for hunting and fishing made the garden into a kind of image of the universe.

The typology of the Roman garden – the famous and fantastic *Horti Luculliani,* the *Horti Casaris,* the *Domus Neroniana* – have come down to us through literary descriptions. They were a complement to the dwelling. "The avenue has hedges of box and rosemary. A young and luxuriant vine casts its shadow... fig trees shade the garden. In front of the covered portico runs a lawn scented with violets. Behind the villa, at one's feet the sea, above the forests. All these views can be enjoyed separately from each window or else confused in a single view," wrote Pliny the Younger in a letter to Gallo.

The idea of the *hortus conclusus* was taken from the theories of Martial and developed in medieval literary sources as well as being realized concretely in monastic cloisters and gardens. Inside a green precinct, the grape vine near a fountain alluded to another life, which in Eden found its proper expression in the happy chromatic distribution of flowers and plants. In Boccaccio's *Decameron* the country could be a refuge from the mishaps of the town: the ideal place for the flowering of idylls and for refined conversations. The humanist's garden inserts itself in the nostalgic dream of Roman villas and in the polemic between the city and the country already present in Petrarch's proposal for a "solitary life." Petrarch had, in fact, selected the place most adapted to repose, far from the anxieties of the city, amid the Euganean hills. He spent his time in more precious activity in the shadow of his vineyard, alternating his studies with poetic creativity. Pietro De' Crescenzi, still thinking about an *hortus conclusus,* suggested the rule for making a country sojourn pleasant and enjoyable: "select a smooth place... and surround it with a wall as tall as is required. In the northern part plant a forest of diverse trees in which wild animals can run and hide themselves... Again make a fish pond there where several sizes of fish can feed... And again it should be understood that many will ornament such a garden with trees that never lose their

*The meeting of Polyphilus and Polia, Francesco Colonna (*Hypnerotomachia Poliphili, *Venice 1499).*

Stefano da Verona. A detail from "The Madonna of the Rose-garden" (Verona, Museo di Castelvecchio). We must not forget that the word Paradise comes from the Greek word meaning garden.

fifteenth century. It is sufficient to recall Stefano da Verona, Carpaccio, Giambellino, Cima da Conegliano, for whom the love of roses, gardens, and orchards appear in such a dominant fashion as if such natural elements had an immense importance in everyday life. Trees of golden apples, scented grasses, flowered meadows, the clear waters of streams in an atmosphere of crystalline air amid music and perfume appear in miniatures, in tapestries, in paintings, as in the treatises and poems. Enchanting scenery reveals itself in a season of eternal spring as if attempting to recapture the pagan "Golden Age" or the Christian's "Earthly Paradise" as in the fresco of the months in the Torre Aquila in Trento. These examples of gardens which have disappeared preserve the characteristics of the "enclosed garden" that still flourishes: high walls, lawns, entwined hedges, rose gardens, bushes, fruit trees like the pomegranate and orange trees, evergreen woods, beds of flowers, herbs and vine pergolas, fountains and canals for the fish ponds or for irrigation.

After the last fortifications had disappeared from the mainland under the republic's pressing policy of expansion and economic renewal, the Venetian aspiration to greenery constrained between water and marble could finally extend itself beyond the closed gardens of Murano, the gardens of the Giudecca and those "visions of flowers" restricted to terraces and city palaces.

In no other place as in *Poliphilo's Dream* did the new thinking about the art of the garden appear so clearly. The island where Poliphilo disembarked is nothing more than an immense garden whose delights are amply described. The circular shape best suited to the habitation of a divinity and the beauty of geometry are united to the fascination of nature in this enchanted place. Nonetheless any theoretical project of "*natura more geometrico demonstrata*" is completely foreign to Veneto culture. Instead the expression of the Veneto sensibility, also found in the *Poliphilo,* is the "loggia overlooking the garden where you can be both in the sun and in the shade," the "green woods" with their "refreshing canals and tremulous rivulets," the "noble rose gardens of festive vermilion flowers." The presence of man is thus recognizable in the skill with which various materials are disposed

greenery such as a pine trees, cypresses, cedars, and even palm trees if they can survive."

Bartolomeo Pagello also allows us to reconstruct the ideal garden of the humanist inhabitant of the villa. "The villa should only contain my possessions and be suited to honest pleasure. It is enough if a single portico runs from the house to a pleasant garden, raised up from the courtyard by only two steps... In the garden are many apple and pear trees, pomegranates and prunes and generous vines. There are many plane trees and clipped box close to the house. A handsome bay tree and a spring sacred to the muses clearer than glass itself."

Poets and writers anticipated the taste for landscape that, among painters, developed in the

*Ludovico Pozzoserrato.
A concert in the garden.
(Treviso, Museo Civico).*

rather than in a rigorous design: the selection of plants, the presence of the waters, the ornamental use of statuary and architecture that civilize rather than violate nature's gifts.

Palladio in particular felt the link between the habitation and its natural environment, whether it was a vast landscape or a setting created by man in such a way that all the elements were recomposed in a single harmony. "Having found the site, happy, pleasant, comfortable and healthy," he said, "the elegant and commodious rearrangement is required" in such a way that "the gentleman will derive great utility and consolation from the villa where he will pass his time in taking care of and ornamenting his possessions, increasing them with his labors and the arts of agriculture. His body will conserve its health and strength easily, taking that exercise on foot and on horseback that the villa affords and where, finally, the soul, tired of the agitations of the city, will be restored and will find consolation." As can be seen, the "great utility" of the country – the new source of wealth for Venetian gentlemen who had invested in lands riches they had acquired from commerce – was to be united with the "consolations" of a new found serenity where those ideals, already propounded by Petrarch and Cornaro, could be revived: "to quietly attend to the contemplation and study of letters" according to the myth of the ancients. "Since for this, the ancient savants often used to retire to similar places where, visted by kind friends and relations, they had houses, gardens, fountains, and other similar amusing places. Above all it was their virtue that here one could easily lead the most blessed life attainable here below because gardens and orchards are the soul and pleasure of the villa."

Water, as in antiquity, assumed a particular value. While the fish ponds had a function that was not only functional but also utilitarian, and the canals and streams created a musical atmosphere, the fountains placed in the key points of the perspectives served to emphasize the forms and proportions of the gardens. Inasmuch as it was the *"fons salutis"* as in ancient cloisters, the fountain's symbolic value was often repeated in the statues that surmounted it. In the same way, the figures completed an allegorical program in the nyphei which often bordered the secret gardens, as at Maser.

Only in the second half of the sixteenth century, did the garden, even though remaining fundamentally within the Veneto tradition, tend to a kind of exhibitionism that demonstrated the nobility and wealth of the landlord in an atmosphere of feudal restoration. "The greater and more spacious gardens are," Scamozzi wrote, "the better they honor the house. And the more fountains of running water and the more trellises and espaliered bay trees, myrtle, and citrus trees and other well-trained plantings."

Varied evidence reflects on the fortune and the splendor of this particular aspect of the *World of the Villas.* We know, for example, that Ottavio Thiene, in his residence at Quinto, enriched his gardens with lime, lemon, orange, and other fruit trees with "a beautiful and clever labyrinth in the centre." Between the seventeenth and eighteenth century gardens became increasingly rich in surprises, labyrinths, open air theaters, follies. They were populated with statues that evoked a mythological or literary culture, as in the park of the Villa Rinaldi at Caselle d'Asolo. Here the unevenness of the land was exploited to create a series of green "backdrops" against a suggestive background of vines which concluded in a circular shape with niches and statues of characters from Ariosto. At Preganziol in the Villa Albrizzi the park, which contained a precious variety of plant life set out according to considerations of color, was divided by avenues and paths populated with statues. This was the place that Pindemonte rechristened the "the green sanctuary."

Up until recently, the park at Catajo could provide for many different species of animals in its vastness. Among the best known were the deer released for the hunt. At the Villa Emo-Capodilista at Selvazzano, the Italian garden was broken up by the distribution of avenues while the intimate link between the interior and the exterior was emphasized by the frescoes of Varotari, who painted false balustrades, leafy pergolas, and the so-called "hall of the vine." The work ordered by Antonio Barbarigo for his residence at Valsanzibio was of grandiose proportions. The gardens were organized according to an imposing scenography with several perspecives, with fountains, lakes, fish ponds and jets that shot up in the middle of pathways, all in such abundance as to distract the visitor from the villa which constituted the center of attention. The art of the garden spread everywhere

in the Veneto, but perhaps there was a particular expansion in the area around Treviso and along the Brenta, where the Venetian city dwellers chose to establish their country residences. Because of the great fashion for holidays in the villas, the gardens were no longer only the goal of the solitary meditative spirit, but now welcomed and delighted the carefree holiday makers and their guests.

Parks were constructed with thick shadows through which woodland gods could be glimpsed and where the noise of some fountain or specially constructed cascade could be heard. Stolls in the park were guided by avenues that intersected according to the principal axes and by the paths that led off them, bringing the visitor to the mysteries of the labyrinth, to the surprises of aquatic jokes and the secrets of the nymphaeum. But we can find another memory of humanistic culture in the pride with which rare and precious

Francesco Bonazza. Pantalone, one of the statues which populate the garden of Villa Widmann at Bagnoli di Sopra.

plants were exhibited. One of the most peculiar elements of the villas in Volkamer's engraved decoration seems to be the greenhouses because of the enthusiasm with which they were planted and the rare varieties that they contained.

Alongside the vegetable garden and the beautiful terrace garden laid out around the axis of the broad staircase, the greenhouses of the Villa Garzadori at Costozza seemed have been held in high esteem. Besides the stables that acted as a backdrop to the park, the Pisani at Stra also built great glass houses that enclosed all the rarest plant specimens. The park of this villa assumed the aspect of a great stage set of nature, with the evocation of ruins following the same theme of fantastic views in painting. Thus the new taste of the century emerged in juxtaposition to the geometric schemes of the Renaissance, suggesting the capricious and the unforeseen with bizarre inventive effects of perspective, of waters, springs

and labyrinths according to the theatrical vocation of a society that, the more it approached its end, the more it exalted noble "appearances."

Only in the case of the villas where the lord loved to surround himself with literary company as, for example, at the now lost Villa Querini at Altichiero, did the gardens still flourish according to sixteenth-century traditions, as a "philosophical" corner, the place of disputations and spiritual growth.

But by the end of the eighteenth century, there appeared a reaction against a rationally organized nature. This was a romantic "naturalism" that had developed primarily in England.

In the "English garden," – which spread quickly in Italy and whose culture was promulgated even by certain Veneto artists and academicians – the ideal returned to a picturesque disorder in nature translated in the construction of tiny lakes, artificial hills, classical or neo-Gothic temples, tortuous paths, false ruins, oriental-style elements (like pagodas), and even the introduction of tropical and exotic plants that gave an unusual note to the nineteenth-century garden. All this suggested the idea of a free environment in which the most diverse plants grow spontaneously, while willow trees, which enjoyed an enormous popularity, suggested a noble melancholy.

Great villas and suburban gardens were born on the country's edge, right next to the city, where, thanks to a reawakened interest in botanic gardens, the exotic aspects and the reconstructions of particular environments gave a special fascination and prestige to the entire layout.

Jappelli's innovations in the Veneto created areas of "spontaneous" nature around the villas that were juxtaposed with the classic Italian garden and participated in, as if by a distant influence, the ancient Persian tradition.

The Veneto villas
of the eighteenth century
in the pages of Carlo Goldoni
The craze for villa holidays

Gian Francesco Costa. The River Brenta, frontispiece of the Delizie del Fiume Brenta espresse ne' Palazzi e casini situati sulle sue sponde dalla sboccatura nella laguna di Venezia fino alla città di Padova *(Venice, 1750-51).*

The Veneto villas had an exceptional chronicler in the eighteenth century. Carlo Goldoni was always an attentive observor of the "World," his declared "Master."

There is no lack of comedies set in the country in Goldoni's work. Some took place in the ancient "feudal" properties and one written in 1752 is even called *Il Feudatario* or the feudatory.

It is the day of taking possession of the fief, and the community of Montefosco is getting ready to take "the oath of vassalage." But the new lord, a profligate young Marquess, in memory of ancient rights, seeks to "enfeoff" the peasants' women.

However, times have changed. The "deputies and syndics" of the "ancient and noble community have decided to "defend the possession of their honor and their reputation" and in the third act

of this comedy, thanks to a solemn beating the Marquess will be forced to gentler attitudes.

But the great feudatories interested Goldoni relatively little. He was the representative of a bourgeoisie, the new managerial class, holding out against the structure of a world headed for its eclipse. Goldoni did not tire of telling the bourgeoisie, especially in the comedy of 1761 called *Le Smanie per la Villegiatura* or The Craze for Villa Holidays, not to exceed the limits of their condition, not to ruin themselves by competing with "the Florentine Marquisses who have fiefs and enormous holdings and offices and grandiose dignity."

He spoke of Florence as elsewhere he spoke of Livorno or Napoli, but in reality he was always dealing with Venice. The model of the older generation was compared to the new generation that let itself be taken in by the "craze for villa holidays," because of the "ambition of the little who wish to impress the great" (as one reads in the preface to that comedy). They knew how to administer the earnings of the country and thus established the period of their visits to the villas in the season of the harvest. "In my times, when I was young," says a character in the same comedy, "one went early to the villa and returned early to the city. Once the wine was made, one returned to the city. But then one went in order to make the wine. Today one goes for amusement and one stays in the country with the cold, watching the leaves dry up on the trees".

Portrait of Carlo Goldoni, an engraving by Giambattista Pitteri from a painting by Piazzetta (Venice, Museo Correr).

"These holidays, which were introduced for the pleasure and profit of the citizenry," writes Goldoni in the introduction to his comedy of 1755 entitled *I Malcontenti,* "have today reached an excess of luxury of expense and of uncomfortable bondage." Even the amusement of a virtuous Arcadia, the natural companion of ancient "good government," is now displaced by the superficial splendors of continual festivity. "I remember my father, who brought with him to the country, learned doctors, men of letters, and musicians... Alas, that's not the fashion now. One wants happy people, happy people. Dance, sing, play jokes, spend happily, spend happily," says a lady, and she is echoed by Roccolinio, a "professional" holiday maker with his fashionable French, "*Allegreman toujour, allegreman toujour.*"

Like the "sponger" Ferdinando in the second act of the *Smanie,* "He was used to going to the country, not for amusement, but as a job."

In the last decades of the eighteenth century the cycle of the seasons and the hours of the day were ignored. A character in a comedy of 1755 titled *La Villegiatura* declares, "One goes on holiday when the autumn is already finished and one turns night into day with gambling, gossip, and amorous intrigue." "There (in Venice) terrific decorum, and here liberty: one plays, one strolls, one gossips, and if every once in a while you get into a jam, here no one says anything. The country seems to permit what the city forbids," says a character in *La Castalda* of 1751.

In this way customs were corrupted and as the bourgeoisie aped the great nobles, the inhabitants of the country were no longer content with their humble life. "The holiday makers bring with them," one reads in the preface to the *Smanie,* "the pomp and tumult of the cities, poisoning the

Francesco Guardi. Detail from a drawing showing the Duke of Polignac's Wedding Banquet at the Villa in Mestre (Venice, Correr Museum).

pleasures of the peasants and the shepherds who take their misery from their landlord's pride."

Recalling phrases from the first two acts and from the preface of the *Smanie:* "Today the country is under greater subjection to the city"; women make for the occasion "an arsenal of things;" the table silver is never sufficient because "in the country one must keep open house" and "troops of friends" come and "there will be gambling, a great feast of dancing." Whoever does not flaunt himself in the country is socially disqualified. "A year without a holiday in the villa! What will they say of me at Montenero? What will they say of me in Livorno? I won't be able to look anyone in the face again." "If she does not go to the country, she will die before the month is out."

No great prophet was needed to guess that "the grandiosity of the villa" would lead to "misery in the city" for the "little ones" who for "ambition" hoped to "make an impression with the great." The products of the country which were already the city dweller's major source of income were no longer sufficient to pay for the luxury of these villa holidays. Here is the significant dialogue between Vittoria and the servant Paolo in the second act of the same comedy:

Vittoria: In the country there will be wheat.
Paolo: There won't even be enough to make the bread we need.
Vittoria: The grapes won't have been sold.
Paolo: Even the grapes are sold.
Vittoria: Even the grapes.

It is no wonder that behind this urban bourgeoisie that does not even take the trouble to look after its own interests, a new category came to the fore that aspired to become bourgeois and supplant the landlords. These were the managers and factors who, living in the country and knowing their work, enriched themselves behind the backs of the old landowners, accumulating enough money to acquire the land on which they had been working. "Poor landowners! These foremen and factors," one reads in the first act of *Castalda* (1751) "they are assassinating us."

The fact that the old landowning class was conscious of its ruin did not attenuate, but rather aggravated the situation. It revealed their moral incapacity to act. Thus Momolo complains in the comedy of 1739 called *Il Prodigo,* which was earlier called *Momolo on the Brenta:* "Certainly no one thinks much of me. They all know the factor. That's because I let him take too many liberties. One day he'll be my landlord. I don't know what to say. I'm so spoiled that it's all right with me to amuse myself without thinking about anything."

Even the servants were aware of how things were going. They recognized their boss in whoever issued orders and had the money to back them: "Where have you taken the grain?" Momolo asks Truffaldino in the third act of the *Prodigo,* and Truffaldino answers "I took the grain from this house and brought it to the boss's granary" "The boss? and who's this boss?" Truffaldino: "The factor." Momolo: "The factor's the boss, you ass?" Truffaldino: "I am not an ass, sir." Even a lowly creature like Truffaldino knew how to defend his dignity before a degraded superior.

The *Castalda,* like the *Prodigo,* took place on the Brenta: "The scene takes place in the villa of Pantalone on the Brenta, the famous resort of the Venetians."

Certainly the fame of these holidays derived from the magnificent villas and the splendid life of the great nobles. But alongside the princely residences there were an increasing number of modest villas of the Venetian bourgeoisie represented by the character of Pantaleone, who invested his earnings in commerce in landed property.

It was natural that the Venetian bourgeoisie took their manners and their scale of living with them to the villas. In the eighteenth century these country houses often reproduced the Venetian house with its central hall and lateral living rooms. They would be given a little character by a modest pediment on the façade, two small statues on the gateposts, recalling, on a bourgeois scale, the dignity of the ancient noble villa.

The villa of the Tiepolo family at Zianigo

Giandomenico Tiepolo. The Walk; this fresco was formely in Tiepolo's villa at Zianigo, and is now in Venice (Ca' Rezzonico).

In 1759 Gian Battista Tiepolo received a conspicuous compensation from the patriarch Daniele Dolfin for the frescoes in a church at Udine. With these new riches Tiepolo could, according to the fashion of the day, construct a villa on their land at Zianigo. This house was probably never used by Gian Battista, who was constantly away on jobs. The frescoes of the villa (now at Ca Rezzonico) were executed by his son Gian Domenico in a period between 1759 to 1797. Little by little significantly different themes and styles succeeded one another according to the changing personal and psychological circumstances of an artist who was gradually freeing himself from his father's teaching.

As in Goya's house, one can understand otherwise undocumented aspects of Gian Domenico through his painting in the Villa at Zianigo. In fact, it was here that he could give free rein to his personal way of seeing, freed from the restrictions of a commission.

In order not to conflict with the dictates of official painting, Gian Battista and Gian Domenico relegated the more unconventional subjects to the guest wing of the Villa Valmarana ai Nani near Vicenza.

Free from agreements or compromises, Gian Domenico took up at Zianigo the theme of the *New World* already introduced at Vicenza, here treating it with greater dramatic effect.

The ceiling of the *portego* or main gallery hall (the most important room on the ground floor) was among the earliest frescoes of the Villa at Zianigo. It represented *the Triumph of Painting* over the other arts which, executed in 1759, was still heavily indebted to his father's model. Still in '59 we see Gian Domenico engaged in the chapel on the ground floor. In a series of frescoes he depicted episodes from the life of San Gerolamo Miani, founder of the Somascho Order to which his brother Giuseppe belonged.

In 1764 the Tiepolos left for Madrid, aware of being artists worthy of celebrating the glories of a court.

Saddened by the imminent departure, Gian Domenico represented an Armido that two friends and companions in arms drag away from Armida. Rinaldo directs his thoughts rather than his glance to her. She is recognizable in the statue that dominates the garden scene. His melancholy is so realistically treated that he seems to personify the artist himself, obliged to leave those beloved places to follow his father's dreams of glory.

This unique literary reference at Zianigo is evidence of a relationship with the same themes

taken from the literature of chivalry at the Valmarana in 1757.

After his father's death and disillusionment with Spain, where Mengs was preferred, and having requested and been refused readmission to the Academy of Venice, Gian Domenico returned in 1771 to his country house, which had remained in his brother Giuseppe's hands.

He set to frescoing the dining room with satyrs and centaurs. There seemed to be a return to the mythical "Golden Age," and to the secret life of the ancients, as a complete break with his father's heroic and divine decorative programs.

From this moment Gian Domenico Tiepolo worked assiduously in his villa, far from the paternal rhetoric which patrons still required of him. Here he could finally express his vision of the world and his artistic personality, no longer bound by the models of mythology and legend. He turned to the world around him with a subtle criticism of society, often sprinkled with sarcasm.

The scene of the *Minuet* and the *Promenade*

seems to document that evasive spirit, fatuous and lacking in moral fiber, that animated eighteenth-century society in the Veneto.

One can distinguish an even more disquieting aspect in the *Promenade.* Characters that head toward a distant goal and who recall the "citizens" of the Revolution are depicted in the background. These characters could represent a society that heads toward new forms bringing with them new hopes. The most significant scene, and undoubtedly the most ironic, is to be found in the fresco of the "New World." The charlatan shows the motley crowd (perhaps because the different classes can find moments of contact only in the world of illusion) fascinating visions from a magic lantern that attract the curiosity of the onlookers seeking ideas, or rather new truths. Attracted to the booth and its evasion of reality and duty are the vulgar peasant and the aristocrat, who crowd together, deprived of an identity, emblems of a decadent society that has forgotten the character of its own appearance. On the left, a Pulcinella stands aloof

observing these people who appear to be the new marionettes.

This fresco is not usual in the art of the Veneto in the eighteenth century. We do not find in it any of the graces of Arcadia or the caprices of the Rococo, nor the heroic and disciplined themes of neoclassicism.

Perhaps one could put the originality of the subject of the New World in relation to the bond that at that time linked Gian Domincio to the

noble Senator Angelo Querini. He was an enlightened spirit, a friend of Voltaire, secretly enrolled in the ranks of Masonry. Even though it did not seek the subversion of authority, the government of the republic, increasingly sensitive to every sort of criticism, had him arrested in 1761. Querini, once freed, founded a cultural circle where men of letters and artists met in his house at Altichiero, not far from Zianigo. He presents many analogies with Tiepolo: both were disillusioned and

Giandomenico Tiepolo.
Pulcinella in love.

Giandomenico Tiepolo.
The Acrobats.

rejected and retired to their properties, seeking to keep alive their independent thought and to flee from a world incomprehensible to them.

The art of Gian Domenico cannot be considered only as an adaptation of his father's art, even if he did conserve, while bringing it to maturity, the character of the language of the vignette.

A last phase in the pictoral cycle at Zianigo is dated 1797 coinciding with the moment of the fall of the republic. The enthusiasm and the illusions referred to by a group of enlightened conservatives are put away. These frescoes represent the "Adventures of Pulcinella." The world that is presented to us is the world of imaginary characters that laugh at every aspect of social life. The Pulcinellas, deprived of any identity by their masks, symbolize a society plunged into ruin because of the aristocracy's incapacity and indifference, where it is possible to survive only through a conscious evasion.

The villas in the nineteenth century and today

The relationship between the city and the country changed definitively with the end of the Serenissima. Venice gradually lost its centralizing force. The mainland acquired its own autonomy.

The customs of the old landlords were not forgotton as the presence of a new class of landlords made itself felt: the peasants and the factors of the ancient nobility, having enriched themselves, managed the lands with a peasant mentality. They are not Venetian or Veneto families but were often Jewish like the Lattes or else of religious orders like the Armenians or else local nobles now related to rich foreign families like the Widmann-Foscari. On one side property was increasingly fragmented, while on the other there was also a process of amalgamation into enormous holdings that paralleled a burgeoning program of industrialization.

This industrial society, with its liberal philosophy founded on physiocracy, affirmed that the origin of wealth was to be found in agriculture and in the "natural" relationships between individuals free of every bond. The urban model of Alvisopoli at Fossalta, with its peasant houses constructed in a row for an industrial type of productivity, was a significant example of the rationalization of agricultural activity in the Veneto.

The Camerini at Piazzola on the Brenta also attempted a fusion between agriculture and industry, while improving upon the social aspect. Their relationship with numerous dependents was impressed with an almost paternalistic spirit that resulted in the construction of dwellings for the peasants and for the workers and in the construction of a railway line that permitted them to reach Padua comfortably and in a short time.

However, in contrast to other regions like Emilia, Romagna, and Lombardy, that industrial type of immense agricultural enterprise never predominated in the Veneto.

Today in the Veneto there are still small and medium-sized industries near the villages so that the peasant-worker can work in the field and is not constrained to abandon the land of his origins. At the same time he can be employed in industrial production in his free hours. This is an organization that recalls that of the eighteenth

Michele Fanoli. Portrait of Giuseppe Japelli, lithograph (Padua, Civic Museum).

century before the advent of machinery and the consequent phenomenon of urbanization. For all its backwardness, it is an industry organized in an elastic fashion that can support crisis better.

There is much evidence of the life that was led in the villas of the Veneto countryside in the nineteenth century. However, one searches in vain for that fusion between economic, social, and cultural aspects that was present in the eighteenth century. In the nineteenth century there occurred a kind of fracture between the theme of wealth and themes of the spirit, almost as if money were a shameful thing to be hidden. Thus, if in Ippolito Nievo's novels the ruin of the villas and the castles

was still a realistic representation of the political and cultural dismemberment of feudal society in the lands bordering on the Friuli, in Fogazzaro the isolated villa immersed in nature could become the ideal environment for the spiritual and romantic ventures of a provincial nobility completely detached from Venice.

The villas were no longer seen as noble residences combined, as in Palladio, with agricultural activity. They served the search for a noble solitude amid green fields and extensive parkland that cleverly reproduced the romantic disorder of nature.

The element characterizing this particular moment in the *World of the Villas* was made up of the great parks that surrounded the buildings, often surpassing them in importance. The architect who, more than any other, revealed himself able to satisfy the romantic aspirations of these new patrons was Giuseppe Jappelli (1783-1852). At first linked to the neo-Gothic movement – as the Pedrocchi at Padua or the Villa de Manzoni at Agordo near Belluno demonstrate – Jappelli showed himself to be particularly brilliant in the planning of parks and gardens, sprinkled with pavillions, glass houses and temples, according to the dictates of the fashion of the day. He usually repeated that, having included in his projects that which could be contained in a limited space, it was equally necessary to make the spectator feel the presence of all surrounding nature.

Landscape seems to prevail in the Villa Fogazzaro Roy at Montegalda, rich in literary reminiscences as the theater of the events narrated by Antonio Fogazzaro in his *Piccolo Mondo Moderno.* There are a number of passages in the famous novel dedicated to the garden, personally cared for by Don Giuseppe Fogazzaro. "Conceived, designed by him, laid out on the rough plain and on the wild hill, embellished little by little, year after year, gazed upon for its flowering in the future, not for it in itself, but for the beloved spirit imparted by the earth against the blindness of men before him."

The villa, once the residence of the Chiericati, was reconstructed radically in 1847 by Antonio Caregaro Negrin, a Vicentine architect often hired to renew and alter the ancient residences of the local nobility according to new nineteenth-century taste. Criticized for this sort of intervention, which was defined by Cevese as "ill-advised devastations," Caregaro Negrin showed himself to be one of the most representative personalities of provincial culture and a forerunner of Art Nouveau. Trained in an environment where both classicism and

romanticism co-existed, the architect brought an eclectic style to maturity without, however, indulging in excessively bizarre solutions. We are thinking of his intervention at Abetone in the Villa Negri de' Salvi, the former residence of the poetess Maddalena Campiglia. Interest was drawn primarily to nature, following the tradition begun by Jappelli, to the picturesque park outlined by staircases, terraces, and greenhouses, dominated by the battlemented towers of the villa, constructed according to the romantic taste for ruins.

The Milanese architect Balzaretto was also an exponent of new, up-to-date artistic ornaments. At Lonigo he built the picturesque Villa of Prince Giovanelli on the ruins of the ancient convent of Ss. Fermo and Rustico, inspired by an eclectic and fantastic culture evident in the entrance and in the vast park.

The last traces of this style can be found in the bourgeois villas that display their little towers like a symbol of the distinction between them and the anonymity of common houses.

When romantic custom gave way to the culture of positivism and science, the proprietors of the villas become the animators of the life in the village, favoring the opening of libraries, academies, and theaters. The province was liberating itself from the city and seeking the documents of its own history and culture.

After the storm of the First World War that had forced many to seek refuge in the country, there began a period in which numerous students became interested in the phenomenon of the villas, publishing works that are still interesting from a historical point of view. Callegari and Brunelli on the Riviera of the Brenta, Fasolo on the villas of the Vicentine territory, and the text of Loukomski dedicated to the *Ville dei Dogi* are among the most noteworthy.

Thus there arose the need to safeguard those buildings which, besides their artistic value, had particular historic interest.

With the advent of Fascism the triumphant D'Annunzio style, well adapted to the taste of the rich bourgeoisie, imposed itself in the villas. The better part of the land owners held important offices under the regime in this period. This ended by causing irreparable harm to the archives kept in the villas. In an attempt to cancel all traces of compromising documents following the fall of Fascism many archives were consigned to flames, depriving us of precious documentation of the past.

Even the countryside did not provide a safe refuge during the Second World War, especially in the terrible period of the Resistance.

In the certainty that the city would never be bombed, there was a massive migration to Venice. The villas deteriorated, abandoned and despoiled of everything that could be carried away. A great part of the artistic patrimony kept in them was thus dispersed and sold to antiques dealers.

To limit the expense of maintenance and in order to make a profit from them, many parks were sold, depriving the buildings of their surroundings.

With the end of the war and with the fervor of the economic recovery, new construction spread everywhere in the Veneto. There grew up a continuous agglomeration where villages were no longer clearly distinguished. Even the villa, which once upon a time stood in isolation surrounded by gardens and fields, was now frequently flanked by buildings of every type, depriving them of their natural space. The fashion for taking one's holiday in the villas changed profoundly.

With the spread of rapid transport and with wealth distribuited in ever widening social strata, the old holiday centers in the country or in the hills were abandoned for the sea or the mountains.

The state of abandonment and desolation was accentuated for old villa buildings situated in locations now out of fashion and extremely costly to maintain in a dignified fashion because of the increased cost of labor.

Thanks to superior economic resources, some landowners did manage to preserve the integrity of the buildings and their decoration. In general, however, the villas were left to a destiny of a total neglect, frequently used for granaries or as barns.

Even just a short time ago, an arch with sixteenth-century frescos in the old garden of the Villa Sailer at Paese was torn down by the new farmer owners to create a throughway for their tractor.

Only recently has that inauspicious custom of ranting against these buildings as symbols of a past luxury or power seemed to abate.

With the publicity given to the Veneto villas for tourism a new stage has been reached. Their historic and cultural importance is being studied and the Agency for the Veneto Villas has been created.

Thanks to the interest of local agencies, a new osmosis has been created between the country and the city. The villas are now considered a part of the common heritage and are being defended and appreciated.

But what role can the villa have in today's world?

It is impossible to stet the old style of life because, along with life itself and a mentality, the economic and political structures are changed. Nonetheless the villa, with its artistic and historic value, can become a symbol of a country, recalling interest to small, forgotten centers to give a new dignity to the country, reminding Italy that "holy agriculture" still has much to teach us.

These symbols of power certainly exploited the peasants' labor but also brought benefits to the country, tracing roads, channeling rivers, reclaiming fields. They could become the new poles of local life. They could be used as schools, municipal offices, libraries, and cultural centers.

Many administrations often supported by the provinces, the region, and the state, have taken this road with excellent results.

Only with the collectivity can these noble buildings, after having been witnesses to a passed civilization, have a new life again in a democratic dimension and be maintained with pride.

*Antonio Canova, Orfeus
and Euridice, sculptures
previously at Villa Valier
di Casella d'Asolo, now
in Venice (Museo Correr).*

Antonio Canova

*Antonio Canova was born
in Passagno in 1757. In 1773,
he moved to Venice where he
developed his artistic talents
under the guidance of
Morlaiter and Marchiori.
It was during this period that
Canova completed two of his
earliest works:* Euridice *and*
Orfeus, *the latter for Villa
Falier, Casella d'Asolo.
Both of these sculptures
demonstrate an air of vitality,
different from the neoclassical
formality of which Canova
became an acknowledged
master.
One of the Counts of Falier
discovered the talents of the
young Canova and came to
his aid as a patron, acquiring
some of Canova's first works
done in soft stone. In 1779
Canova moved to Rome
and there produced some
of his most famous funerary
monuments such as* Genius
of Death *for the tomb of Pope
Clement XIII. The model
for this masterpiece was
for a long time kept at Villa
Barbarigo in Noventa,
Vicenza.
A theme of sensuality can be
noticed in Canova's
masterpieces, particularly
in the group of* Cupid and
Psyche *(1793) and the nude
of Paolina Borghese (1804).
Canova's last years were
centered on the production
of monuments and he died
in 1822.*

Alberto Lembo: The Venetian noble families and their coats of arms

The decision to accompany our treatment of the most important Venetian villas with the reproduction of the noble coat of arms of the respective proprietary family, along with its heraldic description, has been made with a specific purpose in mind: to underscore and display in the most apparent and effective way the ideal of prestige which motivated the noble families of Venice and of the mainland in the building and architecture of their villas.

The ambition to pass on the memory of one's actions to the following generations was, indeed, one of the principal aspirations of these rich aristocrats who used their own wealth, as well as State funds, to collaborate with the leading principles of the new policy of land cultivation which was pushed forward by the *Serenissima* during the course of the fifteenth century.

Their presence, which was a decisive factor in the growth of the mainland communities, was continually underscored and highlighted by the most evident symbols of the prestige of their family *gens,* the coats of arms which were blazoned on the facades of the villas, on the gateway portals, on the parapets around wells, on objects of everyday use and which identified the activity of the nobleman even in the construction of works for public use, of bridges, fountains and cisterns.

The grandeur of the family name and the prestige it had acheived are thus proclaimed through the coat of arms, a visual representation of the history and the glory of one's ancestors.

These emblems, so rich in curious and complexs meanings, underwent numerous changes over the course of centuries with the addition of new entitlements through marriages, inheritances, and patents and investitures of different kinds. In order to guarantee greater uniformity among the noble patents the rule was established that they be drawn, whenever possible, from documents preserved in the State Archive of Venice and presented by all the aristocratic families to the College of Heralds, the *Imperiale Regia Commissione Araldica,* which, after the fall of the Republic, was authorized by the Austrian government to verify local titles and to qualify the Venetian nobility in its standing with the rest of the nobility of the Austrian Empire.

The Venetian nobility created a heraldry distinct, at least in its origins, from that of other Italian regions. It was a heraldry devoid of eagles and lions and of other symbols of power or lordship or of dependence on the Emperor or on other Princes. There were some regulations, eventually overruled, which expressly prohibited the adoption of such symbols.

Many of the coats of arms of the oldest Venetian families can be traced to the marks stamped on the bales of goods to distinguish them from those of other merchants. This explains some of the characteristics of Venetian heraldry which is of an urban and mercantile, rather than feudal, origin. In fact, the Venetian nobility was born and developed with the city itself in a spontaneous process through which, in the beginning, those families were considered "patrician" who were the first to lead in the founding and government of the new State. According to tradition, the "evangelists" are the four families – Bembo, Bragadin, Corner, Giustinian – who subscribed to the act of foundation of the monastery of San Giorgio Maggiore in the year 725. Of the other twelve families, named the "apostolics", there is certain evidence prior to the ninth century, while eight others are from slighty later. From this group of families came almost all of the doges of the first centuries of the Republic as well as the holders of the principal offices of state. The existence of an actual aristocracy, even in the political sense of the rule of a few families, was only made offical, however, only through the reforms of Doge Pietro Gradenigo (1288-1311) who with the closing of the great council, the so-called "Serrata del Maggior Concilio", defined the limits of the patrician class by considering its members only those families whose members were at that time represented in the governing body of the Republic (It happened in some cases that some branches of the same family became patricians while others remained commoners, as appears to be the case of the Tiepolo family). From that time on the major government offices were reserved for the male descendants of this group, as well as the social status of *patrizio veneto,* and with this nobility the possibility of donning the cherished headdress of the Doge.

It was, however, an open aristocracy in the sense that the incorporation of new families remained possible, families who, in addition to resounding ducats for the exhausted coffers of State, brought new blood and fresh energies to the old patriciate. Today the old aristocracy is reduced to a few dozen families: Barbaro, Bembo, Bon, Bragadin, Canal, Cappello, Cicogna, Corner, Dolfin, Donà, Dondi, Emo, Grimani, Gritti, Loredan, Marcello, Memmo, Morosini, Priuli, Querini, Renier, Sandi, Valier, Venier, Zorzi..., all names which recur in the pages of this volume along with those of so many other lines which became extinct over the centuries, but which remain alive in the villas and palaces they built and sealed indelibly with their family coat of arms.

One further point of information: The arms of the Serene Republic as it is reproduced with its "quarters" of dominion and territorial sovereignty is a rather late heraldic construction not in use before the sixteenth century and then only in exceptional circumstances.

In general its use was limited to relations with foreign states, for whom the power of Venice was to be displayed while at the same time affirming its titles to territories no longer held but still claimed as part of the Republic. Internally only the lion of St. Mark was used as a symbol of the state along with the arms of the Doge crowned by the Doge's berretta as a symbol of the reigning serene prince. And on flags, only the lion of St. Mark was depicted.

VENETIAN VILLAS

FROM PETRARCH TO CORNARO

PETRARCH'S HOUSE Arquà Petrarca, Padua

Petrarch's house, here seen with its vineyard, hidden in the ancient Euganean hills, represented the perfect solution to the humanists, who were trying to find, in the countryside, the ideal place to dedicate themselves to learning, far from the confusion and stress of the city.

About the year 1360, Francesco Petrarca, a guest of the Carraresi, Signori of Padua, was able to have à small house, modest but seemly, built for himself at Arqua', near the spring where the villagers went to draw their water. Here, far from his birthplace and the cares of the world, the poet was able to realize his dream of leading a serene existence, absorbed in his studies, among the gentle Euganean hills in intimate contact with nature. He had chosen the small village of Arqua', in order to escape the noise and dust of the city, and to dedicate himself to study, to poetry and other fine

diversions. "The countryside is always lovely, always full of attractions to those who have noble dispositions," he wrote to a friend, "and so I am not only occupied with the ancient and unceasing world of study, which you know so well, but with other household affairs, of which you know nothing. I am very interested in agriculture, and in architecture. I am procuring from every part every sort of tree... I am hurrying to get a room ready for you, so come. I am sure that if you came you would not want to leave again." Petrarch's affection for this area is shown by his will, in which he asks to be buried at the church near his country home. His wishes were respected, and when, an 24 July, 1374, his funeral took place, Arqua' was filled by a huge assembly of nobles, men of the church, scholars and common people, and at its head, Francesco Carraresi, Signor of Padua. It is said that the long canal between Padua and Rivella di Monselice was packed, prow to stern, with the boats of this magnificent funeral procession.

Although the life-style that Petrarch was extolling was completely new and original at the time, it was really a reproposal of the ideals of the ancient, classic world. We only have to remember, as Ackerman does, that alongside the villas of the powerful were those of the men of letters, such as the "Sabine fields" praised by Horace, which "were hidden in the mountains in a spectacular location which seemed to have been created especially for a poet.". Petrarch idealizes nature and rural tranquility and praises the agreeableness of the country and the intimate satisfaction it offers the learned man who devotes himself to his garden and orchard.

Therefore it was in the heart of the Euganean hills, among the lush green slopes, that the advantages and delights of villa life began to be appreciated, that the culture of the villa began to grow. Here was created that particular psychology which, over the following centuries, would guide and inspire the aristocrats and literati, and would make the Venetian provinces richer, more fertile and even more beautiful.

*Previous page: The interior
of Petrarch's house, showing
scenes from Petrarch's life.*

*Petrarch's house.
The entrance hall with
frescoes illustrating Petrarch's
life.*

The poet's study.

PALAZZO DA MULA   The Isle of Murano, Venice

DA MULA
FAMILY

COAT OF ARMS

The Gothic-style facade, fourteenth and fifteenth centuries, of Palazzo da Mula on the Canale degli Angeli. The early villas constructed by the wealthy Venetians for their amusements and pastimes, were situated in the orchards of the nearby islands, and were inspired by the architectural styles of the city.

In the centuries which followed the year 1000, Venice, that vital nucleus of trade and traffic, began to exercise an irresistible fascination. Soon a large throng of dwellings and *botteghe,* or shops, began to spring up around this commercial magnet, whilst the narrow winding canals became even more intricate and lively.

As soon as they had accumulated some money, and had discovered the pleasure of spending it, the busy merchants felt the need to get away from the bustling centre and find a little peace and tranquility in other parts of the lagoon. In the same period, the diffusion of Petrachism and the humanistic culture manifested itself in a renewed love for nature, and of course, gardens.

And so the Giudecca was discovered. There one could relax in the peace of its fragrant orchards, which are clearly documented in Jacopo de Barbari's plan of 1500, where one can make out, along the shores of the island, the beautiful Lonbardesque facades of the villas, whose loggias and porticos opened out onto the gardens behind. One can also clearly see the courtyards with their wells, the vegetable gardens, the orchards and the vineyards that almost completely cover the island.

Equally significant is a German engraving of the Cinquecento depicting the delights of villa life on the Giudecca itself; in the courtyard of some wealthy dwelling several people, in gorgeous clothes, perform dances, whilst in the distance, beyond the wide St. Mark's Basin, one can see the Doge's Palace and the Basilica of St. Mark itself. Even more refined were those noble Venetians who chose as their ideal refuge the island of Murano. Alongside the glass furnaces – whose fumes were believed to purify the air – rose, from the end of the Quattrocento, splendid habitations, the first examples of a tradition that was to carry on throughout the whole of the successive century. Some traces still remain of the frescoes with which Paolo Veronese had

decorated the rooms and facade of one Patrician house, on which other illustrious exponents of Venetian art had also worked, namely Alessandro Vittoria and Vincenzo Scamozzi. But the golden period of Muranese houses, and by house I mean villa, was without doubt the Quattrocento, when the top echelons of Venetian society settled on the island: humanists and literati, magistrates of the Serenissima, patricians and merchants. It was here that the splendid palace of Caterina Cornaro, Queen of Cyprus, arose surrounded by a large garden, alongside the villas and palaces of the most illustrious dogal families of the city.

Of this refined humanistic climate, of this cultured and exclusive world, nothing, however, remains. On the island that is now densely populated, increasing numbers of dwellings have suffocated and invaded those orchards and gardens which at one time characterized the physiognomy of the island, and gave rise to the saying *Murano è a Venezia molto simile ma vi gede piu di amenitade,* (Murano is much like Venice, but there one can enjoy the beauty more).

The last surviving architectural example of that glorious period is Palazzo Da Mula, whose noble facade, elegantly embroidered with quadruple lancet windows and decorated Gothic balconies and walls faced with costly marble reliefs are reflected in the waters of the canals. Unfortunately the interior decorations, the Gothic friezes, and the refined polychromes of the Renaissance decoration have all disappeared, but the garden still possesses a magnificent example of Byzantine art, a round-headed marble arch, decorated with a band of exquisitely carved fantastic motifs.

Thus Palazzo Dal Mula remains the only tangible memory of a particularly happy moment in Venetian history. In fact it was at Murano that the Venetian nobles and humanists enjoyed the tranquility of the surroundings, studying the ancient tracts on

*Palazzo Da Mula seen from
the garden.*

agriculture and reading Petrarch's verses, nursing an increasing desire to get away from the city and its frenetic bustle. Murano witnessed the birth of a new psychology, a renewed appreciation and taste for villa life, that would inspire these Cinquecento Venetians to build their own country retreats overlooking the rivers and canals and in every corner of the hinterland in order to recapture and emulate the delights of these fragrant Muranese gardens.

VILLA DAL VERME Agugliaro, Vicenza

DAL VERME
FAMILY
COAT OF ARMS

Villa dal Verme is an early example of the type of villa that was being built in Basso Vicentino in the fifteenth century. Its elegant Gothic facade used to be reflected in the waters of the Liana canal, but successive risings of the water level meant the construction of higher banks, which unfortunately now partially hide the villa.

Like the other fifteenth-century dwellings, which still survive in Basso Vicentino, its origins seem to be irrevocably linked with the massive land reclamation schemes and canal building which, since the thirteenth and fourteenth centuries, occupied the nobility and populace living in that vast plain embraced by the Berici and Euganean Hills.

Villa Dal Verme seen from the Liona Canal. This house, still Gothic in style, is an early example of a villa constructed by a land reclaimer.

This, in fact, was one of the areas which came under the supervision of the Magistrato ai Beni Inculti, who here carried out several important land reclamation schemes, known as *retratti.* The Liana canal, for example, brought about the economic renaissance of this area, providing a rapid and safe means of communication to the markets.

It was the people of Vicenza who were first to realise the enormous possibilities of drainage schemes to salvage the arable land, at a time when the Serenissima Republic was still far more involved in maritime commerce. So it was along the banks of the Liana, and the other rivers which threaded their way through Basso Vicentino, that there arose some of the oldest villas in the Veneto. The typology of Villa dal Verme – the earliest example of decorated Gothic in the Vicenza countryside – is characteristic, that is it is much more like a city palace than a rural dwelling.

However, as Ackerman says, we must not forget that the villa is "economically a satellite of the city," and this dependence is emphasised, at least initially, by the same shared architectural forms which have been exported from the city into the country. Even though Villa dal Verme lacks agricultural outbuildings, it does possess the two large arches of the groundflow portico, which most probably responded to the needs of country life, acting as a sheltered landing place, a storehouse, and warehouse for the merchandise transported along the Liana waterway.

The three-mullioned window on the river facade.

VILLA SPESSA Carmignano di Brenta, Padua

QUINTO
FAMILY
COAT OF ARMS

Rarely does a place enjoy such good lines of communication as Villa Spessa does: at the meeting point of such important old Roman roads as the Postumia, and near the only place where it is possible to ford the Brenta, it was obviously the perfect site for an important residence.

The villa was built for a certain Giovanni Andrea da Quinto, a middle class Vicentine who had made a lot of money in the wool business and who had begun, in the first quarter of the fifteenth century, to buy up the land around Spessa and Carmignano, excellent for sheep farming and, being well-watered, very suitable for the production of wool.

From an architectural point of view, the building is very much like the palace of a noble citizen, in the Venetian style of the Quattrocento, but which here would form the centre of a proto-industrial, estate. The Quinto family enjoyed a greater freedom of initiative here in respect to those regulations and limits which govern construction in the city, so they were able to put up a large building.

The construction still possessed, however, all the characteristics of a house equipped for practical and utilitarian exigencies; only when it was purchased by the patrician Grimanis in the sixteenth century did it acquire certain aspects of gentrification necessitated by a new and more complex concept of what a villa should represent.

The presence of a small chapel seems to support the hypothesis that a large number of workers' houses – probably built out of poor materials for no trace remains today – had sprung up around this center of activity.

The facade of the small religious building demonstrates the clean forms of that Gothic style onto which Palladio would graft his own pure interpretations.

The confluence of he major communication routes and the nearness of the river Brenta explain the location of this majestic villa, whose owners were connected with the wool industry.

Detail of the facade, showing fifteenth-century decorations.

127

VILLA DALL'AGLIO Lughignano di Casale sul Sile, Treviso

CORNER
FAMILY
COAT OF ARMS

The portico and the facade that overlook the river Sile.

According to literary tradition, this villa was built by Caterina Cornaro and given as a wedding present to Fiammetta, one of her bridesmaids. Bembo tells the same story in his "Asolani." The building belongs to the late Quattrocento, even if some of the elegant capitals might tempt one to anticipate this dating by several decades.

As with Villa Agostini at Cusignana, the formula and typology is still that of a Venetian city dwelling, here ennobled by the perfect harmony of its form and by the elegant four-mullioned window which adorns the main facade. The villa looks over the waters of the river Sile, a nearness which is by no means casual but due to precise needs.

As we have noted before, villas were often built beside a river or canal, almost in symbiosis with the running water, invaluable lines of communication and source of life for the surrounding countryside.

VILLA DA PORTO COLLEONI
Thiene, Vicenza

DA PORTO
FAMILY
COAT OF ARMS

A view of the castle showing the five-mullioned window and crenellations. Surrounded by a wall and flanked by sturdy towers, like the home of a warrior, the villa with its wide open loggias, established a more trusting relationship with nature.

Even though it is rather difficult to place Da Porto Colleoni castle in the logical development of the Venetian villa, this romantic building, with its noble proportions, is extremely interesting and must not be overlooked.

Generally believed to be one of the oldest examples of a villa-cum-castle, it seems to be the result of a long series of modifications, additions and reconstructions, which have not, however, diminished in any way its evocative and highly original character. Apart from the varied construction work which took place between the fourteenth and nineteenth centuries, the sixteenth century saw the addition of the richly painted frescoes, where the festive and triumphant spirit of the Serenissima found its most immediate and admirable expression. Inside a trompe l'oeil loggia, frescoes by Fasolo and Zelotti portray various scenes from Roman history, such as Muzio Scevola, the meeting between Sophonisba and Massinissa, Anthony and Cleopatra, and the Clemency of Scipio.

The tripartite facade, the presence of two sturdy lateral towers, and a similar layout suggest certain parallels with the Fondaco dei Turchi, and more generally, with that typology of construction diffused over all the terra firma in the Quattrocento. The elegantly decorated, Gothic five-mullioned window, which graces the central porton of the complex, also adds to the impression that the building dates from the fifteenth century.

Like a typical medieval castle surrounded by walls and a moat, the complex includes a main dwelling-place, a small chapel, and other, more modest buildings.

Little, however, remains of its feudal and military character, for just beyond the castle walls we have the arcades of the villa, indicating the existence of a lifestyle no longer oppressed by medieval fears. Nevertheless, one can still sense a nostalgia for the days of knights and tournaments, a feeling which has not dulled or diminished over the centuries, for indeed

it was just this type of fortified villa which inspired the Romantic architects of the nineteenth century.

Today the villa houses a most interesting collection of works by Maganza, Maffei, Pietro Vecchia, Langhetti, and Boccacino.

The large salon on the ground floor, with frescoes by Giovanni Antonio Fasolo and Giambattista Zelotti.

Giovanni Antonio Fasolo and Giambattista Zelotti. The Clemency of Scipio.

Giovanni Antonio Fasolo. Sophonisba, pleading with Massinassa, detail.

Giovanni Antonio Fasolo. The feast of Antonio and Cleopatra.

133

Giambattista Zelotti.

Giambattista Zelotti was one of the most famous and highly praised fresco painters in the Veneto in the middle of the sixteenth century. Born in Verona in 1526, he collaborated with Paolo Veronese on the frescoes of Villa Da Porto Colleoni at Thiene and of Villa Soranza, as well as at Venice, in the Doge's Palace (1553-1554) and in the Libreria (1556-1557). He was also active in Vicenza, in the Palazzo Chiericati (1558) and in the Duomo (1572), and was much in demand among the nobility of that time, who often entrusted to him the decoration of their country houses. In about 1557 he completed the enormous cycle of frescoes at Villa Godi at Lonedo; later he worked at Villa Emo at Fanzolo and also at the Malcontenta. In the early 1570's we find him at the castle of Catajo at Battaglia, and in the rooms of the Villa Caldogno at Caldogno. In 1572 he completed the frescoes of Villa Porto at Torri di Quartesolo. In 1575 he moved to Mantova, where he was Prefect of the ducal buildings, and where he died in 1578. Villa Da Porto Colleoni, the large salon, showing scenes from the Clemency of Scipio by Antonio Fasolo and Giambattista Zelotti; at either side of the fireplace there are frescoes by Giovanni Antonio Fasolo portraying Vulcan and Venus.

136

Giovanni Antonio Fasolo.

The amusements, the pastimes, and the delights of villa life found, in the Cinquecento, a careful and sensitive interpreter in the person of Giovanni Antonio Fasolo. Born at Mandello, on lake Como, in 1530, he went to Vicenza when he was still only a boy. He collaborated with Paolo Veronese, on the Venetian church of San Sebastiano (1556) and was later comissioned to carry out the decorations for the Teatro Olimpico (1557-1602) and for the Loggia del Capitanio (1568) at Vicenza, a city where he often worked. He is especially well known for his frescoes in the numerous villas of the province of Vicenza and the neighboring areas: In 1555, together with Zelotti, he painted several scenes in the large salon of Villa Da Porto Colleoni at Thiene; around 1560 he frescoed the open gallery of Villa Roberti at Brugine, and, several years later, worked at Albettone, in the home of the Campiglia family, where part of his important work can still be seen today; lastly, during the 1570's, he was working on the enormous cycle of frescoes at Villa Caldogno at Caldogno, which proved in fact, to be his last work. Fasolo died at Vicenza in 1572.

137

VILLA GIUSTINIAN Roncade, Treviso

GIUSTINIAN
FAMILY
COAT OF ARMS

A grandiose architectural complex of the early Cinquecento, Villa Giustinian's special fascination derives from the double physiognomy which characterizes it.

From the outside it looks like a severe medieval castle, with its crenellations, moat, and massive protective curtain wall with sturdy corner towers. But despite this forbidding

appearance, it is not in fact a feudal nucleus, surviving from the days before the Serenissima annexed the hinterland, but a peaceful country residence, built by Girolamo Giustinian in this way to perpetuate the memory of the ancient home of the Sanzi family.

Therefore, to quote Ackerman, these types of architectural form are "expressions of power and aspirations of class," which for their symbolic value can coexist with "an avantegarde villa of the early Cinquecento," which is how he describes Villa Giustinian.

As soon as one passes over the fake drawbridge the dark medieval atmosphere quickly disappears, and in the center of this fortified space we can see a majestic villa, one of the most emblematical architectural expressions on the Venetian terra firma. No longer a closed, inward-looking defensive structure created in the Middle Ages, but a surprising opening of porticos and airy loggias, an original interpretation of that "open architecture" which for centuries had characterized Venetian buildings, and which, once peace had been restored, would be found all over the hinterland.

A rare example of Lombardesque architecture, Villa Giustinian is made even more beautiful by the delightful pastel-colored frescoes which decorate its facade. With its cordial open porticos it predates Palladio's ingenious inventions by several decades.

The walls of the ancient castle guard the open architecture of the villa, almost as if to emphasize the transformation which has taken place, over the centuries, in the home of a nobleman.

Villa Giustiniani, the sturdy watch towers flanking the fake draw-bridge.

The elegant arched Lombardesque loggia superimposed on the facade of the villa.

QUEEN CATERINA CORNARO'S BARCO Altivole, Treviso

CORNARO
FAMILY
COAT OF ARMS

Polyphilus kneels in reverence before the throne of Queen Eleutevillide, surrounded by her court; (Francesco Colonna, Hypnerotomachia Poliphili *Venice, 1499).*

When the Prince of Lusignano died, his wife, Caterina Cornaro, inherited the dominion of Cyprus. Her reign, however, was short: Venice, fully aware of the island's strategic importance and considering the continuous attacks to which it was subject, entered into discussions with the Queen, and in 1489 finally convinced her to renounce her sovreignty. In exchange she was given the Signoria of Asolo, which she kept until her death in 1510.

After having lived in a sumptuous palace in Cyprus, Caterina was obriously not going to be too happy with either of her Asolan residences, the one an austere castle on top of the hill, and the other a modest little palace in the middle of town; her ambitions were far grander, and her culture much more refined.

So it was in 1490, soon after arriving in Asolo, that she started the construction of a magnificent villa at Altivole, built to the designs of Piero Lugate, where she realized her humanistic dreams, and where art vied with nature to satisfy every longing for spectacular views, color, shade and fragrance. The extensive estate was watered by many small rivers and streams, tributaries of the Piave, which not only irrigated the fields, kitchen gardens and orchards but supplied water for the elegant fountains and for the elaborate water jokes which were used at parties to catch out the unsuspecting guests.

So also at Altivole two different lifestyles existed contemporaneously; alongside that of the agrarian world, with its seasonal labors, harvests, crops and fruits, there was that of the court, a gay and carefree world, inspired by its humanistic love of nature.

The noble residence of Caterina is still known by the name "Barco," a word which Bembo used to signify "Paradise," and it was in this paradise, in this delightful retreat, that the Queen loved to surround herself with her elect court of artists and literati. It was the same Bembo who was so enchanted with the town and its inhabitants, that he invented the word

asolare, which means to pass one's days surrounded by the beauty of nature. The receptions, elegant banquets, and elaborate amusements which consoled her for the loss of her island kingdom, seen to be strangely echoed in the stupendous xylographs that illustrate the *Hypnerotomachia poliphili.* An allegorical romance, interwoven with subtle symbolism and literary references, the "Poliphilo" was the perfect answer to the dreams and cultural aspirations of the late Quattrocento: with its descriptions on gardens, orchards and viridania, of fountains and elegant architecture, it represented a humanistic celebration of beauty, and extolled the most cultured and refined customs of villa life.

Unfortunately, hardly anything remains of the Barco of Altivole, which if it had been conserved in its entirety, would have without doubt constituted the most remarkable example of Quattrocento architecture in the Venetian countryside. It was not long before it embarked on its slow and gradual process of degradation and deterioration, and in 1831 the last towers

and crumbling buildings were torn down, and the fountain eventually found its way to a museum in Vienna.

Only the words of Bembo and the haunting images of the *Poliphilo* remain to testify to the amazing beauty and vastness of the complex; the only surviving architectural testimony of that exquisite and festive world is the elegant Lombardesque loggia, in Nantes stone, which flanked the main building in much the same way as they do in Venetian houses.

The character of the painted decorations on the loggia is surprisingly conservative, especially those of the Oratorium, where the inspiration seems to belong to a tradition and culture far removed from the splendors and pastimes which blossomed at the Court of the Queen of Cyprus.

Garden with the fountain of Venus; Polia makes a laurel wreath for Poliphilus (Francesco Colonna, Hypnerotomachia Poliphili Venice, 1449).

All that is left of Caterina Cornaro's famous villa, the Barco, mentioned in the Poliphilo, *by Fra Giocondo and by Pietro Bembo, is this wonderful Lombardesque loggia.*

Theater historians believe that the great Ruzzante himself recited his works in this loggia, in the summer of 1521.

Recently a monument has been erected in the center of Altivole, in front of the church, to another personage who had a very important role in the history of the Venetian villas; Fra' Giocondo, the great Veronese architect, protagonist of many official building projects undertaken by Serenissima, both in the field of hydraulic engineering and of civic construction. The monument to Fra' Giocondo in this very place is very apt, and fits in well with the memory of the villa that Caterina Cornaro was building in those same years.

Both the architect and the Queen were inspired by the highest standards of culture and learning, and they were both protagonists in one of the most memorable and fascinating periods in the history of the villa.

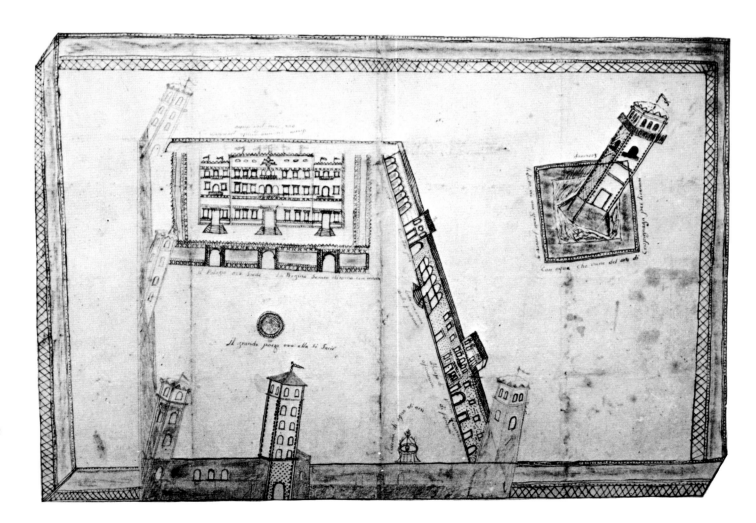

Plan of Caterina Cornaro's villa at Altivole, a drawing from the seventeenth century (Asolo, Civil Museum).

Barco of the Queen Caterina Cornaro, a fifteenth-century loggia with traces of elaborate frescoed decorations, and a detail of a capital.

144

VILLA TIRETTA AGOSTINI
Cusignana di Arcade, Treviso

AGOSTINI
FAMILY
COAT OF ARMS

Blessed with remarkably elegant proportions and a high standard of workmanship, this fifteenth-century villa seems to constitute the link in that intermediate phase between the traditional Venetian house exported to the countryside and the harmony of Palladio's designs, with its noble flight of steps leading up to the entrance of the simple but fine facade.

Thus it seems to be an example of the evolution, and here I quote Ackerman, "from the stoic morale of Cato and Verrone, who saw in the countryside the means of purifying oneself of the contamination of the city, to the ideals of Pliny the Younger, who praised the pleasures of villa and country life."

At one time the severe simplicity of the building was embellished by frescoes of historical scenes and imitations of ancient reliefs, portraying the values and ideals that the owners wished to convey. These decorations have long since vanished, and nothing is left to disturb the equilibrium of the bare walls and the erudite distribution of space.

It is especially in the Marca Trevigiana, a region very dear to the hearts of the Venetians, that we can find such successful interpretations of the architectonic type of house-cum-warehouse, so common in the capital. The arcades of the porticos, which in Venice served as a sheltered place to load and unload merchandise that had come from every corner of the world, here, in the villas of Trevigiana, were built to receive more humble wares, farm carts loaded with the produce and fruits of the rich Trevigiano earth.

This villa, still reminiscent of the fifteenth century, recaptures the style of the old Venetian house-cum-storehouse, with its portico for the loading and unloading of merchandise.

146

PALAZZO ALLA CORTE known as "Villa Ottavia"
La Costa di Rovolon, Padua

COAT OF ARMS

This building, now known as Villa Ottavia, is at Rovolon, on those slopes of the Euganean hills which look onto the setting sun. Here we have a page of history which is of exceptional importance, closely linked to the developement of the Venetian villas.

It must not be forgotten that the Paduan Benedictine Order was chiefly concerned with the countryside rather than with the city, instigating well organized agricultral projects, and more important, extensive land reclamation schemes. Naturally here they worked together with the Paduan and Venetian nobles, until the Magistrati dei Bene inculti assumed the definitive systemization of the territory.

In 970 Bishop Gauslino had endowed the monastery of Santa Giustina in Padua with extensive lands, including several churches, and amongst these was the church of San Giorgio in Rovolon. More land in the same area was purchased in 1441, and this included the hamlet of La Costa with the houses of Giovanni Parisino, where at one time had existed a fortress belonging to the Counts of Padua.

The Rector had his residence and administrative offices here, in the Palazzo alla "Corte," whilst another functionary acted as official at the "Corte del Vegrolongo," in the neighborhood of Bastia, where the monks owned another 700 fields.

At the "Court of Rovolon," in the 1500's, the monks collected the rents and the tithes – the half and tenth part of the grain, the third and tenth part of the vegetables, the half and

tenth part of the wine "brought in grapes to press at the Court of Vegrolongo."

Angelo Portenari, in his book *Della Felicità di Padova* (1623) talks about the hills of Rovolon, "which towards the west is planted with vines and trees, and which has a gracious outlook over the plain," and the places which "have by the same monks been embellished and made very beautiful, and for delightfulness can be compared with any place near Padua."

Apropos this last remark, it is interesting to know that the Palace of Rovolon, with its marvelous setting, was also used as a country retreat for the monks from the abbey at Padua, and in fact this is still the function of the ancient palace today.

The main body of the building, which echoes the typical style of the Venetian house, is embellished by an elegant portico, providing access to the villa and to the open Lombardesque loggia that overlooks the valley.

THE CORNARO LOGGIA AND ODEON Padua

CORNARO
FAMILY
COAT OF ARMS

Even though today it forms part of the urban texture of Padua, this architetonic complex was originally a suburban redidence, built on the ruins of an old dwelling that Alvise Cornaro had inherited from his maternal uncle, Alvise Angelieri, together with the vast property of Codevigo. Alongside these buildings – which were perhaps spared the fifteenth-century *guasto,* or blitz, (when all the buildings near the city walls were torn down for defence purposes), because of their nearness to the Basilica of St. Anthony – ran a small river, which was a useful means of communication to Venice.

After succeeding his uncle, Alvise occupied himself principally with the construction and decoration of those buildings designed for amusement and the arts, where, very soon, there would be meetings of friends and foreigners, attracted by the intellectual pleasures offered by this great patron of the arts.

A devout student of classical civilization, and closely connected with the lively world of Rome, Alvise Cornaro personally oversaw the realization of the two buildings: the Loggia, a perfect proscenium that witnessed the dialogues and plays of Ruzzante, amongst others, and the Odeon, built for concerts, for a more refined enjoyment of music.

Especially in the months of winter, the Paduan residence would play host to the most varied collection of cultural events. With the arrival of better weather, the whole court transferred to the country, either to Codevigo, or more often to the Villa at Este, documented by Cornaro himself. In the *Dialogue della vita sobria* we can find an accurate description of the banquets and performance that took place in those Paradisian hills. No trace, however, remains of the theater he is said to have built at Lorea. For the building of the Loggia and the Odeon Alvise Cornaro availed himself of the work of Giovanni Maria Falconetto, an architect who was very active in Padua and the surrounding province: it is to him that we owe

several of the majestic city gates and also the completion of the Monte di Pietà, where his Renaissance style blends so harmoniously with the superb medieval structure of Giovanni degli Eremetani.

It is thanks to Cornaro that Falconetto also obtained the commission to design the Villa dei Vescovi at Luvigliano. In the Loggia and the Odeon, however, it is very difficult to distinguish between the *invenzioni* of the architect, and those of his great patron.

This architectonic complex in Padua brings us almost to the middle of the sixteenth century, in fact to the dawn of the vast Renaissance movement, of which, in a few decades, Palladio himself would become part, after having carefully assimilated the humanistic lessons of Alvise Cornaro.

Facade of the Odeon, a building designed for musical performances.

150

To know more about the history of theater in the villa, we can do no better than look at the example provided by Alvise Cornaro; a patron of writers and artists, the friend and patron of Ruzzante, his own residence in Padua was actually designed as a theater. His other villas, scattered around the countryside, also played host to numerous recitals and plays, amusements which were much appreciated after a day's hunting.

No traces remain today of these theaters, but it has been suggested that the Arch of Este designed by Falconetto, the only surviving remnant of the villa built by Cornaro in this town, could have had a double function, that of an imposing entrance and also of a classical frons scenae. Later on when the baroque theatrical taste of the seventeenth century became more grandiose and spectacular, the whole architectonic structure of the villa itself became involved; the exclusive gatherings, isolated in the countryside, designed for the pleasure of just a few noblemen, disappeared. The villas themselves were now conceived scenographically, each and every element contributed to the performance, as we shall see at Piazzola sul Brenta. But the love for these "theaters in the greenery" so much enjoyed during the Renaissance, soon flowered again, inspired by the Arcadian culture: pastoral fables and hunting scenes, feasts and balls, all found their ideal ambience in the garden.

There were very many theaters in the villas during the eighteenth century, and great was the prestige of the noblemen who could offer plays and performances to his own guests in his own villa. The Widmanns, above all others, were especially successful in this field; at their villa at Bagnoli di Sopra, Carlo Goldoni himself presented some of this plays, which he watched in the company of his noble friends.

The loggia of Villa Cornaro, with the portico that provided an ideal scenographic background for theatrical performances.

VILLA DEI VESCOVI
Luvigliano di Torreglia, Padua

PISANI
FAMILY
COAT OF ARMS

Villa dei Vescovi, designed by Giovanni Maria Falconetto in the heart of the Euganean hills.

Giovanni Maria Falconetto.

Giovanni Maria Falconetto, an architect and painter born at Verona in 1468, had an important influence on the development of the villa in the Veneto. The first phase of his artistic career was dedicated essentially to frescoes, and he worked in the church of Saints Nazano and Celso (1497-1499) and in the Calcasoli chapel at Verona. After moving to Padua in order to be able to enjoy the patronage of Alvise Cornaro, he distinguished himself as an architect, designing the Loggia and the Odeon (1524) for his patron, and the city gates of San Giovanni (1528) and Savonarola (1530). Again for Cornaro he built the Villa dei Vescovi at Luvigliano, one of the first examples of Venetian architecture to be inspired by Ancient Rome. He also designed Villa Cornaro at Este, of which only the triumphal Arch, built of Nantes stone, remains. The actual date of his death is uncertain, but it took place around the year 1540.

Before Palladio's ideals regarding the design and construction of villas spread around the Venetian hinterland, the country residences were of a very varied physiognomy, being the result of the owner's wishes and of course influenced by the presence *in loco* of existing architecture.

This was the situation at Luvigliano where in 1529, Giovanni Maria Falconetto was commissioned by the Bishop of Padua to build a summer residence on the foundations of a medieval castle. Falconetto received the commission through the devices of his friend and patron, Alvise Cornaro, who was the administrator of Pisani, the Bishop of Padua.

Situated in an open valley which was the form of an amphitheater, deep in the heart of the Euganean hills, the Veronese architect built the princely residence on different levels, its massive rectangular structure is relieved by the sudden and unexpected openings of porticos and loggias.

The whole complex possesses a sense of noble monumentality: the elegant balustrades, the turns of the wide steps that connect the various floors, the walled courtyard with its classic arcades, are all elements of Falconetto's particular conception of a villa.

Built of the materials from the ruins of the castle, the villa has a most charming and elegant interior: all the rooms are frescoed with floral motifs, refined Mannerist mythological groups, executed in brilliant colors, the work perhaps of Lambert Sustris, a Flemish painter.

Without doubt Alvise Cornaro's presence was very important in the history of this villa, both as administrator of the Bishop, and as friend of the architect: "And if a gentleman or private person desires to know how to build in the city, come to the Cornaro house in Padua; if he wants to build a villa, go to Codevigo and to Campagna; he who wants to build a palace worthy of a prince, must go to Luvigliano."

All of the above mentioned buildings were

Villa dei Vescovi, the main façade. The glorification of the triumphal Roman spirit is an indication of the cultural level of the Vescovi of Padua, the owners of this Villa.

The steps and the terraces which extol the wonderful position of the villa, dominating the valley.

by Falconetto: although the palace at Luvigliano had little resonance in the Veneto, and is of no consequence in the history of the Venetian villas, it nevertheless represents a particular cultural moment: what prevails is that triumphant Roman spirit, which was to influence the architecture of Sanmichele, if not that of Palladio.

157

ARCO DI VILLA CORNARO Este, Padua

CORNARO
FAMILY
COAT OF ARMS

"I go in April and May, and again in September and October, for several days to enjoy my hill in the Euganean mountains, and in the most beautiful part I have my fountains and gardens, and above all my comfortable and beautiful rooms. Here I can still have enough breath to do a little hunting, such that is suitable to my age, easy but very pleasurable."

So wrote Alvise Cornaro, protagonist and tutelary deity of the history and culture of the Venetian villas, describing his *villegiatura,* or holidays at his villa at Este. "It is the man of the city," as Ackerman says, "who idealizes life in the country, and who, if he possesses the necessary means, purchases a property in order to enjoy it. This need is of a psychological nature rather than a utilitarian one; it is a need which is essentially psychological." Cornaro's love of art and architecture dovetailed perfectly with his idyllic conception of the country, but even more profound was his love for *la santa agricoltura,* or blessed agriculture, which he viewed realistcally as the true basis of wealth and prosperity.

The only surviving remnant of a magnificent noble residence, this arch, designed by Giovanni Maria Falconetto, still manages to convey an idea of the beauty of Alvise Cornaro's retreat in the Euganean Hills.

So at Codevigo, where the Cornaros had already carried out various land reclamation projects, they created a complete village from almost nothing, separating the land from the water, bringing in entire peasant families to work on the salvaged land, building roads, houses, and even a temple where all could gather to offer their thanks to God.

It was the abundant wealth derived from this well organized agriculture that permitted Alvise Cornaro to construct his famous residence in Padua, where the Loggia and the Odeon are testimonies of the culture, ingeniousness and initiative of the great Paduan, and also of the skill of Giovanni Maria Falconetto, the architect who worked for and was advised by him. Here the aristocratic and learned friends of Cornaro would listen to the dialogues and plays of Angelo Beolco, better known as Ruzzante, who was often a guest at Cornaro's villa at Este, too.

Hardly anything remains of this once splendid residence, the theater there that was built "in imitation of the ancients" vanished long ago, the villa with its six fields of vineyards and gardens has been demolished, and the only piece of architecture left standing is the entrance arch to the garden, an elegant testimony of the art of Falconetto – who, whote Vasari, collaborated on many projects with Alvise Cornaro – and of the exquisite taste of his patron.

Built of gold, crumbling Nantes stone, the arch is decorated with a centrally placed mask, and with Victories in the spandrels. The obvious classical inspiration and the grandeur of this triumphal arch are not simply tributes to empty rhetoric or erudite magniloquence, thanks to the delicate elegance of its shape, and especially to the soft warm colors of the Nantes stone which relieves the severe architecture.

The sole survivor of a noble complex, the arch still evokes memories of this amazing retreat built by Cornaro at Este, with its glorious gardens, terraces and spacious villa.

159

VILLA TRISSINO Cricoli, Vicenza

TRISSINO DAL VELLO D'ORO
FAMILY
COAT OF ARMS

The growing appreciation for the type of lifestyle which was possible when one owned a country villa, that lifestyle so warmly praised by Petrarch and later by the humanists, led to construction of many elegant surburban dwellings in the fifteenth century, homes which were within easy reach of the city, yet which enjoyed the tranquil surroundings of the countryside.

The tragic events of the Cambrian war rudely interrupted this trend, indeed many villas were torn down in the *guasto* for defence reasons, and Venetian society experienced a period of crisis and decadence.

The first architectural manifestation of the successive cultural and economic renaissance in the province of Vicenza seems to have been the villa built by Giangiorgio Trissino, poet and humanist, dilettante architect, a product of the lively cultural atmosphere of Rome. This villa, built at Cricoli, near Vicenza between the years 1530 and 1538, seems in many ways to be almost a portrait of its owner, reflecting his literary tastes and his preference for the classical world: Trissino, as we now know, took an active part in the planning and designing of the villa, suggesting various architectonic solutions which have an obvious Roman derivation, and composing the Latin and Greek inscriptions which at one time formed the friezes which decorated the rooms of the villa.

Absolutely symmetrical, the facade consists of two massive towers which flank and form a marked contrast to the completely Renaissance polychrome central section. It was during the construction of the house that Trissino happened to meet and fall into conversation with one of the many craftsmen who were working on the site, a certain stone dresser by the name of Andrea di Pietro della Gondola, and this was to be the beginning of a famous and fruitful relationship. It was Trissino who gave Andrea the humanist name of Palladio, and who introduced him into the aristocratic circles of Vicenza, where he was to meet many of his future clients, and where he was able ot

experience that refined intellectual climate which had developed around the "Accademia Ocriculana," which met at the villa and included some of the most fervid geniuses of the time. One of Trissino's projects was to develop a language that would be totally free of dialectical inflections, a language that would be pure and universal. In this he did not succeed, but his discovery and disciple was destined to become one of the greatest and certainly the most imitated architects throughout the world, of all time.

Vincenzo Catena. Portrait of Giangiorgio Trissino (Paris, The Louvre).

A major figure of the humanist culture of the sixteenth century, Giangiorgio Trissino assisted with the planning of his villa (1530-1538), which would be the seat of a refined academy.

160

Giangiorgio Trissino.

Poet and humanist, and one of the most worthy exponents of Italian culture in the early part of the Cinquecento, Giangiorgio Trissino, (born in Vicenza in 1478), enjoyed remarkable fame in his life, and was praised by such people as Ariosto and Aretino. He always combined a profound commitment to political and civil matters (leaning towards the Holy Roman Emperor, rather than to Venice) with a large variety of cultural interests, as his literary output shows. At his villa at Cricoli there gathered together some of the most ardent geniuses of the time, who started the famous Trissinian or Oricolan Academy.

Notwithstanding his undoubtled merits in the field of humanistic studies, perhaps he will be remembered above all as the discoverer and patron of Andrea Palladio. It was thanks to his brilliant instruction, that the humble stone cutter from the workshop of Bartolomeo da Sossano was able to emerge from anonymity, and become one of the great men of the Cinquecento. Trissino, after meeting Andrea while he was doing some work at Cricoli, immediately recognized his enormous talents. He chose for him the significant name of Palladio, instructed him personally, introducing him to the world of the classical art, guiding him in his discovery of the monuments of ancient Rome, encouraging him in his studies of treatises, and lastly, introducing him into the most cultured and refined circles of the time.

Giangiorgio Trissino died in Rome in 1550.

162

THE HISTORY AND CULTURE OF THE
VENETIAN VILLAS

FROM SANSOVINO
TO PALLADIO

VILLA GARZONI
Pontecasale di Candiana, Padua

GARZONI
FAMILY
COAT OF ARMS

Symbolic example of the villa of a land reclaimer; this large imposing white building proclaims the wealth of the Garzoni family, who initiated a series of land reclamation projects in the area.

When, in the fifteenth century, Venice had triumphantly conquered the terra firma, many estates belonging to the local nobility were appropriated by the Serenissima, and then auctioned off to the highest bidder. This was to be the fate of 1500 fields of the estate owned by the Dal Verme family at Pontecasale. Put up for sale in 1440, the land was purchased by one Luigi Garzoni, a member of a very wealthy Venetian banking family.

One hundred years later, evidently inspired or stimulated by the general climate of patriotic fervor, the Garzoni family undertook various land reclamation and drainage projects, and eventually, as by now was the custom, commissioned the construction of an important residence, destined to be a symbol or espression of the family's wealth and prestige.

The major artists working at Venice at that time were consulted, and the task of designing the building was entrusted to the famous Jacopo Tatti, known as Sansovino, who as Vasari

writes: "Made the palace of Signor Luigi de Garzoni langer than the Fondaco dei Turchi, on every side, by thirteen paces, and with much comfort, for the water runs all through the palace, which is adorned with four very beautiful figures by Sansovino, the said palace is at Ponte Casale in the country." The villa faces south, and its impressive facade rises abruptly from the flat surrounding plain, and is reached only after climbing an imposing flight of steps.

A solemnity, a monumentality of Roman inspiration seems to permeate this noble architecture, which, however, unlike the villas built by Palladio, was to remain a splendid deviation destined to have no imitators, being perhaps too aulic for the surrounding countryside, even through it was precisely this that had inspired the Garzonis to invest their money there and leave this monument to their successors.

Two large wings reach out from the central body, spanned by the ten arches of the magnificent atrium, which perhaps inspired Palladio's addition to the Basilica of Vicenza. By crossing this airy opening, full of light, one reaches the delightful internal courtyard whose marble pavements hide a reservoir of rain water, this not only guaranteed the water supply, but cooled and refreshed the villa itself.

One of the largest and best preserved architectonic complexes, Villa Garzoni also boasts some wonderful fireplaces with marble caryatids by Sansovino and his school, but Vittoria's firedogs and the precious furniture by Ammannati, were sold in the 30's by the Counts Donà dalle Rose.

With its mass of statuary and extensive parkland this building is certainly comparable with the most magnificent palaces of Europe, even though it does lack the large ornate garden which would have made this admirable villa even more glorious and charming.

Villa Garzoni, the hanging courtyard with its loggia crowned by statues.

The central part of the two-storied facade is animated by a double order of five arches, separated by half-columns, as in the facade of the Libreria Marciana.

The parties that surround the hanging courtyard, with a well curb sculptured by Jacopo Sansovino.

VILLA GODI Lonedo di Lugo, Vicenza

GODI
FAMILY
COAT OF ARMS

Villa Godi, whose severe form dominates the beautiful rolling foothills of the Dolomites, is one of Palladio's first documented works. Dating from just before his Roman experiences, Villa Godi seems to be imprinted with a profoundly Venetian style. It could be seen as a sixteenth-century reproposal of the traditional twin-towered house that was built all over the province of Vicenza in the fifteenth century. The structurally unitary construction of the various parts, which would later be typical of Palladio, are still only in an embryonic stage here, and the central spine of the villa seems to be inserted rather than integrated into the building.

Illustrated in the *Quattro Libri,* Villa Godi is a large construction with two tower-like blocks which convey a sense of strength and solidarity. Ackerman describes it as an example of a centralized cubic villa, "which is in clear contradiction with nature." And it does, in fact, lack that cordial rapport which usually existed between Palladio's villas and their environment. The building is surrounded by a large park (which was landscaped in the nineteenth century by Antonio Carego Negrin) and seems to clearly express the ambitions and prestige of its *committente,* Girolamo Godi, who, as Palladio notes, spared no expense in order to achieve a perfection of form.

The entrance to the house is particulary interesting. A steep flight of steps, enclosed by two projecting wings, leads up to a balustrade balcony, which in turn leads into a tripartite portico.

The interior of Villa Godi is in complete contrast to the exterior, and seems like the inside of a jewel casket, richly and even sumptuously decorated. Indeed, some of the foremost fresco painters of the time worked here, artists such as Gualtiero Padovano, Giambattista Zelotti, and Battista del Moro who filled the various rooms and the belvedere loggia with an exuberance of figures, scenes and

This villa, with its severe and imposing squared masses, is one of Palladio's first works, constructed before his visits to Rome, which inspired the artist to strive after the elegant equilibrium of classical architecture.

IN LONEDO luogo del Vicentino è la feguente fabrica del Signor Girolamo de' Godi pofta fopra vn colle di bellifsima uifta, & a canto un fiume, che ferue per Pefchiera. Per rendere quefto fito commodo per l'vfo di Villa ui fono ftati fatti cortili, & ftrade fopra uolti con non picciola fpefa. La fabrica di mezo è per l'habitatione del padrone, & della famiglia. Le ftanze del padrone hanno il piano loro alto da terra tredici piedi, e fono in folaro, fopra quefte ui fono i granari, & nella parte di fotto, cioè nell'altezza de i tredeci piedi ui fono difpofte le cantine, i luoghi da fare i uini, la cucina, & altri luoghi fimili. La Sala giugne con la fua altezza fin fotto il tetto, & ha due ordini di feneftre. Dall'vno e l'altro lato di quefto corpo di fabrica ui fono i cortili, & i coperti per le cofe di Villa. E' ftata quefta fabrica ornata di pitture di bellifsima inuentione da Meffer Gualtiero Padouano, da Meffer Battifta del Moro Veronefe, & da Meffer Battifta Venetiano; perche quefto Gentil'huomo, ilquale è giudiciofifsimo, per redurla a quella eccellenza & perfettione, che fia pofsibile; non ha guardato a fpefa alcuna, & ha fcelto i più fingolari, & eccellenti Pittori de' noftri tempi.

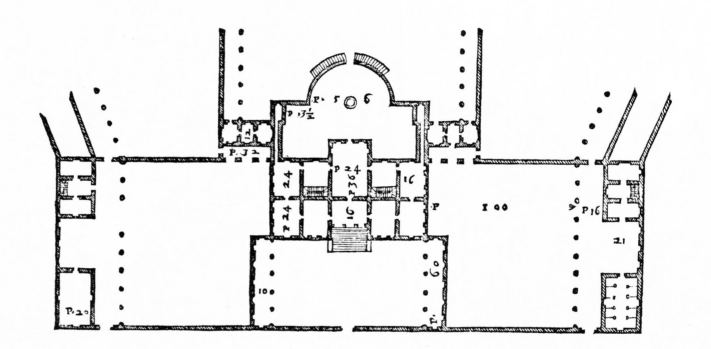

II   A SANTA

decorations which sometimes seems excessive.

Whole walls are hidden beneath caryatids and trompe l'oeil columns, classical scenes, mythological figures or military triumphs, or else they open up like windows on to the vast and luminous trompe l'oeil landscapes of Gualtiero Padovano, as if to capture forever an idealized rapport with nature. Trophies of war and various allegories complete the decorations, and here one can make out the noble figure of Securitas, an obvious reference and celebration of the peace finally achieved after the dark and terrible period of the Cambrian War, after which it was once more feasible and possible to build villas in every corner of the Venetian countryside.

The loggia of the villa with frescoes by Gualtiero Padovano overlooks the garden and the surrounding hills.

The circle of frescoes inside the building were carried out between the years 1552 and 1553, and represent the first example of villa decoration conceived on a large scale.

173

*Villa Godi, Salon of the
Muses, with frescoes by
Battista dell'Angelo, known
as del Moro, which portray
the Muses with Poets;
monumental caryatids
support the trabeation.*

177

VILLA PIOVENE Lonedo di Lugo, Vicenza

PIOVENE
FAMILY
COAT OF ARMS

Villa Piovene enjoys a magnificent setting, dominating as it does the deeply furrowed plain of Astico, and possessing a lovely nineteenth-century park.

Its actual attribution to Palladio is somewhat controversial but there is no doubt that it was he who at least inspired it, especially when one looks at the pronaos or portico spanned by six Ionic columns. The Piovene residence was completed in 1740 by Frances Muttoni, one of the most faithful and sensitive heirs to the Palladian tradition, who also designed the airy *barchesse,* or agricultural wings, and the truly monumental flight of steps which eventually leads up to the portico.

One of the most interesting aspects of this

As well as enjoying a superb setting, the architectural complex is remarkable due to the contrast between the sober, classical style of the main building and the animated Baroque style of the entrance gate and steps.

Beyond the gates one can see a flight of steps leading up to the Palladian villa; the statues that adorn the magnificent entrance, the steps, the the garden are the work of Orazio Marinali's workshop and Valsodan stonemasons.

From the loggia one can gaze over the plendid landscape of the Vicenza plain; the portico was added in 1740 by Francesco Muttoni.

On the following pages: The scenographic flight steps which follow the slope of the hill; it was probably built at the beginning of the eighteenth century, at the same time as the entrance portico.

villa is the striking and exciting contrast between the peaceful sobriety of the main building, which is splendidly elegant, and the Baroque animation and decorative profusion that characterizes the entrance gates and, beyond them, the imposing steps that follow the contour of the hill, and are adorned with noble statues, vases and picturesque groups of figures.

179

VILLA PISANI Bagnolo di Lonigo, Vicenza

PISANI
FAMILY
COAT OF ARMS

Built by Andrea Palladio on the bank of the navigable canal and center of an enormous agricultural estate, this villa, with is magnificient triumphal arch, proclaims the authority and prestige of the Pisani family. The Roman classical, and Mannerist inspirations, noticeable in the ashlar-work of the arches, the semi-circular steps, and the pediment, marry well with the traditional Venetian dovecotes, an example of Palladio's constant search for beauty combined with usefulness.

Not far from Lonigo, at the point where the old Roman road crosses the river Gua, there stands the severe facade of the Palladian Villa Pisani. Signors of the surrounding territory, a wealthy family made even wealthier by their organized agricultural activities and by their introduction of specialized cultivation, the Pisanis had already had a palace, which is now the town hall built for them at Lonigo. They now thought it was necessary to have a place in the country, on their estate, a dwelling with ample store-houses, granaries and other agricultural buildings which would form the nucleus of their agricultural operations. Palladio was thus asked to design a complex which would not only be functional and practical, but which would also convey a sense of authority and prestige suitable to the feudal power which the Pisani exercised over Lonigo and the surrounding area.

The villa, built in an area which already bore the traces of many ancient settlements, manages to preserve the memory of the pre-existing medieval castle, with its two stocky towers and ashlar-work which, as Ackerman points out, still manages to signify a military or public function, whilst from the river it appears almost to be a triumphal arch.

The classical portico of the rear elevation, shown in the *Quattro Libri* but unfortunately never completed, was to have opened out onto the rear courtyard, almost as if to celebrate the establishment of Renaissance culture in the countryside.

The enormous agricultural wings formed the nucleus of the Pisanis intense agricultural activity and flourishing commerce. Before they were destroyed by wartime events, these agricultural wings, spanned by never-ending Doric colonnades, were said to have enclosed a space as big as St. Mark's Square.

Palladio remarks that the large salon on the piano nobile is inspired by a Roman house. It was here where the Pisanis, as representatives of the Serenissima, carried out their public duties.

Frescoes of allegorical groups decorate the main salon, whilst in another room on the same floor there are traces of frescoes portraying the delights and amusements of life in a villa.

182

SECONDO.
DE I DISEGNI DELLE CASE DI VILLA DI ALCVNI
nobili Venetiani.   Cap. XIIII.

47

LA FABRICA, che fegue è in Bagnolo luogo due miglia lontano da Lonigo Ca
ftello del Vicentino, & è de' Magnifici Signori Conti Vittore, Marco, e Daniele fra
telli de' Pifani. Dall'vna, e l'altra parte del cortile ui fono le ftalle, le cantine, i granari, e fimili altri luoghi per l'ufo della Villa. Le colonne de i portici fono di ordine Dorico. La parte di mezo di quefta fabrica è per l'habitatione del Padrone: il
pauimento delle prime ftanze è alto da terra fette piedi: fotto ui fono le cucine, &
altri fimili luoghi per la famiglia. La Sala è in uolto alta quanto larga, e la metà più: à quefta altezza
giugne anco il uolto delle loggie: Le ftanze fono in folaro alte quanto larghe: le maggiori fono lunghe un quadro e due terzi: le altre un quadro e mezo. Et è da auertirfi che non fi ha hauuto molta
confideratione nel metter le fcale minori in luogo, che habbiano lume viuo (come habbiamo ricor-
dato nel primo libro) perche non hauendo effe à feruire, fe non à i luoghi di fotto, & à quelli di fopra,
i quali feruono per granari ouer mezati; fi ha hauuto rifguardo principalmente ad accommodar bene l'ordine di mezo: il quale è per l'habitatione del Padrone, e de' foreftieri: e le Scale, che à queft'ordine portano; fono pofte in luogo attifsimo, come fi uede ne i difegni. E ciò farà detto ancho per
auertenza del prudente lettore per tutte le altre fabriche feguenti di un'ordine folo: percioche in
quelle, che ne hanno due belli, & ornati; ho curato che le Scale fiano lucide, e pofte in luoghi commo-
di: e dico due; perche quello, che uà fotto terra per le cantine, e fimili ufi, e quello che uà nella parte
di fopra, e ferue per granari, e mezati non chiamo ordine principale, per non darfi all'habitatione de'
Gentil'huomini.

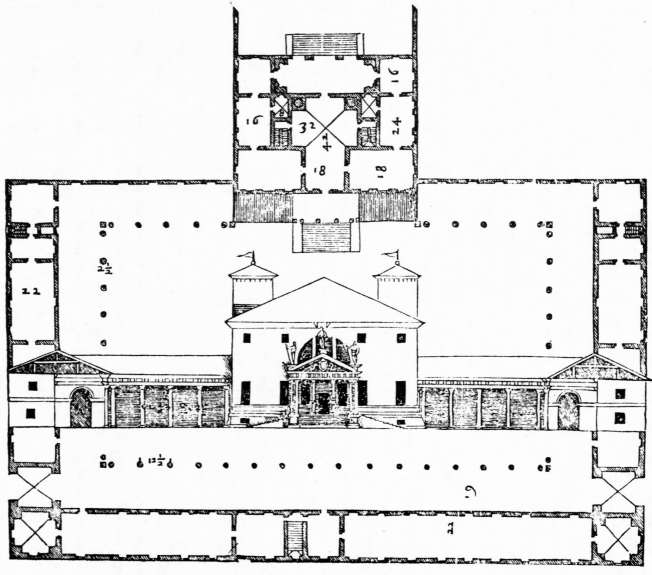

*Andrea Palladio. Description,
plan and view of Villa Pisani
di Bagnolo* I Quattro Libri
dell'Architettura, *Venice,
1570, book II, chapter XIV).*

Villa Pisani. Main salon, with thermal window and painted decoration from the fifteenth century.

VILLA THIENE Quinto Vicentino, Vicenza

THIENE
FAMILY
COAT OF ARMS

Excessive ambition seems to have been the main motivation behind the architectural project for Villa Thiene. In 1514 Adriano and Marc'Antonio Thiene commissioned Palladio to build what would have been a huge villa on their property at Quinto Vicentino. The brothers were dilettante architects and the plans show that the villa was clearly inspired by the public baths and magnificent villas of ancient Rome. Only a very small part of the original scheme was ever completed, and this only after many difficult years, further proof of the Thiene's exaggerrated aspirations.

In 1740 the descendants of Adriano and Marc'Antonio resolved to at least finish that part of the building which had been begun, and so they turned to Francesco Muttoni who, as has been mentioned earlier in this book, was one of Palladio's most faithful followers, but who nevertheless found it necessary to modify the initial project considerably.

The vicissitudes of this villa might well be compared with those that beleaguered the Trissino's villa at Melodo, another partially completed project, another expression of a particular moment of perhaps excessive exhaltation and utopian ideals which led Palladio quite astray from his usual simplicity and functionality. There is little doubt that the architect, as well as his clients, had been strongly affected by the climate of euphoria when in his *Quattro Libri* he obviously exaggerates the amenities of the site, which he claims is "very beautiful indeed, as on one hand there is the Tessina, and on the other a large tributary of the same river. "No doubt certain fluvial alterations have taken place over the intervening centuries, but even then it seems extremely improbable that either river ever possessed the qualities so warmly attributed to them by Palladio.

Of all the interior decorations carried out by Giovanni De Mio, only those on the vaulted ceiling of one room have been conserved, portraying various mythological scenes from the classical world such as "The struggle between the Lapithae and the Centaurs," "The Amazons coming to the aid of Troy," and "The Labors of Hercules."

The exterior walls of the villa, or rather what was built of it, has been left unplastered, and they reveal that knowledgeable use of terra cotta, the accurate choice of materials, and the great technical ability which contributed to the fame and duration of Palladian architecture.

I DISEGNI, che feguono fono della fabrica del Conte Ottauio Thiene à Quinto fua Villa.
Fù cominciata dalla felice memoria del Conte Marc'Antonio fuo padre, e dal Conte Adriano fuo
Zio : il fito è molto bello per hauer da una parte la Tefina, e dall'altra vn ramo di detto fiume affai
grande : Hà quefto palagio vna loggia dauanti la porta di ordine Dorico : per quefta fi paffa in vn'altra loggia, e di quella in vn cortile : il quale ha ne i fianchi due loggie : dall'vna, e l'altra tefta di quefte
loggie fono gli appartamenti delle ftanze, delle quali alcune fono ftate ornate di pitture da Meffer
Giouanni Indemio Vicentino huomo di belliffimo ingegno. Rincontro all'entrata fi troua vna
loggia fimile à quella dell'entrata, dalla quale fi entra in vn'Atrio di quattro colonne, e da quello nel
cortile, il quale ha i portici di ordine Dorico, e ferue per l vfo di Villa. Non ui è alcuna fcala principale corrifpondente à tutta la fabrica : percioche la parte di fopra non ha da feruire, fe non per falua-
robba, e per luoghi da feruitori.

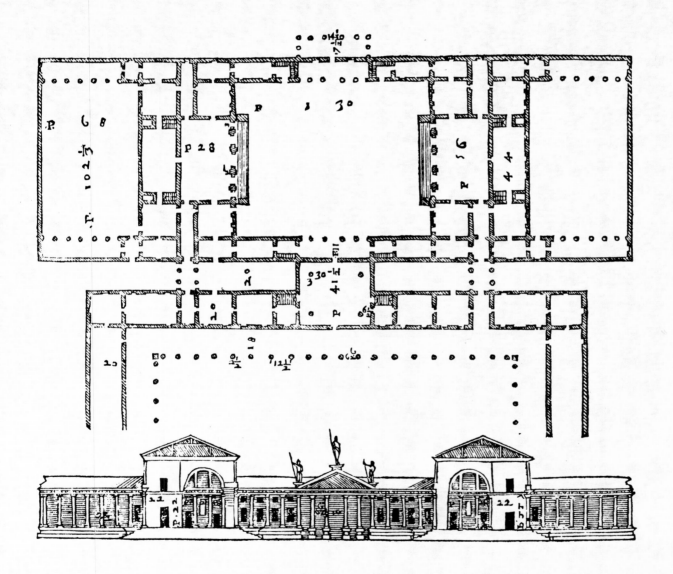

IN LONEDO

This is the only concrete evidence of the enormous project which Palladio had designed to satisfy the grandiose ambitions of one of the most noble Vicentine families.

*Andrea Palladio. Description, plan, and elevation of villa Thiene, (*I Quattro Libri dell'Architettura, *Venice, 1570, book II, chapter XIV).*

VILLA POJANA Pojana Maggiore, Vicenza

POJANA
FAMILY
COAT OF ARMS

Palladio's plans for Villa Pojana manage to answer two basically different needs. On the one hand he conveys the old military traditions of the owner's family, and on the other their comparatively recent but very intense interest in agriculture.

Highly distinguished in the arts of war and totally faithful to the Serenissima whatever the emergency, the Pojana family had for centuries exercised a jurisdiction that was almost feudal over the surrounding area, and this powerful military background is expressed by the severity and austere purity of the villa built by Palladio for Bonifacio Pojana in the years 1548-1549. It was not only the family that enjoyed military connections, but the whole area, which had for many years supplied the Venetian army with its cavalry.

However, with the arrival of more peaceful times, and with the renewed enthusiasm for what Alvise Cornaro called "blessed agriculture," also the Pojana began to discover the joys and benefits of their country estate.

They now became involved in the land, just as Marcus Billenius, a Roman centurion from the battle of Azio who is mentioned on a stone tablet found at Pojana, had done centuries before.

With Villa Pojana, which is slightly elevated and so well proportioned as to seem smaller than it really is, Palladio's spirit of synthesis appears to have achieved its maximum expression: a Roman serliana dominates the facade, whilst beautifully simple linear pilasters support the pierced arch.

Palladio himself documented the "interior decorations" by Bernardo India, Anselmo Canera and Bartolomeo Ridolfi. In the atrium, elegant stucco frames, whose floral designs entwine around trompe l'oeil reliefs, enclose monochromes of river gods, while here and there appear patches of sky populated with other deities. The bust of Bonifacio Pojana looks down from over the main entrance, and above him are the family's coat of arms and military trophies.

Other decorations depict Pompeian scenes with the backgrounds and landscapes strewn with picturesque ruins and broken columns, whilst monochromatic figures of warriors stand watch in the trompe l'oeil niches. The most significant fresco of all can be found in the central hall: a family from classical times, dressed in tunics and togas, kneel in front of an altar whilst the paterfamilias extinguishes the torch of war at the feet of the statue of Peace which stands on the altar. It is a clear allusion to that peace so painstakingly and painfully achieved, which would finally allow the Venetians to enjoy the delights of the terra firma.

Andrea Palladio. Description,
plan, and elevation of Villa
*Pojana (*I Quattro Libri
dell'Architettura, *Venice,*
1570, book II, chapter XIV).

58   L I B R O

IN POGLIANA Villa del Vicentino è la sottoposta fabrica del Caualiér Pogliana: le sue
stanze sono state ornate di pitture, e stucchi bellissimi da Messer Bernardino India, & Messer Anselmo Canera pittori Veronesi, e da Messer Bartolomeo Rodolfi Scultore Veronese: le stanze grandi
sono lunghe vn quadro, e due terzi, e sono in uolto: le quadre hanno le lunette ne gli angoli: sopra i
camerini ui sono mezati: la altezza della Sala è la metà più della larghezza, e uiene ad essere al pari
dell'altezza della loggia: la sala è inuoltata à fascia, e la loggia à crociera: sopra tutti questi luoghi è il
Granaro, e sotto le Cantine, e la cucina: percioche il piano delle stanze si alza cinque piedi da terra:
Da vn lato ha il cortile, & altri luoghi per le cose di Villa, dall'altro vn giardino, che corrisponde a det
to Cortile, e nella parte di dietro il Bruolo, & una Peschiera, di modo che questo gentil'huomo, come quello che è magnifico, e di nobilissimo animo, non ha mancato di fare tutti quegli ornamenti, &
tutte quelle commodità che sono possibili per rendere questo suo luogo bello, dilettenole, & commodo.

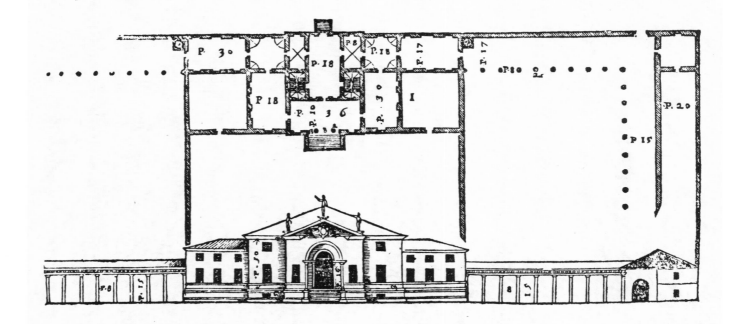

193

The Emperor's Salon with
a sacrifical scene by Anselmo
Carera; the elder of the group
shows the right way to his
people by extinguishing the
torch of war on the altar
of peace.

Anselmo Carera. Detail of
the ceiling of the Emperor's
Salon, showing a battle scene.

PALAZZO CHIERICATI Vicenza

CHIERICATI
FAMILY
COAT OF ARMS

A building designed to express prestige and nobility. Constructed at the entrance to the city near the ancient quay of the Bachiglione, this Palladian palace seems to repropose the typology of the "maritime villa" often found in classical scenes. The motif of the internal courtyard with its porticos and loggias typical of Palladian palaces, is here moved to the facade, with the uninterrupted repetition of columns, just halted on the second floor, where there are the windows of the main reception room.

Perhaps the positioning of the chapter dealing with Palazzo Chiericati in the *Quattro Libri* is not merely casual: one of the last palaces built in the of Vicenza, it comes immediately before the section devoted to villa contruction. In effect the elevation, with its double orders of colonnades and multiple opening which involve the external space, seems to be a reproposal of the ideal villa of the classical world. The man who commissioned the building was Girolamo Chiericati, a member of that "generation of the great Utopia" who frequently turned to Palladio to interpret and realize their own ideals.

One of the supervisors of the loggia of the Basilica, Chiericati was to enjoy a close and fruitful friendship with Andrea Palladio. Encouraged by the prevailing climate of euphoria and high ideals, they collaborated on the ambitious project of requalifying urbanistically the big empty area known as the "Isola", decentered with respect to the traditional "magnets" of the city, not cluttered by any medieval buildings, in fact just a wide open space. This was obviously the ideal site for Chiericati's new palace, creating a new architectonic nucleus from which one could structure and organize the whole area. Several important buildings rose up in rapid succession (the Cogollo house, the Teatro Olimpico and the Palazzo Piovene) and this was also the place where the lines of communication between Venice and Vicenza, and Padova and Vicenza met, both by road – crossing the Ponte degli Angeli (also by Palladio) – and by water, by means of the Bacchiglione.

The Pianta Angelica clearly shows the presence of a city gate in this area; so from the wide porticos and loggias of the Palazzo Chiericati one could watch the arrival of the boats from Venice, which, from time to time drew out the authorities and the Vicenza populace to welcome the new captains, to watch the embarkation of the press-gang and to

IN VICENZA sopra la piazza, che uolgarméte si dice l'Isola; ha fabricato secondo la inuen
tione, che segue, il Conte Valerio Chiericato, cauallier & gentil'huomo honorato di quella città. Hà
questa fabrica nella parte di sotto una loggia dauanti, che piglia tutta la facciata : il pauimento del
primo ordine s'alza da terra cinque piedi: il che è stato fatto sì per ponerui sotto le cantine, & altri luo
ghi appartenenti al commodo della casa, iquali non sariano riusciti se fossero stati fatti del tutto sot-
terra ; percioche il fiume non è molto discosto ; sì anco accioche gli ordini di sopra meglio godes-
sero del bel sito dinanzi. Le stanze maggiori hanno i uolti loro alti secondo il primo modo dell'altez
ze de' uolti: le mediocri sono inuoltate à lunette ; & hanno i uolti tanto alti quanto sono quelli delle
maggiori. I camerini sono ancor essi in uolto, e sono amezati. Sono tutti questi uolti ornati di com-
partimenti di stucco eccellentissimi di mano di Messer Bartolameo Ridolfi Scultore Veronese; & di
pitture di mano di Messer Domenico Rizzo, & di Messer Battista Venetiano, huomini singolari in
queste professioni. La sala è di sopra nel mezo della facciata : & occupa della loggia di sotto la parte di mezo. La sua altezza è fin sotto il tetto : e perche esce alquanto in fuori; ha sotto gli Angoli le
colonne doppie, dall'una e l'altra parte di questa sala ui sono due loggie, cioè una per banda; lequali
hanno i soffitti loro, ouer lacunari ornati di bellissimi quadri di pittura, e fanno bellissima uista.
Il primo ordine della facciata è Dorico, & il secondo è Ionico.

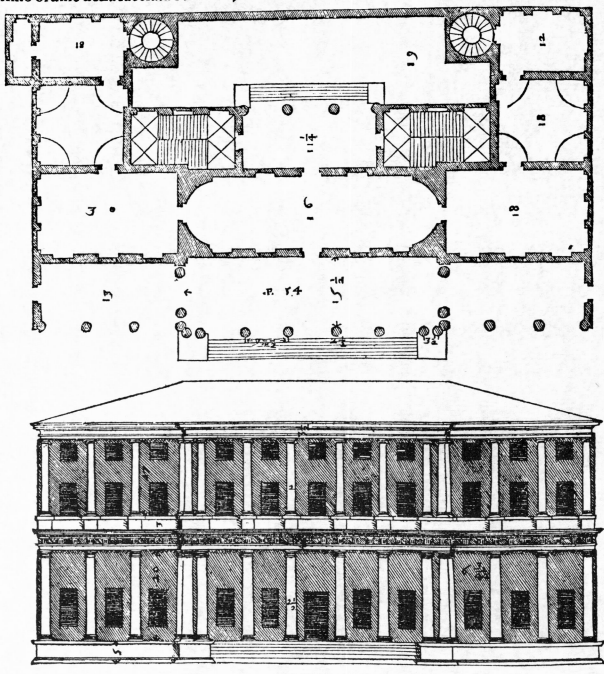

SEGVE il disegno di parte della facciata in forma maggiore.

comment on the latest political and social news.

So as it stood such an important and busy place, the Palazzo Chiericati was also designed to represent and express the "civilized face" of the city. Therefore it is nice to think of the artist and his client designing the new palace not merely as a stoa or *frons scenae,* but as a building which functioned as the perfect backdrop for any one arriving in Vicenza by water.

In the scenes that have survived from antiquity there frequently appear buildings with porticos and columns overlooking the sea. These "maritime villas" represent the idealised structure of a classic port. This probable relationship between the palace and the waterway in front of it was understood, in the eighteenth century, by Canaletto, who in one of his famous "Capriccii," placed the maritime villa on the Grand Canal, with the facade turned towards water - exactly as the Vicentine architect had planned.

*Andrea Palladio. Detail of the facade of Palazzo Chiericati (*I Quattro Libri dell'Architettura, Venice, 1570, book II, chapter III).

VILLA PISANI Montagnana, Padua

PISANI
FAMILY
COAT OF ARMS

The Palladian Villa Pisani stands beside the city gate which greets the traveler who has come from the direction of Padua. The facade of the building, which resembles a city palace, ennobles the outskirts of this small provincial town. The rear of the house is much more like that of a country villa, for the portico and loggias open out onto orchards and gardens.

Under the right section of the villa runs a stream, which, in the past, after it had cooled the rooms and furnished the house with water, fed the ancient Carraresi water mills, documented since the Middle Ages, over which the Pisani seemed to enjoy a particular

jurisdiction. Given these two important advantages, i. e. the control of hydraulic energy and the use of the water mills, it would seem very probable that Villa Pisani was a very early example of a villa connected to an industrial activity.

The present Palladian building does not completely correspond to the original project, as shown in the *Quattro Libri,* which would have revolutionized the town planning of Montagnana, upsetting the medieval fabric and order of the city. Two wings were to have extended from the main body of the house, running right up to the city walls, culminating

A rare example of a villa connected to an industrial activity, this building by Andrea Palladio controlled the waters of the Fiumicello which besides cooling the rooms in the summer, powered the city's water mills. The facade which looks out on the street resembles a palace, despite the presence of various elements which are typical of a villa, such as the pediment and the double order of columns, which here however are partially enclosed by the walls. Only on the opposite facade where the double loggia looks out onto the garden, does the building assume the appearance of a real villa.

LA SEGVENTE fabrica è appresso la porta di Montagnana Castello del Padoano, e fu edi-
ficata dal Magnifico Signor Francesco Pisani : ilquale passato à miglior uita non la ha potuta finire.
Le stanze maggiori sono lunghe un quadro e tre quarti : i uolti sono à schiffo, alti secondo il secondo
modo delle altezze de' uolti : le mediocri sono quadre, & inuoltate a cadino : I camerini, e l'andito so
no di uguale larghezza : i uolti loro sono alti due quadri : La entrata ha quattro colonne, il quinto più
sottili di quelle di fuori : lequali sostentano il pauimento della Sala, e fanno l'altezza del uolto bella, e
secura. Ne i quattro nicchi, che ui si ueggono sono stati scolpiti i quattro tempi dell'anno da Messer
Alessandro Vittoria Scultore eccellente : il primo ordine delle colonne è Dorico, il secondo Ionico.
Le stanze di sopra sono in solaro : L'altezza della Sala giugne fin sotto il tetto. Ha questa fabrica due
strade da i fianchi, doue sono due porte, sopra le quali ui sono anditi, che conducono in cucina, e
luoghi per seruitori.

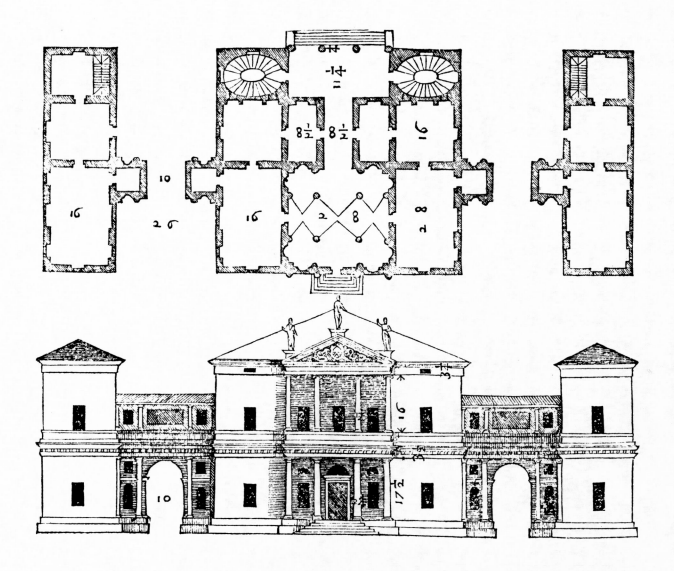

LA FABRICA

Andrea Palladio. Description,
plan, and elevation of Villa
Pisani of Montagnana
(I Quattro Libri
dell'Architettura, Venice,
1570, book II, chapter XIV).

Villa Pisani, the facade of the house with its porticos and loggias, which overlook the garden.
The main salon of Villa Pisani with one of the sculptures by Alessandro Vittoria, mentioned by Palladio.

Alessandro Vittoria.

Sculptor, decorator, and medallist, Alessandro Vittoria was born in Trento in 1525 in Verona. In 1543 he entered Sansovino's workshop, and from then on worked mainly in Verona. Together with the Tuscan maestro he worked on the decorations in the Libreria Marciana and on the tomb of Doge Francesco Vernier at San Salvatore. He was especially talented at portraits, and often worked on the decoration of merchants' palaces and patrician villas. He was active in Villa Pisani at Montagnana and in Villa Duodo at Monselice, whilst his presence at Maser is still controversial, even though the wealth of sculpture that decorates Villa Barbaro and the nymphaeum behind it is very much in his style. Vittoria died in Venice in 1608.

in two triumphal arches, one of which would have partially obliterated the moat that encircles the walled city. Perhaps the historic conscience of the Montagnana community would not allow them to stand by and let the medieval physiogomy of their beautiful city be eroded, or

perhaps it was a choice dictated by reasons of defence, and, even in these times of peace, of the fear and diffidence, which a the begining of the century, had forced the Venetian cities of the hinterland to carry out the drastic demolition scheme, or *guasto*, to protect their city walls.

202

VILLA BADOER Fratta Polesine, Rovigo

BADOER
FAMILY
COAT OF ARMS

One of the most precious and beautifully conserved of all Palladian villas is in the small town of Fratta, which lies in the Polesan plain. This expanse of land was the object of many reclamation and drainage schemes, as can be seen by the numerous rivers and canals which thread their way across the fields. It was here, in the middle of this rich and fertile plain, on the land which they had salvaged from the swamps, that the Badoer commissioned Palladio to build them a country residence.

With its harmonious proportions, Villa Badoer is arranged around a small circular courtyard: the main body of the house and the two amazingly elegant curved wings of the outbuildings are complemented by the rhythmic movement of the colonnades, which confer a noble yet restrained beauty to the whole complex. Here we do not find the majestic structure of some of the other Palladian villas, as it lacks the usual symbols of prestige and *sacralità,* such as cupolas, pinnacles, and akroterion statues. Here, instead, their place had been taken by simplicity, by refined harmony and sober elegance. Similarly, the agricultural wings of Villa Badoer cannot be compared with the agricultural wings of other Palladian villas, where the agricultural utilitarian aspect is more

Built in an area subject to many land reclamation schemes, this villa by Andrea Palladio is almost like a temple built to celebrate the victory of man over the swamps.

A noble flight of steps leads up to the elegant Ionic loggia of the main house, maybe as a protection from the frequent floods of this area. The two semi-circular "agricultural wings," a motif dear to Palladio, seem to protect the serene harmony of this architecture.

LA SEGVENTE fabrica è del Magnifico Signor Francesco Badoero nel Polesine ad vn luo
go detto la Frata, in vn sito alquanto rileuato, e bagnata da un ramo dell'Adige, oue era anticamen-
te vn Castello di Salinguerra da Este cognato di Ezzelino da Romano.   Fa basa à tutta la fabrica
vn piedestilo alto cinque piedi: a questa altezza è il pauimento delle stanze: lequali tutte sono in solaro, e sono state ornate di Grottesche di bellissima inuentione dal Giallo Fiorentino   Di sopra
hanno il granaro, e di sotto la cucina, le cantine, & altri luoghi alla commodità pertinenti: Le colonne delle Loggie della casa del padrone sono Ioniche: La Cornice come corona circonda tutta la casa.   Il frontespicio sopra loggie fa vna bellissima uista: perche rende la parte di mezo più eminente
de i fianchi.   Discendendo poi al piano si ritrouano luoghi da Fattore, Gastaldo, stalle, & altri alla
Villa conueneuoli.

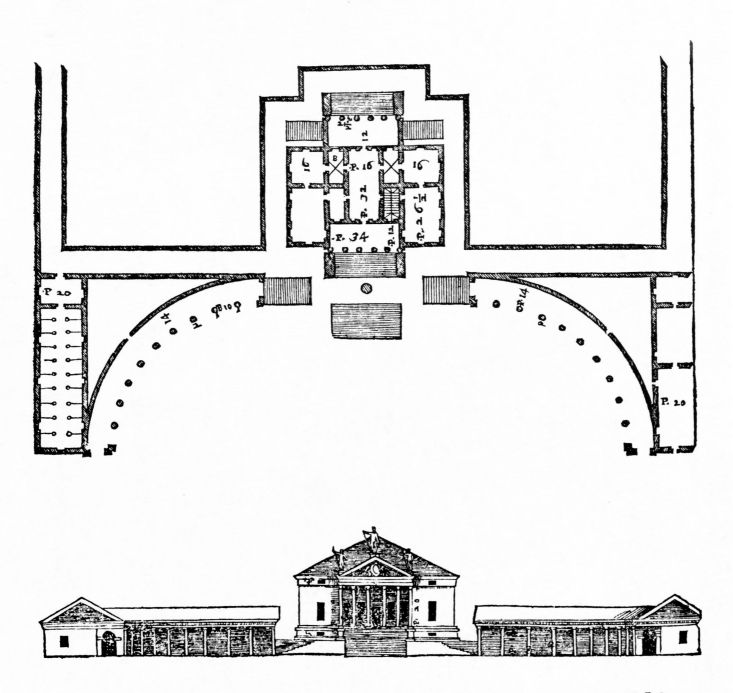

IL MAGNIFICO

*Andrea Palladio, description, plan, and elevation of Villa Badoer (*I Quattro Libri dell'Architettura, Venice, 1570, Book II, chapter XIV).

openly stated; nor has one the sensation that
the architect felt that these outbuildings had to
correspond to the enormous area of land
rendered productive by the Badoer family.
It seems that in this case Palladio was not
motivated by concrete necessity and
functionality, but inspired rather by superior
motives of harmony and proportion which
found expression in one his most noble

creations, almost a scale model of what he had
wanted to create at Melodo.

For Ackerman, who stresses the continuity
of the ideals and architectonic typology of the
villas, a Gallic-Roman villa, recently uncovered
in French Gaul "seems to anticipate the type of
villa with an entrance flanked by two quadrants
of a circle, re-introduced by Palladio in works
such as Villa Badoer at Fratta Polesine, and

then repeated in innumerable houses and villas throughout Europe and America."

The villa was built for Francesco Badoer in 1556 and the patrician family lived there until 1678, when the last Badoer bequeathed it to a Morosini, together with all its lands. Richly decorated by Giallo Fiorentino, whose frescoes have been carefully uncovered and restored, the villa is without doubt the complete and organic expression of Palladian genius. And here, as in perhaps few other places, it is the unity which results from a successful combination of various delightful particulars which makes this architecture so utterly fascinating.

Villa Badoer, the surrounding wall and the stairs leading to the piano nobile.

VILLA BARBARO Maser, Treviso

BARBARO
FAMILY
COAT OF ARMS

Jacopo Sansovino. Presumed portrait of Andrea Palladio (Venice, St. Mark's Sacristy, detail of bronze door).

The history of the Venetian villas takes up an entire chapter in the history of architecture, as do the Greek temples, the chatêaus of the Loire, and the skyscrapers of New York. And the name which occurs most often in this chapter is naturally that of Andrea Palladio.

Whenever wars cease and that sense of tranquility, which is produced by a feeling of wellbeing, starts to be diffused, this is the moment when man builds villas-in the country, on the hills, along the banks of the rivers, beside lakes, near the sea. The many and different waves of this phenomenon can be counted and are easily recognizable, for they all share one constant factor the presence, either more or less direct or conscious, of ancient Rome. "Venetia" – as Andrea Palladio wrote in his preface to his *Quattro Libri,* is the sole remaining example of the grandeur and magnificence of the Romans."

The aristocratic Venetians, reading Cato, Columella, Varrone, and any other author who had written about classical agriculture, and whose works were being willingly reprinted by wise Venetian publishers, knew very well that the villas they were planning to build had to be in proportion to the enormous area of arable or cultivated land which surrounded them. This was not true just for the volume of agricultural work, but also for the actual organism of the estate, so the villa became the element of synthesis which was necessary to demontrate the extent of their possessions.

The owners of the Venetian villas, noblemen and farmers at the same time, were men who had attained the highest level of human dignity, who are not only known through history and literature, but also by portaits painted of them by Titian, Vittoria, and other artists of Cinquecento Venice. As Palladio claimed, the villas resemble their owners, they are in fact portraits. "If you want to know the character and mind of the owner, observe with attention how he has built his house" – so reads an inscription on the wall of a villa near Vicenza.

Many Venetian clients had the good fortune to find in Andrea Palladio an architect who knew how to interpret and realize their dreams of culture and glory in a concrete way. The

quitessence of his poetry had its roots in Padua, the city of Alvise Cornaro, in the classical culture and in an intellectual structure based on *esperientia,* which leads to *scientia,* which in turn leads to the study of those mysterious laws which govern the harmony of the world. At that moment a new ethic was born, no longer bound by medieval constraints and inhibitions, man now exulted in himself, considered himself capable of wonderful things: "He must strive to imitate in his creations," as Ackerman says, "the supreme rational order which permeates the divine creation."

During his visit to Rome Palladio was continuously stimulated not only by the ancient monuments and ruins, which he sketched and measured, but also by the buildings designed by Bramante, Raphael, and Michelangelo. His personality, however, remained independent and autonomous, and, we may add, completely Venetian. He was an ideal citizen at that magic and exhilarating moment following the Peace of Bologna (1529-30) when, Florence and Rome having collapsed, the city on the lagoon reached the apex of its splendor. Just as sumptuous palaces rose up along the sides of the Grand Canal, so in the countryside, reclaimed and salvaged by the Venetian and local landowners, arose the splendid villas of the great Venetian families: of the aristocracy, of the rich merchants and soldiers of fortune, and of the humanists and men of the church. The habit of spending a long time in the country to administer one's estates united them in their ideals and needs, of which Palladio would be their interpreter.

The most famous and well preserved of the Venetian villas is that which the Barbaro brothers had built for them at Maser, near Asolo, in the heart of the Marca Trevigiana. Not far from Altivole, where one could still see Caterina Cornaro's Barco, is the hill where the Barbaros chose to construct their home. It is neither at the top of the hill, nor at the bottom, but halfway down the gentle slope, and the peaceful atmosphere makes one think of a landscape by the school of Giorgione. One could even say that the architectonic and decorative example provided by Villa Barbaro represents the synthesis of all the ideals of the Venetian culture on the terra firma in the sixteenth century.

The grandiose complex was designed for Marc'Antonio and Daniele Barbaro, sons of Francesco who, besides leaving an enormous patrimony, had had the idea of creating a type of monument at Maser for his descendants, and this explains why his name, as well as those of his sons appears on the front of the villa. Daniele and Marc'Antonio had evidently formed a *fraterna,* in order to keep the family fortune intact, but entrusting the administration to the elder son, who also had the task of providing an heir to secure the continuation the line. The first son, Marc'Antonio, Procurator of San Marco de Supra, had served as the Republic's Ambassador to France, Constantinople, and England. He had also held the post of Procurator of the Arsenate and "Proveditore al Sale", so he had become a man of great importance in the public life of Venice. His brother Daniele was, instead, a man of the

Paolo Veronese. Portrait of Daniel Barbaro, on the table the Libri dell'Architettura *the result of the collaboration of this noble scholar with Palladio. (Amsterdam, Rijksmuseum).*

LA SOTTOPOSTA fabrica è à Mafera Villa vicina ad Afolo Caftello del Triuigiano, di Monfignor Reuerendifsimo Eletto di Aquileia, e del Magnifico Signor Marc'Antonio fratelli de' Barbari. Quella parte della fabrica, che efce alquanto in fuori; ha due ordini di ftanze, il piano di quelle di fopra è à pari del piano del cortile di dietro, oue è tagliata nel monte rincontro alla cafa vna fontana con infiniti ornamenti di ftucco, e di pittura. Fa quefta fonte vn laghetto, che ferue per pe-fchiera: da quefto luogo partitafi l'acqua fcorre nella cucina, & dapoi irrigati i giardini, che fono dal-la deftra, e finiftra parte della ftrada, la quale pian piano afcendendo conduce alla fabrica; fa due pe-fchiere co i loro beueratori fopra la ftrada commune: d'onde partitafi; adacqua il Bruolo, ilquale è grandifsimo, e pieno di frutti eccellentifsimi, e di diuerfe feluaticine. La facciata della cafa del pa-drone hà quattro colonne di ordine Ionico: il capitello di quelle de gli angoli fa fronte da due parti: i quai capitelli come fi facciano; porrò nel libro de i Tempij. Dall'vna, e l'altra parte ui fono loggie, le quali nell'eftremità hanno due colombare, e fotto quelle ui fono luoghi da fare i uini, e le ftalle, e gli altri luoghi per l'vfo di Villa.

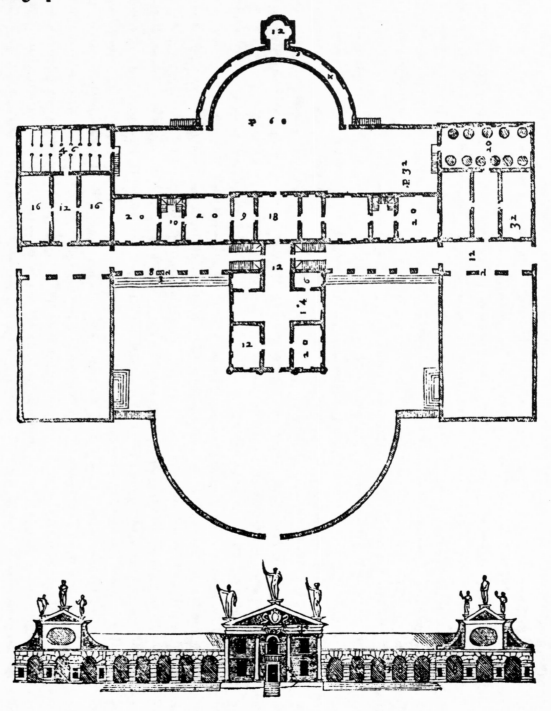

Andrea Palladio. Description, plan, and elevation of villa Barbaro at Maser (I Quattro Libri dell'Architettura, Venice, 1570, Book II, chapter XIV).

GG 2   LA SEGVENTE

church, of science and of culture. Asked by the Republic to assume the Patriarchate of Aquilea, he took part in the Council of Trent in 1562-1563, but cultural obligations always took precedence over political and religious ones.

Friend of artists and literati, from Bembo to Alvise Cornaro, from Varchi to Della Casa and Sperone Speroni, and painted by Paolo Veronese, Daniele Barbaro had not only published the *Pratica della prospettiva* and other studies, but also the translation and commentary of Vitruvius' *Trattato,* with illustrations by Andrea Palladio.

We have mentioned the political activities of the Barbaro brothers and earlier in the book we talked a little about the Cinquecento notion that a villa resembled its owner, well even though it may be true that at Maser there is the constant presence of Marc'Antonio, the villa bears even closer resemblance to Daniele, who as we remember was a source of inspiration to Palladio when they were working together on that edition of Vitruvius.

The choice of site for the villa (not on the crest of the hill, like a castle, nor in the middle of a plain, like the villas which formed the nucleus of an agricultural activity) is perfect for the Renaissance man, both for the ease of access, and for its distance from the dark woods, the unhealthiness of the swamps and the fogs of the plains. This choice was determined by the earlier presence of the Barbaros in the area, and by the fact that that hill had already been chosen as the ideal site for a home. Maybe in the intervening years they might have built a castle here, or perhaps a religious building with a place to bury their dead. The presence of the spring which gives its name to the locality, and to which Scamozzi refers to as that "beautiful spring of Maser," would seem to suggest that at one time there was a temple here, or at least somewhere where the local people could worship the gods of the place.

It is this same spring which determined the

site of the Palladian complex. As with many villas, the spring at Maser constituted the nucleus and power supply, the Greeks would say *omphalos* of the habitation. Water, in fact, came to assume a profound significance and was connected with ancient tales, myths, which claimed that he spring was that unique link between this life and the past. When Palladio is discussing Maser on his *Tratto,* he doesn't waste time talking about ideals, values, and the language of art, which he rightly condemns as unworthy of mention, but discusses at greater length than usual the spring, whose water, having supplied the needs of the villa, feeds the fish ponds which are located in front of the southern facade, and also irrigates the gardens and the orchards which extend along the hill.

Villa Barbaro faces south – as do most country houses which do not have to cope with the problems of roads, squares, and neighbors – in obedience to the laws of nature and of astrology, to the benefit of the inhabitants and

*Andrea Palladio. Frontispiece of the Second Book (*I Quattro Libri dell'Architettura, *Venice, 1570).*

to the benefit also of the crops stored in the spacious granaries. This "solar" location of Maser is also influenced by the architectural organisation of the buiding which, in order to use the official areas of the villa to the best advantage, interrupts the horizontal development and pushes forward the more decorated central section, as if to present itself to the visitor and welcome the guest. The presence of the semi-columns and the tympanum at the center of the villa accentuate the symmetry of the building, clearly a classical reference, whilst the corner towers of the dovecotes, allude to a medieval tradition that had really outlived its function of attracting doves and other fowls to, eventually, the lord's table. The right hand dovecote in fact houses the sun-dial, connecting the villa to the world of the stars, so important to the life of Renaissance man. But let us stop and look at the facade of the villa, so like one of those temples discussed and illustrated by Palladio in one of the chapters of his *Quattro Libri dell'Architettura.* "In all the villas and also in some of the city houses I have put a frontispiece on the forward facade where the principal doors are because such frontispieces accentuate the entrance to the house and add very much to the grandeur and magnificence of the work, being thus made more eminent than the other parts. Besides they prove to be especially useful for the builder's coat of arms, which are usually put on the middle of the facade, as can be seen in the remains of the temples and other public buildings."

The visitor who approaches the balcony of the first floor, turns round and looks towards the inside, with his back to the landscape, receives the same impression as he who turns towards the presbytery of a holy building. The most sacred and holy part of the house is the central salon, called the Olympus Salon, whose vaulted ceiling possesses the mystical significance of a dome, and whose decorations, which were entrusted to Paolo Veronese, convey the

principal messages of Maser. Beyond the north wall there is a secret internal courtyard where we can find the famous spring. This sacred place is not dedicated to the fortunes of the Barbaro family, but to the local divinities. It is only at this point that the visitor pauses; having passed through the "nave" and the "presbytery," he has at last reached the shrine of the temple. The water, gushes out of the rock and is collected in a circular bowl, which is at the centre of a Roman inspired nympheum. Its fame and importance arise more from the secret messages it bears concerning the spring and on the decoration of the grotto, than from the sculpture of the nymphaeum itself, which was probably the work of Daniele Barbaro. Above the nymphaeum Paolo Veronese has portrayed a young queen, who, as she is accompanied by a lion, has been interpreted as the allegorical figure of Venice.

The vaulted Salon of Olympus, which we have compared to a profane presbytery, is the urbanistic, as well as the spiritual centre of the villa. To the right and to the left stretches an enfilade of rooms, anthropomorphically symmetrical like the trancepts of a cruciform church.

Up till now we have discussed the ideals, values, and the significance of the heroic glorification at Maser and of the Barbaro family, but this building is also a significant example of those practical aspects which so interested Palladio. As well as being the beloved home of its clients, Maser also functioned as what was termed a *villa dell'utile,* or a working farm. The two porticos that flank the central portion, as well as being stylistically functional, also serve as agricultural wings, designed to house the farm carts and agricultural implements, to protect the hay from the weather – sheltering it from the sudden storms and from the fierce sun – and, especially, to preserve the precious crops.

Anyone who has visited a Palladian villa

Beyond the slope of the garden stands Villa Barbaro whose central section is flanked by two lateral wings with dovecotes. Yet these elements, typical of villa architecture originally connected to agricultural activities, are here sublimated in a superior and ideal unity which makes this Palladian masterpiece the typical residence of a great humanist to whom the countriside represents not so much profit, but a place to enjoy his literary pursuits.

218

and has admired the nobility of the architecture and the wealth of decoration inside is always surprised, if not shocked, to find hardly any information about the said art in the *Quattro Libri.* "The cellars, the granaries, the stables and other outbuildings of this villa," writes Palladio of Villa Emo di Fanzolo, "are at one end and at the other of the main house and at these extremities there are two dovecotes which are useful to the owner and an ornament to the place, and one can go everywhere under cover, which is one of the most desirable things in a villa. Behind this building there is a square garden of eighty Treviso fields, through which runs a river, which makes the site beautiful and agreeable. It has been decorated with painting by Messer Battista Venetiano." That's all, nothing else. He says much the same for Villa Finale and for the other buildings with porticos used for agricultural purposes.

Here is the description of Maser from the *Quattro Libri:* "The building below is at Maser, a Villa near Asolo Castello del Trevigiano, of Monsignor Reverendissimo Eletto di Aquilea and of magnifico Signor Marc'Antonio, the de Barbari brothers. That part of the building which projects forward, has two levels of rooms. The floor of the upper story is at the same level as the pavement of the courtyard at the rear, where the mountain has been cut away and there is a fountain decorated with infinite amounts of stucco and paint. This spring makes a small lake that serves as a fish pond. From here the water leaves and flows into the kitchen, and then it irrigates the gardens which are to the right and the left of part of the road, which, slowly climbing, leads up to the building. It (the water) then makes two fish ponds with their drinking troughs above the public road, from where it parts, and waters the garden that is very large and full of excellent fruit trees and various bushes. The facade of the house has four columns of the Ionic order; the capitals and the corner ones face in two directions. I found these

temples and how they are made from the book on temples. On the one side and on the other there are loggias, whose extremites have dovecotes, and under these there are places to make wine, and the stables, and the other outbuildings for the use of the villa."

Here again we can see that the writer makes

absolutely no reference to the sculptors and painters who carried out decorations of the villa. This has suggested the existence of ill-feeling on the part of the architect, especially toward Paolo Veronese, but of this we have no record. James Ackerman is right when he claims that the two artists were in fact made for one another, both inspired by classical ideals, by the arts of ancient Greece, even if Veronese showed a love of decoration, which might seem incomplete contrast to the sober and pure vision of Andrea Palladio.

In the *Quattro Libri,* printed in Venice for

and 1562 refer to periods when Daniele Barbaro was in residence at the villa, where Paolo Veronese had finished his cycle of frescoes in 1561, again referred to in the documents.

Palladio's genius is so sublime that one tends to forget the utilitarian aspect of his architecture; similarly, the enchanting elegance of Paolo Veronese transports our thoughts into the world of ideals.

Harmony and gaiety were the gifts offered by the Venetian artists of the Cinquecento, a century troubled and tormented by the crisis of the Reformation and by the tumultuous world

the first time in 1570, no mention is made of the church, or Tempietto, at Maser, which was completed ten years later. There is some discussion among the critics as to the dating of the main building, which is certainly after Palladio's visit to Rome with Daniele Barbaro in 1554. Various documents dated 1558, 1559,

of politics. Palladio and Veronese perhaps suffered less than anyone from the anguished mysticism of the new religiosity, proposing the serenity of a vision which praises the values of life of a new Golden Age. Where else can one find examples of such harmony? Harmony of the building and its surroundings; harmony between the present and the past; harmony between the architecture and its inhabitants.

In the main salon of the villa the fantastic frescoed landscapes are framed by white columns. These alternate with real windows, which look out onto real landscapes. This trick gives greater veracity to the painting, while at the same time ennobling the landscape which fades away into the distance. The concept of harmony re-emerges here too, this time between the interiors and the external world, almost a friendly contest between beautiful reality and picturesque romantic fantasy.

The harmonious connection between this architecture and that of the classical world which arose in the plains and hills of Italy is accentuated in the frescoes, one of which reproduces, among the glorious and evocative ruins of the past, Villa Barbaro itself.

Many of the frescoes portray heroic deeds and ancient allegories common to classical mythology and cosmology. Alongside the symbols of Virtue, Faith, Charity, Justice, Temperance, and Strength we find the gods of a more pastoral aspect, such as Diana, Ceres, and of course Bacchus. The other inhabitants

Marc'Antonio Barbaro, just back from Fontainbleu favored the French style, evident in this nymphaeum, where maybe he himself worked as an amateur sculptor.

of Olympus are also here: Mars and Venus, Vulcan and Saturn share the walls with the Madonna della Tazza and other sacred figures. This obviuosly means that at Maser the Christian world and the pagan one were not in antithesis, but in harmony, merged together, reflecting the broad cultural outlook of the owners of the villa and their guests, who believed in the Christian religion, but also considered themselves to be the true spiritual heirs of the ancients.

The Salon of Olympus is not only dedicated to mythological and sacred images, but there are also "real" people who remind us of the every day life of the villa. The most famous and striking of these is without doubt is the hunter coming in from the woods with his dogs. And almost as if to indicate a precise subdivision

of the chores of running a villa we have a female figure carrying a tray who seems to be the tutelar deity of the house.

There are many other lively and interesting subjects on the walls of Maser: a small child, a dog sniffing around to see whats going on, a young servant, objects placed here and there as if by chance. From the servant's bearing and elegant clothes we may safely assume that he has been honored with the post of personal servant to his master, so he doesn't have to work in the fields with the others. A noblewoman pauses to look down from a balcony. Near her are some children who play with a monkey and a parrot, pets of the rich at that period, whilst two young boys read a book. The fact that these figures are painted life size of course accentuates the illusion; the same is true

Villa Barbaro, details of the garden populated by statues of gods and goddesses.

224

for the gods in the frescoes, who are an example to mortals, and who protect them throughout their earthly life.

The attention of a visitor to Maser is continually drawn by a thousand and one things; everywhere there are trompe-l'oeil monochrome cameos, banners, trophies, and arms that evoke past feasts and battles, plus brushes and other utilitarian objects that appear in no other villa; and that give the impression that Villa Barbaro has really been lived in.

Sometimes a vine is painted in the frescoes. This is a motif made famous by a painter from the classical world, and can be seen as a symbol of the sort of lifestyle led at the villa, never out of touch with the world of nature.

Other ceilings, especially that of the central cupola, depict astrological scenes which prophesy the future of he who is born under the influence of that sign. Another Barbaro, a certain Emolao, wrote several texts concerning the influence exercised by the stars on the life of men, and the whole Barbaro family was very much taken up with astrology. Also here we are dealing with harmony: the harmony that exists between life and destiny. The serpent that coils

Paolo Veronese. Figures looking over the edge of the trompe l'oeil balcony of the Salon of Olympus.

From the trompe l'oeil door a gentleman comes in from the hunt with his dogs.

Paolo Veronese.

One of the most famous Venetian painters of the Renaissance, Paolo Veronese has left many examples of his genius, especially in the frescoes of the Venetian villas, thus creating a genre which his followers and disciples admired and imitated. Paolo Caliari was born in Verona in 1528; at the age of 20 he painted his first documented work, followed by the decorations of Villa Soranza, near Castelfranco. After arriving in Venice around 1553, he achieved great fame with the canvases destined for the ceilings of Ducal Palace, and with his decorations for the church of San Bastiano. Apart from his large canvases portraying "The Wedding-Feast of Cana," "The Banquet of Gregory the Great," "The Guests in the House of Levi," his portraits and allegorical and mythological paintings are also very well known. From time to time he worked as a fresco-painter and decorator in the Venetian palaces and villas. Circa 1560 he executed one the most significant cycle of paintings in the Veneto, by frescoing the rooms of Villa Barbaro at Maser, which proved a source of inspiration for most of the artists working in the Venetian villas in the second half of the Cinquecento. Paolo died in Venice in 1588.

227

Villa Barbaro, Salon
of Olympus; in the vaulted
ceiling the heavenly gods with
the signs of the Zodiac; in the
centre the allegory of Divine
Wisdom with a serpent
symbolising Eternity;
in the lunette are portrayed
"Summer" and "Autumn."
In the detail, a young boy
holding a book looks over the
trompe l'oeil balustrade.

around itself in the centre of the Olympus
cupola is a symbol of eternity, whereas the
female figure, who seems to be the vertex of all
the decoration in the villa, has been interpreted
as the image of Divine Wisdom. This is a
religious symbol, and the allegory of Venice,
painted on the small cupola over the spring, is
a political symbol.

All these details and symbols combine to
make Maser the synthesis of all the ideals which
inspired the creation of the Venetian villas, but
this particular example has remained untouched
by the evolution of time. It has not been part of
that historical continuity that has characterised
other, even more modest villas. Maser was built
as a temple to art, culture, and harmony, and

so it has always remained. It has always had an exclusively aristocratic character; no village or town has ever grown up around its walls, even though the right conditions for such future development did in fact exist. Some years after the completion of the villa, Palladio was asked to return to Maser. He had expected to construct various other buildings but was now commissioned to design a small church, which would be know as the "Tempietto."
The inscription on this church reads: "ANNO DOMINI NOSTRI JESUS CHRISTI MDLXXX / ANDREAS PALADIUS INVENTOR MARCUS ANTONIUS BARBARUS PROCURATOR FRANCISCI FILIUS."

"Palladio," writes Wittkover, "was faced

*Villa Barbaro, Salon
of Olympus; between the
Corinthian columns are
frescoed landscapes with
mountains and rivers. The
sober modern furniture was
designed especially not to
detract attention from the
frescoes and architecture.*

*Salon of Bacchus, fireplace
by Alessandro Vittoria with a
classical inscription invoking
serenity:* Ignem in sinu ne
abscondas. *In the centre
of the side wall is a fresco
depicting a villa and its
avenue with carriages and
horsemen.*

with the problem of directing a centrally planned church. The temple of Maser, with its austere classical portico, is modeled on the Pantheon, the most perfect example of a centrally planned building in antiquity. Palladio's plan for Maser was a perfect circle with chapels on the four axes. Volumetrically it is a cylinder, surmounted by a hemispherical cupola. The walls have been left bare, there is absolutely no painting, and the decoration is exclusively sculptural. If Alberti had been able to see the Tempietto, he would surely have been able to sense the 'Divine Presence'." This building was constructed outside the villa walls on the other side of the public road, so it could be used by the villagers.

With other villas this sort of "proposal" would have instigated the development and have been the matrix of an inhabited area, but not at Maser. The Tempietto still stands alone opposite the villa, for it was precisely the attachment of the Barbaros to the integrity of their home and their possession, which defeated any intentions of a social character which Palladio may have had. As the Barbaro and their descendants were able to hold on to the land surrounding the villa, it became a unicum to which no other building was able to aspire: a symbol, perhaps, too perfect for every day life, an unrepeatable, and so particularly fascinating ivory tower.

Andrea Palladio.
The Tempietto di Maser, a
circular plan derived from
classical models; on the
facade appears an inscription
with the name of the
committente, *or client,*
the Procurator of St. Mark,
Marc'Antonio Barbaro.

VILLA EMO Fanzolo di Vedelago, Treviso

EMO
FAMILY
COAT OF ARMS

In this building the two components which characterize Palladio's villas – the traditional Venetian barchesse with their dovecotes, and the culture of Rome, clearly seen in the main building, are combined by his ingenious feeling for light and landscape.

The villa of the "magnifico signor Leonardo Emo" at Fanzolo is perhaps the building that corresponds with the greatest clearness to those ideals of concreteness and functionality characteristic of Palladian planning. "The cellars, the granaries, the stables, and the other places of the villa" – writes the Vicentine architect in his *Quattro Libri* – are on each side of the main house, and at their extremities are two dovecotes which are useful for the owner and ornament the place, and everywhere one can go under cover, which is one of the principal things looked for in a villa."

The building, which develops horizontally, almost stretching itself out over the large plain, is flanked by two dovecotes that, however, are not just simple utilitarian buildings, but romantic allusions to ancient medieval towers.

This Palladian villa was constructed on the enormous property which Leonardo di Giovanni Emo bought from the Barbaro family after the battle of Cambrai in 1509, and which was later inherited by his grandson-nephew Leonardo di Alvise. In 1535 or 1536 the Emos were able to buy a stretch of water, the Barbarigo "seriola," a sort of tributary of the Brentella canal, and they then started work on the reclamation and drainage of their territory, maybe on the advice of Alvise Cornaro. This perhaps paved the way for the construction of the villa by his successors, the heirs of "that generation of fathers" inspired and guided by Cornaro, and faithful to the ideals of "blessed architecture."

In fact it was precisely in that period that the Emos, being able to utilize the abundant supplies of water, introduced the cultivation of maize, a cereal much richer than the sorghum which had formed the basic food of the peasants up till then.

Architectonically the villa of Fanzolo appears similar to that of Maser, with that

A FANZOLO Villa del Triuigiano diſcoſto da Caſtelfranco tre miglia, è la ſottopoſta fabrica del Magnifico Signor Leonardo Emo. Le Cantine, i Granari, le Stalle, e gli altri luoghi di Villa ſono dall'vna, e l'altra parte della caſa dominicale, e nell'eſtremità loro vi ſono due colombare, che
apportano utile al padrone, & ornamento al luogo, e per tutto ſi può andare al coperto: ilche è vna
delle principal coſe, che ſi ricercano ad vna caſa di Villa, come è ſtato auertito di ſopra. Dietro à
queſta fabrica è vn giardino quadro di ottanta campi Triuigiani: per mezo il quale corre vn fiumicello, che rende il ſito molto bello, e diletteuole. E' ſtata ornata di pitture da M. Battiſta Venetiano.

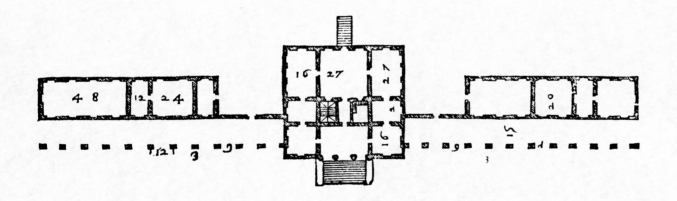

DE I

Andrea Palladio. Description, plan, and elevation of Villa Emo at Fanzolo (I Quattro Libri dell'Architettura, Venice, 1570, Book II, chapter XIV).

241

Detail of the portico, with the dovecote.
The central body of the villa falls into line with the straight side wings, in harmony with the surrounding flat countryside.

arrayment of porticos which creates a perfect fusion between the main building and the agricultural parts. Built between the years 1554 and 1565, with a precision of measurement rare in the Renaissance period, it was used for the Emo-Grimani wedding celebrations, and probably completed especially for this occasion.

The highest motives that inspired the building of villas in the Cinquecento seem to co-exist in complete harmony at Fanzolo; on the one hand the main residence possesses a tremendous dignity that is not excessive or exaggerated but still maintains a certain aristocratic sobriety, whilst on the other hand the *barchesse* and the other outbuildings in no way detract from the nobility of the central portion. When talking about this villa and Villa Barbaro at Maser, where Palladio "transformed

Villa Emo, the central body of the villa crowned by a tympanum that bears the coat of arms of the Emo family, who still own the villa. "The covered ways of the villa are made for those who enter and for the animals, and in such a way as to be connected to the house of the owner, who can go to every place under cover: so that neither the rain nor the fierce sun of the summer will bother him when he goes to see his stores, it will also be very useful to cover the wood and many other things of the villa." (Andrea Palladio, I Quattro Libri dell'Architettura, *Venice, Book II, chapter XIV).*

Villa Emo, the salon, with frescoes by Giambattista Zelotti: trompe l'oeil architectonic structures frame the scene portraying Scipio giving Aluccio his wife back; at the sides, symbolic portrayals of Earth and of Water, with naked captives and trophies of war; underneath, monochromes of triumphal processions.

Eulogy to the agrarian life

The dualism between the city and the country, theorized since the times of ancient Rome, seemed to have deeply interested the humanists of the Quattrocento and Cinquecento. Petrarch had already recounted the advantages of living in the country as opposed to life in the bustling, frenetic city. In the country passions are exalted, man finds redemption from the negative influence of the city, home of vices and corruption, and virtue triumphs. In fact it is virtue which distinguishes a gentleman, which raises him up and confers prestige upon him; it is not by accident that in the frescoes of the villas one often finds tribute to the virtuous behavior of the great men of the past, such as Alexander the Great and Scipio.

the *barchesse* into loggias on the two sides of a temple," Ackerman notes the "various messages" transmitted by the architect "on the theme of the villa:" "While his geometric axial forms make a subtle contrast to the organic world, the total composition extends out to embrace the surrounding area, while its cupolas and the sacred pediment of its facade possess their own sense of urbanity and communicate, and thus at the same time celebrate, the social status of the family by means of classical know-how and religious tradition. Palladio often unites some elements from a normal agricultural farm to these characteristics."

Inside the villa, Zelotti's paintings correspond perfectly to the ideals that guided the inhabitants of the villa: the scenes and people portrayed allude, in fact, to those historic or mythological episodes that constituted an irreplaceable fundamental ethic of the culture of the Venetian villas.

In the isolation of the country and the agrarian world passions are overcome and vices are defeated: the villa becomes a place of virtue that influences those who are fortunate enough to live under its roof, offering the choice of peace and tranquility, study, or industry, from which wealth is derived. This seems to be the scheme of things, which, prompted by the Emo, form the message of Zelotti's frescoes.

In the main salon examples of the Virtue and Chastity of the ancients are recalled by the "Episodes of Scipio;" while in the hall one is reminded that by "Prudence" one obtains "Abundance" and "Wealth."

In the Salon of the Arts one is encouraged to cultivate the studies of Astronomy, Poetry, Music, Sculpture, Architecture, and Painting. Above the fireplace are references to the Seasons that regulate all the activities of the countryside. In the other rooms characters and scenes from mythology give the artist ample opportunity to demonstrate his skill at landscapes and pastoral scenes.

Giambattista Zelotti. Fresco
potraying the murder
of Virginia, in the salon
of Villa Emo.

Giambattista Zelotti. Fresco
in the salon of the Arts, with
the figure of Astronomy.

250

Villa Emo, Salon of the Arts, frescoes by Giambattista Zelotti with the allegories of Poetry and of Music; above the door, the green monochrome figure of summer.

251

*Villa Emo, the Salon
of Venus, frescoes by
Giambattista Zelotti, with the
scene showing a goddess
helping the wounded Adonis.*

Giambattista Zelotti. Venus tries to prevent Adonis hunting.

Giambattista Zelotti. Detail from a painted decoration with a grotesque and the Emo' family's coat of arms.

Giambattista Zelotti. Doorway with the allegorical figures of Prudence and Abundance, the vaulted ceiling of the vestibule is decorated with a pergola of vines.

Salon of Venus, above the fireplace a fresco by Giambattista Zelotti showing Venus wounded by love.

VILLA ZENO al Donegal Cessalto, Treviso

The façade of Villa Zeno which looks onto the road. When compared with the plans of Palladio, one notices immediately the absence of the thermal window.

The rear of the villa that looks out over the countryside.

Describing the villas of various Venetian noblement Palladio informs us that "the Magnifico signor Marco Zeno (who was the podestà of Vicenza) has built according to the project that follows, at Cessalto, a place near to Motta, a castle of the Trevigiano." That which was built, was a villa raised up on a slightly elevated base, as the area was obviously prone to flooding. Today the villa does not bear much resemblance to the engraving in Palladio's *Secondo Libro,* and it is true that this is partly due the architect himself, who made various modifications during the actual construction of the villa. Unfortunately these modifications did not stop with Palladio, but are still being carried out, and the latest proposal is to transform the villa into a dairy, naturally with the addition of a few unsuitable outbuildings and sheds!

To complete the tragic tale, the marvelous agricultural wings that embraced the courtyard, together with their inevitable dovecotes, gardens, and courts, and all those other things that a villa needs and which Palladio provided, have totally vanished.

IL MAGNIFICO Signor Marco Zeno ha fabricato fecondo la inuentione, che fegue in Ce-
falto luogo propinquo alla Motta, Caftello del Triuigiano. Sopra vn bafamento, il quale circonda
tutta la fabrica, è il pauimento delle ftanze: lequali tutte fono fatte in uolto: l'altezza de i uolti delle
maggiori è fecondo il modo fecondo delle altezze de' volti. Le quadre hanno le lunette ne gli angoli, al diritto delle fineftre: i camerini appreffo la loggia, hanno i uolti à fafcia, e cofi ancho la fala: il
volto della loggia è alto quanto quello della fala, e fuperano tutti due l'altezza delle ftanze. Ha quefta fabrica Giardini, Cortile, Colombara, e tutto quello, che fa bifogno all'ufo di Villa.

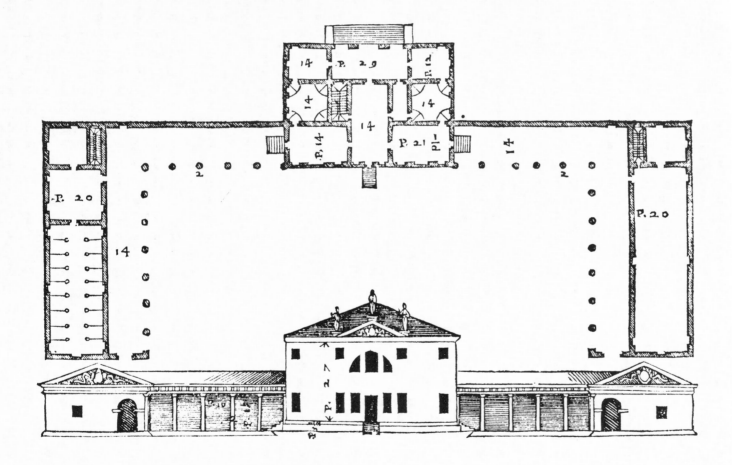

GG   NON MOLTO

Andrea Palladio. Description,
plan and elevation of Villa
Zeno at Cessalto (I Quattro
Libri dell'Architettura,
Venice, 1570, Book II,
chapter XIV).

VILLA FOSCARI known as "La Malcontenta" Mira, Venice

FOSCARI
FAMILY

COAT OF ARMS

Not far from Venice, on the banks of the Brenta, stands the magnificent Palladian Villa Foscari, perhaps better known as "the Malcontenta;" the first of a series of villas that flowered in the terra firma during the rule of the Serenissima. Today that green plain, salvaged centuries ago from the mosquito-ridden swamps by Venetian landowners, is again in danger, this time not from floods but from continuous encroachment by the industries of Marghera, whose fumes suffocate and corrode the very fabric of the villas.

When Albert Landsberg bought the villa, it was being used for the cultivation of silk worms, which he promptly stopped in time to save some of the frescoes. Fortunately times have changed and today there are a sufficient number of people who are aware of the immense historical and artistic value of our enormous architectural patrimony.

Without doubt one of the most fascinating of all Palladian buildings, la Malcontenta is reflected in the waters of the Brenta, which give it life and make it even more beautiful. Rivers were very important indeed in the past, as they were a very popular and economic means of communication. "If one can build on a river," writes Palladio, "it will be very convenient and beautiful since one can always reach the city with little expense..., and the view is very beautiful, and very easily and with great ornament one can water the possesions, the gardens, and the kithen gardens, which are the life and the recreation of the villa."

Palladio solved the problem of high water and flooding by placing the piano nobile on a base which both enhances the majesty of the building and lets it be seen from afar. "This building is raised eleven feet above the ground," Palladio, in fact, writes.

The Brenta, so important in the history of the villa, also determined its siting, thus changing the usual building typology, for the principle facade faces north to overlook the river, presenting the dignity and solemnity of its Ionic loggia to its guests and travelers passing by. On the south side however, Palladio breaks up the massive block of the building with different shaped openings, which let the early afternoon light inundate the lofty interior.

The typical sobriety of Palladian masterpieces is at last encountered in the sides of the building; the extremely sparing distribution of cornices and openings and the graduated use of ashlar-work contribute much to the beauty and harmony of the whole complex.

The villa is richly decorated with frescoes: Battista Franco started those in the Salon of the Giants, which remind of the Mantuan paintings of Giulio Romano, and they were completed by Giambattista Zelotti, painter of the grotesques and landscapes, that can be reconstructed or at least visualised from the descriptions of Ridolfi. Mythological scenes alternate with Allegories of the Arts and of Virtue, with the usual references to villa life symbolised by "Astra showing Jove the pleasures of the Earth."

Built around 1560, the villa was mainly used for official receptions, within easy reach of the city it entertained many honored guests, including Henry III in 1574.

NON MOLTO lungi dalle Gambarare ſopra la Brenta è la ſeguente fabrica delli Magnifici
Signori Nicolò, e Luigi de' Foſcari.   Queſta fabrica è alzata da terra undici piedi, e ſotto ui ſono cu
cine, tinelli, e ſimili luoghi, & è fatta in uolto coſi di ſopra, come di ſotto. Le ſtanze maggiori hanno i
uolti alti ſecondo il primo modo delle altezze de' uolti. Le quadre hanno i uolti à cupola : ſopra i ca
merini vi ſono mezati : il uolto della Sala è à Crociera di mezo cerchio : la ſua impoſta è tanto alta dal
piano, quanto è larga la Sala : la quale è ſtata ornata di eccellentiſsime pitture da Meſſer Battiſta Ve
netiano.   Meſſer Battiſta Franco grandiſsimo diſegnatore à noſtri tempi hauea ancor eſſo dato prin
cipio à dipingere una delle ſtanze grandi, ma ſoprauenuto dalla morte ha laſciata l'opera imperfetta.
La loggia è di ordine Ionico : La Cornice gira intorno tutta la caſa, e fa fronteſpicio ſopra la loggia, e
nella parte oppoſta.   Sotto la Gronda vi è vn'altra Cornice, che camina ſopra i fronteſpicij : Le ca
mere di ſopra ſono come mezati per la loro baſſezza, perche ſono alte ſolo otto piedi.

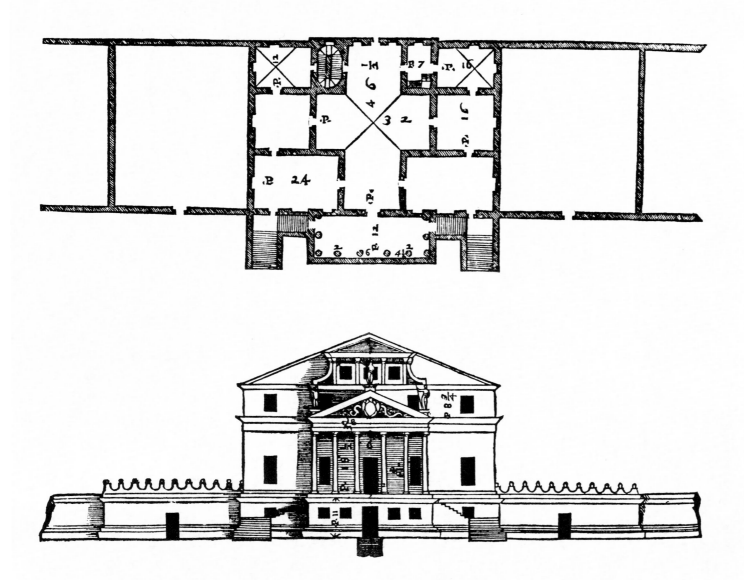

LA SOTTOPOSTA

*Andrea Palladio. Description, plan and elevation of Villa Foscari (*I Quattro Libri dell'Architettura, *Venice, 1570, Book II, chapter XIV).*

Palladio's beautiful and noble architecture seems to welcome the travellers who come down the busy Brenta. Even today Villa Malcontenta is like a Roman dream come true, overlooking the waters of the canal, which, as more and more patrician residences were built along its banks, became a sort of Grand Canal for those who fled from Venice for their villeggiatura.

261

Villa Foscari or "La
Malcontenta," the facade
overlooking the river.
The double flight of steps
leads up to the solemn
portico, reminding one of the
Parthenon and other ancient
monuments studied
by Palladio.

The southern aspect of the
villa. The lack of decorative
elements shows up the purity
of the linear values of this
southern facade.

On the following pages:
Interior of the main salon
which is in the form of a
cross. The large windows
looking out towards the south
flood the enormous room,
which is two storeys high,
with brilliant light.
On the walls there are traces
of frescoes by Giambattista
Zelotti with allegorical and
mythical subjects, framed by
trompe l'oeil architectural
motifs such as columns and
niches.

Villa Foscari, salon of the Giants with frescoes left unfinished by Battista in 1561, the year of his death.

Giambattista Zelotti, detail of a grotesque fresco, perfectly conserved, in the small rooms of the villa.

Giambattista Zelotti. Tradition has it that this female figure is of "The Malcontenta."

267

VILLA SARACENO Finale di Agugliaro, Vicenza

SARACENO
FAMILY
COAT OF ARMS

In this part of the province of Vicenza one can find the oldest examples of Venetian villas, from the Gothic construction of Villa dal Verme to the noble architecture of Cà Brusà. Palladio's Villa Saraceno at Finale is also an early example of his work and is characterized by a sobriety of elements that make this one of his simplest and purest architectural achievements.

Villa Saraceno stands near the Liona canal, whose waters also reflect the facade of Villa dal Verme. It is built on a base, as the surrounding plain was often threatened by flooding.
The territory around the house had previously been unhealthy mosquito-ridden swamps, but now was particularly fertile arable land.

One of the existing murals portrays an allegorical figure who has nothing to do with mythology or Christianity, but who is admirably suited to the functional spirit and pragmatic character of those men who built the Venetian villas, it is of course the "Allegory of Wealth."

The upper floor is taken up by a vast granary where victuals were stored. It would have been difficult to conserve these in the wooden thatched buildings generally inhabited by the poor peasants. So the construction of such large villas was justified by the practical necessity for storage, and nowhere is this more evident than in the example of Villa Saraceno, which is distinguished by the minimum of architectonic and decorative embellishments.

This villa, built beside a canal which helped salvage the surrounding territory, is one of Palladio's simplest and purest architectural projects, and proof that the poetry of the villa does not consist solely of splendid noble statements, but of a language which stems from the peace of the countryside.

DE I DISEGNI DELLE CASE DI VILLA DI ALCVNI
Gentil'huomini di Terra Ferma.   Cap. XV.

D VN luogo del Vicentino detto il FINALE, è la seguente fabrica del Signor Biagio Sarraceno: il piano delle stanze s'alza da terra cinque piedi: le stanze maggiori sono lunghe vn quadro, e cinque ottaui, & alte quanto larghe, e sono in solaro.   Continua questa altezza ancho nella Sala: i camerini appresso la loggia sono in uolto: la altezza de' uolti al pari di quella delle stanze: di sotto vi sono le Cantine, e di sopra il Granaro: il quale occupa tutto il corpo della casa. Le cucine sono fuori di quella: ma però congiunte in modo che riescono commode. Dall'vna, e l'altra parte ui sono i luoghi all'vso di Villa necessarij.

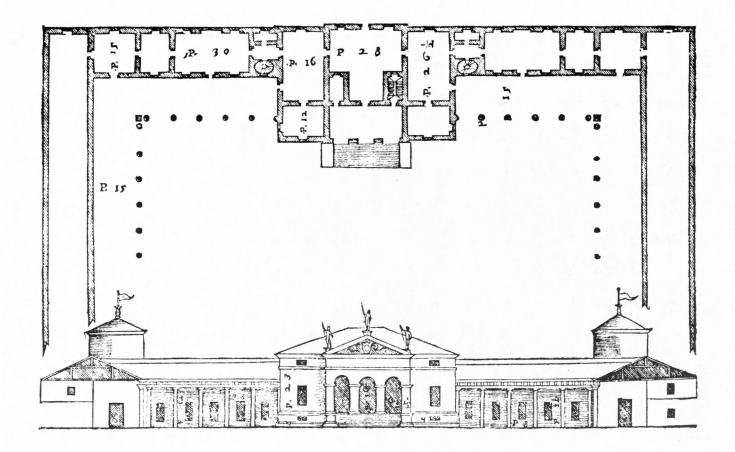

I DISEGNI

*Andrea Palladio. Description, plan, and elevation of Villa Saraceno at Finale (*I Quattro Libri dell'Architettura, *Venice, 1570, Book II, chapter XV).*

VILLA REPETA Campiglia dei Berici, Vicenza

REPETA
FAMILY

COAT OF ARMS

The extremely original villa at Campiglia and the words with which Palladio describes it are usually juxtaposed to the egalitarian inspirations of Anabaptism, which were extremely popular in and around Vicenza at that time. However, the most authentic motive behind the construction of this villa was probably inspired by a culture that was even higher; one thinks immediately of the Academy founded by Giangiorgio Trissino, whose model and inspiration was the world of the ancient Greeks and their serene and harmonious culture.

The plans of Francesco and Mario Ripeta's villa show exactly how a building can overcome and sublimate every practical motive. In fact, it seems to allude to the secret dreams of the Venetians. Only at Campiglia can we find a perfect and total expression of those egalitarian ideas, of that profound sense of hospitality so dear to the elect circle of Trissino and so foreign to the exclusive world of Alvise Cornaro.

In his writings Palladio quite often returned to various aspects of the Greek civilization, as in Chapter IX of his *Secondo Libro* for example, where, when talking about Greek homes he comments, "they provided the guests with a place to stay, and furnished them with every thing necessary for living, so that the guests were free in every respect to feel that they were in their own homes."

Not surprisingly, such dreams were short lived: the refined ideals of Trissino collapsed, his hopes of founding a Hellenic culture were proved to be only an illusion. The egalitarianism, the open-mindedness and the social values which inspired the villa all disappeared. When, in fact, the Palladian buiding was completely destroyed by fire in 1672, very different criteria governed its rebuilding. The inscription on the front of the "new" villa is very revealing, claiming that the new physiognomy of the villa is in obedience to the *elegantiorem cultum* of the eighteenth

century. Indeed, the massive structure, which used to have more floors than it has now, has very little in common with the pure vision of the Francesco Repeta and Palladio.

The present villa follows the layout of a Venetian palace, but instead of a portego, there is a salon with a cupola, almost sixty feet high, like a grandiose temple, which does in fact correspond to the decisively *signorile* and feudal character of the building. Construction was carried out during a period of intense refeudalization, and the Repeta family, long distinguished in the arts of war and who had enjoyed feudal privileges in the area since 1217, wanted to build on their own domain a residence worthy of such a great and powerful family, a severe and solemn home suitable for the head of an army.

In front of the villa there is an enormous, perfectly conserved curtain wall, formed of false arcades, which makes one think of a Roman circus where the soldiers could carry out their drills and maneuvers, performances in which the Repetas had always distinguished themselves.

The serene and harmonious world of the Greeks, praised by the Trissinian Academy, inspired Villa Repeta, now replaced by a seventeenth-century building dedicated to the family's military activities. Giovanni Antonio Fasolo. The Game of Tric-Trac, detail, (Albettone, Villa Campiglia, later Negri de Salvi).

LA FABRICA sottopoſta è in Campiglia luogo del Vicentino, & è del Signor Mario Repe-ta,ilquale ha eſequito in queſta fabrica l'animo della felice memoria del Signor Franceſco ſuo padre. Le colonne de i portici ſono di ordine Dorico: gli intercolunnij ſono quattro diametri di colonna: Ne gli eſtremi angoli del coperto,oue ſi ueggono le loggie fuori di tutto il corpo della caſa,ui uanno due colombare,& le loggie. Nel fianco rincontro alle ſtalle ui ſono ſtanze,delle quali altre ſono de-dicate alla Continenza,altre alla Giuſtitia,& altre ad altre Virtù con gli Elogij, e Pitture, che ciò di-moſtrano, parte delle quali è opera di Meſſer Battiſta Maganza Vicentino Pittore,e Poeta ſingolare: il che è ſtato fatto affine che queſto Gentil'huomo, il quale riceue molto uolentieri tutti quelli, che vanno à ritrouarlo ; poſſa alloggiare i ſuoi foreſtieri,& amici nella camera di quella Virtù, alla quale eſsi gli pareranno hauer più inclinato l'animo. Ha queſta fabrica la commodità di potere andare per tutto al coperto; e perche la parte per l'habitatione del padrone,e quella per l'uſo di Villa ſono di vno iſteſſo ordine ; quanto quella perde di grandezza per non eſſere più eminente di queſta ; tanto que-ſta di Villa accreſce del ſuo debito ornamento, e dignità,facendoſi vguale à quella del Padrone con bellezza di tutta l'opera.

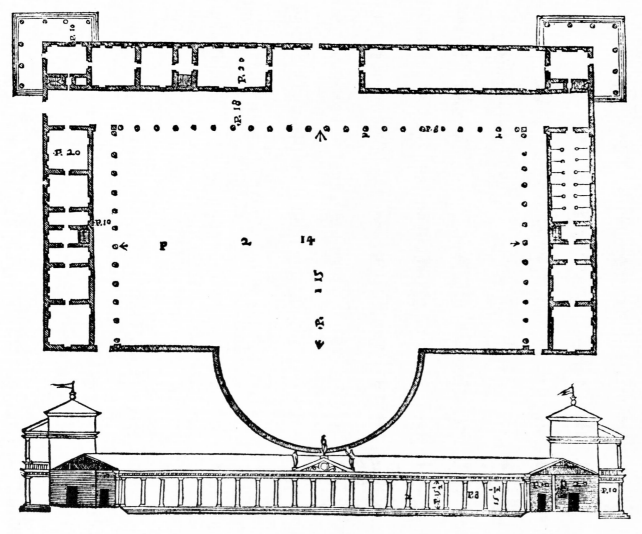

LA SEGVENTE

Andrea Palladio. Description, plan and elevation of Villa Repeta at Campiglia dei Benci. (I Quattro Libri dell'Architettura, Venice, 1570, book II, chapter XV).

VILLA CALDOGNO Caldogno, Vicenza

CALDOGNO
FAMILY
COAT OF ARMS

Despite the absence of precise documentation regarding the authorship of this building, the compositive rhythms which echo other documented works by Palladio – such as the relief of the three ashlar-work arches on the otherwise plain wall, the tympanum, the original polygonal steps – are all elements which suggest that this is another example of Palladio's work.

In about 1565, Angelo Caldogno, a Vicentine aristocrat and friend of Andrea Palladio, commissioned the architect to build a villa to the north of Vicenza, in the heart of an area long dominated by the presence of his family. Even though it does not appear among the pages of the *Quattro Libri,* its solid architectonic structure and the simplicity of its exterior, elegant in its purity, suggest the hand of Andrea. So much so that it does not seem wise to attribute this house to Piero di Nanto as several historians have done. Its Palladian paternity would seem only to be confirmed by the friendship that existed between the architect and the noble Vicentine, but apart from this historical fact, by the undeniable artistic quality of this villa and its affinity with

other documented creations of Palladio.

The principal prospect of the house is particularly significant, with its three great arches, strongly outlined by the ashlar-work cornice that spans the portico, its only decorative element. Moreover, the simplicity and bareness that characterise the surface of the walls suggest an ideal parallel to Palladio's early works, particularly that of Villa Saraceno at Finale.

The interior decorations are especially beautiful and were for the most part executed by Giovanni Antonio Fasolo, who, in the loggia and main salon, illustrates the amusements and pleasures of life in the villa. The frescoes of the loggia are dedicated to depicting those very pleasant days spent playing cards and listening to concerts, or indeed dancing and banqueting.

Zelotti also worked at Villa Caldogno where he painted "The History of Scipio and Sophonisba," whilst later on, with the portrayal of Pastor Fido, Carpioni, would introduce a motive dealing with a literary theme.

Of particular interest are some figures with carefully painted physiognomy, probably portraits of the more important members of the Caldogno family.

273

Giambattista Zelotti.
Frescoes in the Scipio salon,
framed by a large arch, the
scene shows Scipio giving
Aluccio his wife back.

277

VILLA CORNARO Piombino Dese, Padua

CORNARO
FAMILY
COAT OF ARMS

The villa that Palladio designed in about 1553 for the Venetian nobleman Giorgio Cornaro has had a difficult and tormented history. In his will, dated 1570, Cornaro requests that a certain sum of money should be put aside "as long as the construction of the palace continue:" a significant codex that lets us understand that once the building of the villa had begun, his heirs had to respect the wishes of their predecessor and finish it. This codex is also an example of the importance of the concept of continuity to the Venetians, a concept particularly praised by all those involved with the history of the Venetian villas, from Alvise Cornaro to Palladio himself.

Still unfinished in 1582, the villa was enhanced with an upper loggia in 1596, and only in a drawing dated 1613 do we see it in its final form. Probably the superimposition of constructive phases and the series of modifications can explain the weakness of the architecture, scarcely homogeneous, devoid of any truly harmonious agreement between its various parts.

Built more as a suburban residence than a working "villa-farm," it is characterized by the presence of two piani nobile, one on top of the other, an unusual occurrence for a country villa but often found in the city.

The villa stands near a river and possesses a garden with flower beds and fish ponds. The principal prospect, divided up by columns that are too slender and marked by a scarce agreement between the floors, looks out onto the road. In fact, it almost seems part of it, as do many Settecento villas. Flanked by other dwellings, the Cornaro residence somehow contradicts the usual "princely autonomy" of the other Palladian villas.

In the interior there are portraits of the Cornaro family attributed to Camillo Mariani: an example of self-celebration which is an exception to the usual iconography.

Alongside tha main house are the usual agricultural buildings that at one time, as can be seen in an eighteenth-century drawing, were dominated by a dovecote.

A classic example of "open architecture," characterized by porticos and loggias, the Cornaro's villa has become, despite its evident stylistic incongruities, one of the most widely imitated models of English and American Palladianism.

Facing the public road, this villa, whose double order of culumns confers on it the dignity of a palace, is one of the most imitated models of English and American Palladianism.

LA FABRICA, che fegue è del Magnifico Signor Giorgio Cornaro in Piombino luogo di Caſtel Franco. Il primo ordine delle loggie è Ionico. La Sala è poſta nella parte più a dentro della caſa, accioche ſia lontana dal caldo, e dal freddo : le ale oue ſi ueggono i nicchi ſono larghe la terza parte della ſua lunghezza : le colonne riſpondono al diritto delle penultime delle loggie, e ſono tanto diſtanti tra ſe, quanto alte : le ſtanze maggiori ſono lunghe un quadro, e tre quarti : i uolti ſono alti ſecondo il primo modo delle altezze de' volti : le mediocri ſono quadre il terzo più alte che lárghe ; i uolti ſono à lunette : ſopra i camerini vi ſono mezati. Le loggie di ſopra ſono di ordine Corinthio : le colonne ſono la quinta parte più ſottili di quelle di ſotto. Le ſtanze ſono in ſolaro, & hanno ſopra alcuni mezati. Da vna parte ui è la cucina, e luoghi per maſſare, e dall'altra i luoghi per ſeruitori.

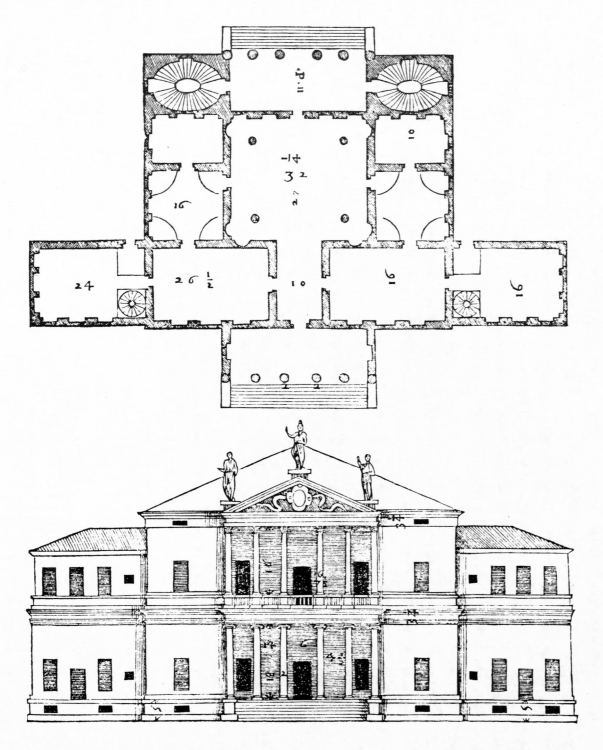

LA SOTTOPOSTA

Andrea Palladio. Description, plan, and elevation of Villa Cornaro at Piombino Dese (I Quattro Libri dell'Architettura, Venice, 1570, book II, chapter XIV).

Villa Cornaro, as seen from the garden.

Salon of the four columns, detail; in the niche is a lady from the Cornaro family, statue in plaster by Camillo Mariani.

VILLA ALMERICO CAPRA
known as "La Rotonda" Vicenza

ALMERICO
FAMILY
COAT OF ARMS

The villa was conceived by Palladio as a monument to the client. Paolo Almerico from Vicenza, Apostolic Referendary of Popes Pius IV and Pius V. Built on top of a hill, this villa, crowned by a dome like a Greek temple, is characterized above all by the motif of the Ionic pronaos, or portico, which is repeated on all four sides, almost as if to underline its celebratory character.

This is the most famous and well known of all Palladian villas, considered by the architect as a city residence, because it was built on the immediante outskirts of Vicenza, and was devoid of all agricultural functions.

The acropolic position, crowning a small hill, makes it a stunning belvedere which looks out, thanks to its four equal prospects, over all the surrounding landscape, and admirably realizes the Palladian ideal of "see and be seen."

The client, Paolo Almerico, was a man of the church, being Apostolic Referendary to Popes Pius IV and Pius V. He had lived in Rome and wished to realize his dreams of ambition, his desire to win the respect and admiration of his fellow citizens. Ackerman must have had La Rotonda in mind when he wrote: "The mythical dimension of the ideology of the villa frees it from the concrete limitations of a utilitarian and productive nature and makes it the perfect place to demonstrate the creative aspirations of both the client and the architect."

Inspired by the most noble examples of Rome and crowned by a dome, like a sacred temple, the villa still possesses a completely Venetian character, thanks to its cordial relationship with the surrounding landscape. If therefore appears as a living vibrant presence, with none of the coldness and rigidity of an exclusively architectural taste.

In fact, the Rotonda was designed to appear as the top of the hill upon which it was built: the steps follow the natural slope of the hill and the dome crowns the villa just as the villa crowns the hill. Thus the classical elements become almost an emanation of the landscape; the pronaos surmounted by a tympanum is no longer the vertex of a hierarchy, as it is repeated on all four sides, letting the visitor enjoy the countryside from every point of view. The culmination of the villa is thus the dome, which Palladio had studied at Rome, particularly in his idealized reconstruction of the Baths of Caracalla, as a dominant element also in profane buildings.

La Rotonda, pronaos, seen from the side. Here one can clearly see the architectonic values of the villa.

One of the four facades, the entrance drive is flanked by statues.

On the following pages: Two details of the pronaos, with statues attributed to a pupil of Vittoria, Agostino Rubini. In the tympanum, the coat of arms of the Capra, the family who bought the villa from the Americos.

Often referred to as Villa Capra, it actually is an expression of the culture of Paolo Almerico, who already possessed a princely palace in the

city, but who wanted to build a monument to his personality in this charming countryside. Such a desire is only comprehensible when seen against the background òf a particular climate that was widespread in the sixteenth century, and that had more or less affected all of Palladio's clients.

Almerico's desire to perpetuate the glory of his *gens* was but a short-lived dream, his son sold the villa to the Capra family, the ideals

284

MARIVS CAPRA
GABRIELIS F

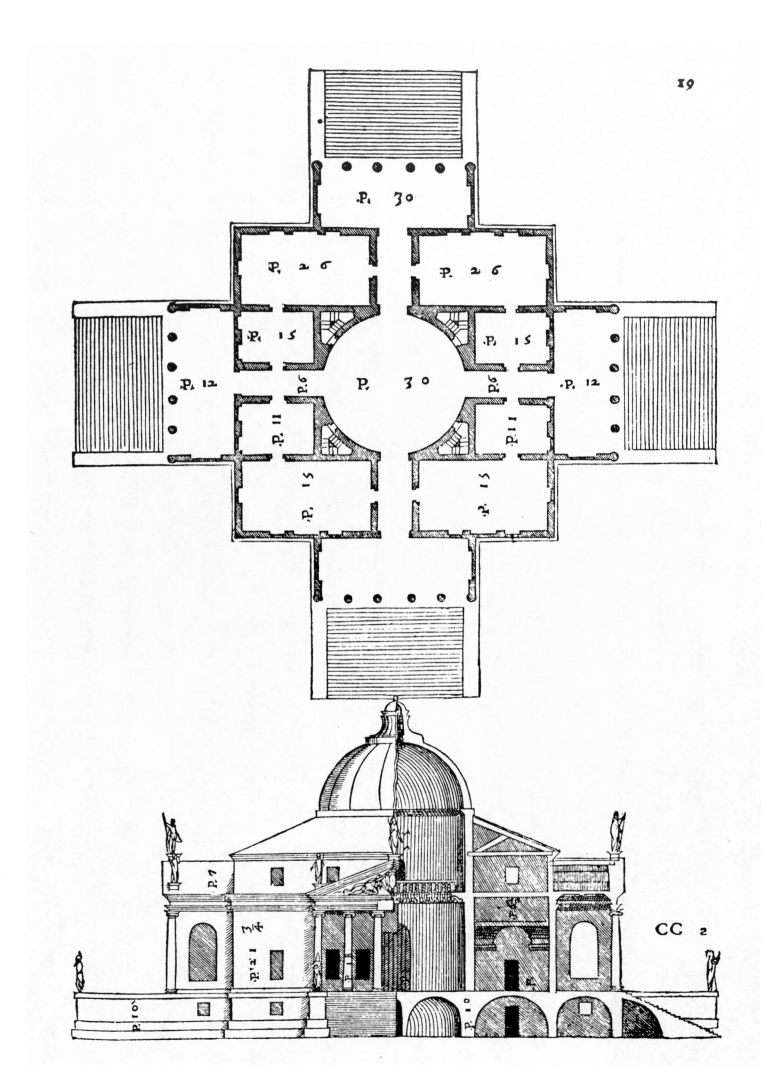

*Andrea Palladio. Description, plan, and elevation of Villa Almerico (*I Quattro Libri dell'Architettura, *Venice, 1570, book II, chapter III).*

"Today I have seen a splendid villa called La Rotonda, half an hour away from the city, on a beautiful hill... Maybe art has never before reached such a level of magnificence... Thus the villa can be admired from every part of the region, and also the view which can be admired from the inside is one of the most delightful. One can see the Bachiglione flowing, bringing the boats down from Verona to the Brenta..." (Wolfgang Goethe, Viaggio in Italia, 1816-1817).

changed rapidly and the inscription put up by the new proprietors deprived the Rotonda of its idealized function as a lay and profane monument, placing it instead firmly in the category of traditional country villas. The Capra, who had bought up all the surrounding land, thought more of their new union with the country than of the glory of their family. Here is the inscription that the new proprietors had placed on the facades of the villa: "MARIUS CAPRA / GABRIELIS F. // QUI AEDES HAS ARCTISSIMO/PRIMOGENITURAE / GRADUI SUBIECIT // UNA CUM OMNIBUS CENSIBUS / AGRIS VALLIBUS ET COLL / BUS CITRA VIAM

MAGNAM // MEMORIALE PERPETUAE MANDANS / HAEC DUM SUSTINET / AC ABSTINET."

A more realistic vision has therefore taken over, which, during the Seicento, stresses the economic value and functionality of the architectonic complex, without however, disturbing the original structure of the building. The agricultural outbuildings, designed by Scamozzi, were in fact constructed at a much lower level, hidden away from sight. Thus, in conclusion, this villa, conceived as a monument to a noble aristocrat, assumed in time the perequisites corresponding to the ethics and

View of the villa with one of the four symmetrical Ionic pronaos.

the most lively Venetian tradition, becoming symbolically, the Queen of the Venetian villas.

Only later and at various different times were the interior decorations carried out, with the introduction of trompe l'oeil architectural perspective which exaggerated and dulled the original Palladian spirit. One should mention the frescoes of Anselmo Canera, the great dome decorated by Alessandro Maganza, and later decorations by Ludovico Dovigny. The stucco work on the ceilings is especially beautiful.

On the facades and on the parapets of the balustrades are statues by Albanese and Lorenzo Rubini, as documented by Palladio himself.

A statue that crowns the lodge at the side of the Rotonda's entrance drive, perhaps of Pyramus committing suicide.

La Rotonda detail of pronaos with statues attributed to Agostino Rubini.

On the following pages: one of the corridors leading to the central salon and the grandiose dome which crowns it. This is the first example of a civilian building with a dome, usually reserved for churches and temples. The proportions studied by Palladio based on squares and circles are according to arithmetical and musical relations, learned allusions to the philosophical and artistic reunions which took place in this villa. The frescoes with allegorical figures are by Alessandro Maganza.

291

La Rotonda, the central salon with frescoes by Ludovico Dorigny and by an unknown quadraturista *who multiplies illusionistically the architectonic effects of the building.*

294

VILLA SEREGO
Santa Sofia di San Pietro in Cariano, Verona

SEREGO
FAMILY
COAT OF ARMS

Adapting himself to the military traditions of the Veronese aristocracy and interpreting the Serego's aspirations to power, Palladio conceived this villa using the intensely expressive strength of the materials and the buildings which recall his experiences of the architecture of ancient Rome and the mannerism of Giulio Romano.

Santa Sofia di San Pietro in Caraino takes its name from the ancient church of Santa Sofia, already annexed to a previous villa that Antonio Della Scala had given to the *condottiere,* Cortesia Serego; the documents which supply this information also mention a high dovecote, a cistern, a wine press, and other agricultural equipment.

Saving the church, Palladio started construction of the present villa sometime between 1560 and 1570, probably the project had a long gestation period (some say it started as early as 1551).

The building complex is surrounded by a large park, and the whole is outstandingly beautiful, as Palladio himself notes in the *Quattro Libri:* "situated in a wonderful position, that is on top of a hill that is very easily climbed and it looks out over part of the city and it is between two small valleys; all the hills around are very pleasant and full of very good water, so therefore this building is adorned with gardens and marvelous fountains..."

The villa is a rather unusual example of Palladio's work; always as receptive to the various exigencies and aspirations of his clients as he was to the varying landscapes. In this villa he managed to express the military character of this Veronese family, erecting an edifice which, had it been completed according ot its plans, would have resulted in a massive architectural complex, with three courtyards, nestling in the hilly surroundings.

The only part of the project that was actually built brings us back to one of those three principles that inspired Palladio's work: durability. Time, in fact, has hardly affected the plaster, and the rudely cùt rocks piled up one on top of another, which form the columns, are almost harsh and primitive in their massive solidarity. The plastic density of the ashlar-work on these columns, which are all the same order, expresses a grandeur and strength equalled only by Michelangelo. Palladio was obviously

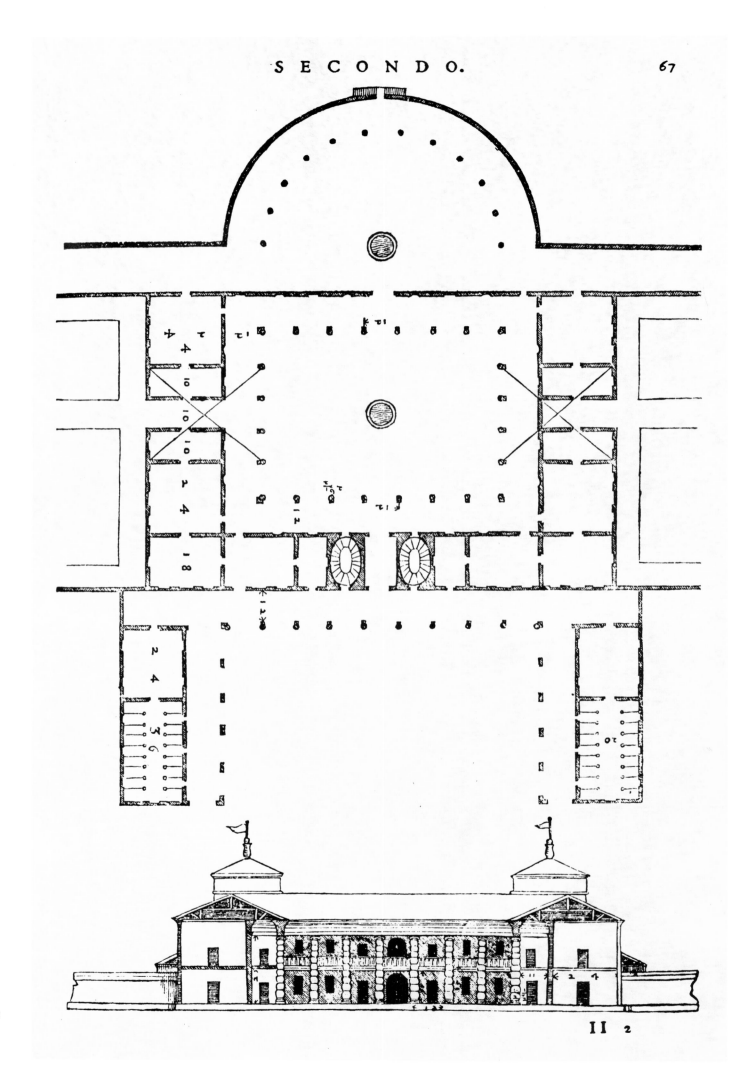

*Andrea Palladio. Plan, and description of Villa Serego at Santa Sofia (*I Quattro Libri dell'Architettura, *Venice, 1570, book II, chapter XV).*

thinking of these "stones not cleaned" when he wrote that "the villa needs elements that are straightforward and simple rather than delicate."

More than anything designed by Sanmicheli or Giulio Romano, Villa Serego makes us think immediately of the buildings of ancient Rome.

Inside the old chapel of Santa Sofia there are frescoes dating from the Trecento.

Villa Sarego, the "stone not cleaned" underlines the sheer weight of the material, in contrast with more well known forms of Palladio.

VILLA CAMPIGLIA NEGRI DE' SALVI Albettone, Vicenza

CAMPIGLIA
FAMILY
COAT OF ARMS

The spread of Romanticism in the nineteenth century brought about much rebuilding and sometimes even demolition of the old villas, carried out on the orders of owners who felt that their homes had become inadequate and no longer fulfilled the needs of those modern, different times.

The most famous protagonist of such "tampering" in the Vicenza area was a certain architect called Antonio Caregaro Negrin, who, in 1842, was commissioned by the Negri de' Salvi to "gothisize" their residence at Albettone. Fortunately one ground floor room of this Quattrocento building, which had belonged to the noble Campiglia family, was saved. This had been frescoed by Giovanni Antonio Fasolo between the years 1560 and 1570 with scenes depicting various aspects of life in a villa and which were especially interesting and delightful because of the elegance of the figures and the naturalness of their poses.

The frescoes portraying "Music," "Games," "the Chase" were heavily repainted by Giovanni Busato in 1858. Only recently have careful restorations returned them to their original charm and vivacity.

In their fascinating entirety, the cycle of frescoes at Albettone provide us with the most complete image of what life was like in the villa of an aristocratic Venetian, a style of the life which lasted throught the whole of the Settecento. Alongside the equestrian pursuit of hunting and the games that helped pass the time in the villa, music represented the call of the arts.

Many of these villas acted as true academies, as was noted by Palladio himself when describing Villa Repeta in Campiglia, not far from Albettone.

From the ancient dwelling of the Campiglia, restored in the Ottocento, was saved one room in which Giovanni Antonio Fasolo had painted various episodes and amusements from villa life.

Giovanni Antonio Fasolo. Detail from "The Concert."

On the following pages: "The game of Tric-Trac" and "Three gentlemen playing flutes."

THE HISTORY AND CULTURE OF THE
VENETIAN VILLAS

SCAMOZZI'S VILLAS AND OTHER SIXTEENTH-CENTURY VILLAS

VILLA OBIZZI called "Il Catajo" Battaglia, Padua

OBIZZI
FAMILY
COAT OF ARMS

Evoking remote legends, the Catajo castle, which rises up at the foot of the Euganean Hills near Monselice, constitutes one of the most extraordinary architectural complexes of the Venetian mainland. Erected around 1570 by the *condottiere* of the Venetian Republic, Pio Enea degli Obizzi, whose name derives from the invention of a kind of firearm (the *obice,* or howitzer), the castle clearly reflects the military ideals of the man who had it built. The crenellated turrets, triumphal arches, drawbridge, and the massive, austere structure of the central part eloquently allude to the art of war to which Enea degli Obizzi and his guests devoted their lives. Nevertheless, the present-day structure of the building does not fully correspond to the original design, which tradition maintains was drafted by Obizzi himself.

For the fresco decorations – even the facade was painted, as one can see in the print by Volkamer – Obizzi turned to Giambattista Zelotti and to other artists who, in the various rooms, retold episodes from Roman history and more recent war scenes in which the Obizzis had figured prominently. Now deprived of the decorative finishings which once softened its forms, the facade presents itself in all its massive severity. To the original main block new architectural complexes were later added, and it became necessary to flatten further the surrounding hills to facilitate transportation to nearby centers.

The Courtyard of the Giants, constructed in the seventeenth century, was the site of numerous jousts, while the theater housed spectacles and dramas. The work of expansion was carried on by subsequent owners, members of noble families who enriched the castle with whimsical structures and displays, such as the nineteenth-century decoration of the chapel in German Gothic style.

The Catajo stands as a testimony of the endurance of chivalric nostalgia over the centuries. The castle gained particular prestige when works of art, antiques and precious musical instruments were collected in its rooms; unfortunately, however, these collections were broken up at the end of the last century and are now scattered in various foreign museums.

Pal: del N.H. Obizzo alla Bataglia.

Erected around 1570, this castle-villa, symbol of the endurance of chivalrous sentiment over the centuries, faithfully mirrors the military ideal of the man who commissioned it, Pio Enea degli Obizzi, condottiere in the service of the Serene Republic.

Joseph Cristopher Volkamer, engraving representing the fruit of a cedar as an example of the citruses cultivated in the greenhouses of the Catajo (Continuation der Nurnbergischen Hesperidum, 1714). On the villa's façade one can still see the frescoes of Giambattista Zelotti, which have since disappeared.

*Tradition has it that the
original idea for the immense
castle came when a
noblewoman, delighted by the
landscape, expressed the
desire to have on that spot
a "tower with three or four
small rooms."*

LXII

la parte interiore della Lima verrucosa.

*Another of the villa's facades,
with the hill behind it.
Engraving by Volkamer.*

310

VILLA EOLIA Costozza di Longare, Vicenza

TRENTO
FAMILY
COAT OF ARMS

The ceiling of the hall of Villa Eolia, with frescoes attributed to Giovanni Antonio Fasolo. In the middle is Aeolus, in the niches the allegories of the Four Seasons flanked by Olympian deities on chariots drawn by animals sacred to them.

Two details portraying Mars and Venus.

Among those villas whose proprietors included Renaissance humanists, we find the wonderful Villa Eolia or "Prison of the Winds" at Costozza. It was built, according to Renaissance architect Andrea Palladio, by the remarkable gentleman Francesco Trento who, by using a network of wind-ducts, took advantage of the intermittently cool and warm air of the caves and galleries of the nearby Berici hills to make more pleasurable the scholarly gatherings held there, which brought together some of the most celebrated figures of the time. Palladio writes: "... as there are in the same hills as said Villa a number of very large caves... in which some very fresh winds originate, these Gentlemen, by means of underground passageways that they call wind-ducts, convey [these winds] to their houses, and with pipes similar to these ducts they convey the cool wind to all of their rooms, closing them and opening them as they please to obtain more or less coolness, depending on the season" (from *The Four Books of Architecture,* 1570)

The scholars gathered at Villa Eolia thus could always enjoy a mild atmosphere, thanks to the air coming up from the cryptoporticus below and flowing into the house through a grating in the floor. Originally the name Eolia belonged to the underground hollow, and on its entrance door one still reads today: AEOLUS HIC CLAUSO VENTORUM CARCERE REGNAT AEOLIA.

Outside, the building has an extremely simple, unadorned surface, in marked contrast with the decorative richness of the interior. Divided by painted, illusory architectural elements, the walls contain vast landscapes, while above, in the cross-vault, is a sky peopled with deities according to the seasons and the Zodiac. The entire decorative display seems to converge toward the center of the dome where, enclosed in an octagon, hovers the radiant image of Apollo-Helios, symbol of the neo-Platonic culture that inspired the iconography of the room. These frescoes, evidently inspired by Veronese, are the work of various painters, though mostly of Giovanni Antonio Fasolo, one of the most famous fresco painters of the Vicenza region.

Of particular significance is the cryptoporticus – also painted in fresco by Fasolo – which seems to express the will to establish a new, almost osmotic relationship with the underground realm. Overturning the motif that inspired the Rotonda, whose architectures crown the countryside, Villa Eolia seems ideally to embrace and dominate the more mysterious and recondite forces of nature.

VILLE ASOLANE Asolo, Treviso

CONTARINI
FAMILY
COAT OF ARMS

The Casa Longobarda: an eccentric artist took pleasure in building for himself this little villa, which combines some of the most disparate elements of the mannerist style.

The "Casa Longobarda"

Because of the erroneous inscription on the facade, the Asolo residence of Francesco Grazioli – an architect of the early Cinquecento – was called the "Casa Longobarda." On the memorial tablet is written, in fact, "MAGISTER FRANCISCUS GRAZIOLUS NATIONE LONGOBARDUS," but the latter adjective actually means "Lombard," not "Longobard," as a number of features of this highly original construction will attest.

An atypical chapter in the history of villas, it has often been ignored by scholars, perhaps because of the whimsicality, decorative excess, and surprisingly proto-Baroque features of this early Cinquecento work of architecture.

Francesco Grazioli, who worked in Asolo and perhaps had a hand in the Barco of Caterina Cornaro, shows himself to be a rather eccentric personage who rebelled against custom. In his residence he brings together a great variety of cultural references and artistic elements which merge and accumulate, creating a totally original composite that is perhaps more curious and amusing than of great value. An effectedly archaic style derived from Lombard Romanesque characterizes the reliefs of the balconies and their typically medieval iconography, which are superimposed on an equally extravagant architecture. Partly borrowed from the precedents of Giulio Romano (who at the time was working in Mantua at the Palazzo del Te) and the engravings of Serlio, which already enjoyed widespread fame, the construction nevertheless is very personal and unusual in its final result.

Amusement and a taste for surprise and originalty seem to have guided Grazioli in this "fantastic" work of architecture intended solely for his personal use. And aside from purely stylistic considerations, the Casa Longobarda is also of especial interest to us because it constitutes one of the earliest examples of a villa built by an architect for himself and his family. It was a new custom that spread rapidly in the first half of the 1500s in Italy: the progressive social rise of artists – no longer considered humble craftsmen but honored for their genius – enabled them to build and acquire rich homes, a sign of rank and prestige. Though small, the Grazioli residence also embodies this new reality, and it resembles more the small villa of a gentleman than the house of an artisan. Indeed, it used to stand at the periphery of the town, a suburban villa full of delights, and although not surrounded by a park or garden, it gives onto a vast horizon, fertile countryside and rolling green hills. Vincenzo Scamozzi, in

his 1615 work entitled *The Idea of a Universal Architecture,* said this about the house: "The villa is delightful in my opinion, perhaps because from it one sees the hills, mountains, valleys and countryside adorned with trees."

Villa Contarini

On one of the most agreeable of the Asolian hills stands, by itself, the villa that the Contarini family had built in the 16th century. It was given the name "the Villa of the Armenians" when the fathers of a religious order that had moved from the East to Venice, to the Island of San Lazzaro, gained possession of it in the early 1700s.

The Cinquecento edifice's facade still bears the frescoes of Lattanzio Gambara, which present Biblical stories in the compartments between the windows, monochrome figures of the Virtues, and, in the feigned balustrades, a series of trophies, helmets and busts.

One curious feature of this villa is the underground corridor which, by running through the summit of the hill, makes for a "secret" passage from the Cinquecento building to a small, picturesque eighteenth-century villa (known as "Il fresco") framed by very tall cypresses.

315

VILLA MOROSINI CAPPELLO Cartigliano, Vicenza

MOROSINI
FAMILY
COAT OF ARMS

Inspired by Palladio's lessons, the villa has been attributed to Francesco Zamberlan, known for having collaborated with the master.

On the following page: detail of the facade, with the loggias and columns that distinguish this architecture.

Not far from Bassano, on the left bank of the Brenta, stands a very original villa, unique in all of Venetia for the boldness of its architecture. Built around the end of the 1500s for an unidentified member of the Morosini family, the villa is distinguished by the portico that runs along its entire exterior, an unbroken series of columns that create a charming play of light and shadow. Two avant-corps (projecting elements), halfway along the two longer sides, momentarily break the rhythm, marking the entrance to the manor house.

The propitious scenic location seems to have had a particularly strong influence on the architect as well as his client, both of them obviously sensitive to nature's charms and intent on realizing a beautiful lookout onto the ever-changing surrounding landscape. It is quite possible that the nearby river was what suggested the idea for the vast colonnade, which is reminiscent of the classical architectural prototype known as the "maritime villa."

We do not know how he interiors were furnished, although one is led to believe that they probably corresponded to a vision of heroic exaltation. If we knew more about the history of this noble family, we might perhaps know as well the circumstances that led to the creation of so monumental a building. In 1861, Cabianca-Fedele Lampertico wrote, in his book *Vicenza and its Territory*, "In Cartigliano there is a palace, formerly belonging to the noble Cappello family, which is magnificent for the immensity of its rooms and its theater and innovative for the order of porticos that surround the entire building."

VILLA BARBARIGO
Noventa Vicentina, Vicenza

BARBARIGO
FAMILY
COAT OF ARMS

The villa that the dogal Barbarigo family built at Noventa Vicentina in the late 1500s stands as one of the most emblematic expressions of the "villa culture" that for centuries characterized the Venetian countryside. Indeed, this villa embodies the deepest significance and noblest purpose of the patrician villas on the mainland, which were seen as symbols of the Venetian aristocracy and destined to become cornerstones of the surrounding territory. If over the course of time much of the villa's original significance has been lost, its role as the pulsating heart of local life remains nevertheless alive and tangible. What is most striking even today is how the town of Noventa developed and organized itself around this exceptionally unified architectural complex. In particular, there are the two wings of annexes, cadenced by Tuscan columns, which enclose a large grain market-square, a reminder of the once-thriving farming industry, now transformed by the monument to the was dead which rises up at its center.

Two very clear and precise intentions seem to have guided the Barbarigos in this undertaking: the quest for revenue – their land holdings were vast in the region – and the desire for political affirmation. Both intentions are represented in the frescoes adorning the villa, and next to scenes of battle and scenes exalting the glory of the *gens,* we find mythological representations celebrating deities connected to agriculture. The subjects of these paintings, attributed for the most part to Antonio Foler and Antonio Vassillacchi (called "l'Aliense"), have led us to call the Noventa villa the "Villa of the Doges", a title which Loukomski erroneously gave to all the villas of the region. Aside from the portraits of the Doges Marco and Agostino Barbarigo, there are representations of other members of the dogal house in various other rooms, next to celebrations of their deeds in peace and in war, performed in the name of Venice and Saint Mark.

The title of "Villas of the Doges" that Loukomsky gave to the villas of Venetia is particularly applicable to Villa Barbarigo at Noventa, especially because of its portraits of the Barbarigo doges and its cycle of frescoes depicting in the wartime and peacetime deeds of this family.

318

RESIDENZA MUNICIPALE

319

Portrait of the doge Agostino Barbarigo. By Antonio Vassilacchi, known as Aliense.

A Barbarigo ambassador being received by a King. Fresco by Aliense in the Hall of the Ambassadors in Villa Barbarigo.

While the decorations on the top floor are devoted to the celebration of culture and the arts, especially those done by Luca Ferrari da Reggio, the frescoes on the first floor have a primarily "political" function. In the *Hall with the Portrait of the Doge Marco*, we see the meaningful allegories of *Peace triumphing over destroyed arms, Wisdom,* and *Obedience,* virtues which lead to *Fame*. In the *Hall with the*

Portrait of the Doge Agostino, on the other hand, we find allegories of *Beauty, Love, Fame, Fortune* and *War*.

As with the building's architecture – solemn and majestic with the colonnades that distinguish both the main body and the annexes – what matters most in the paintings is the display of political prestige by these "talking walls," which are like an open book on the

Probable portrait
of Francesco Barbarigo,
son of doge Agostino.
By Aliense.

Fresco of the Battle of
Lepanto, in the crosshall
of Villa Barbarigo.

glories of the Barbarigo family. As Andrea
Palladio said in his *Four Books of Architecture*
(1570), "... the Architect should realize above all
that great Gentlemen, especially those of the
Republic, require houses with loggias and
spacious, ornate rooms, so that in these places
they can entertain those who are waiting to
greet the patron, or to ask him for help, or for
favors."

VILLA CONTARINI Piazzola sul Brenta, Padua

CONTARINI
FAMILY
COAT OF ARMS

The history of the villa of Piazzola, formerly a fief of the Carraresi and assigned to the noble Contarini family in 1413 after the Venetian expansion onto the mainland, is complex and full of significance. In order to increase their own prestige and jurisdiction over the area, the Contarini built a magnificent villa which was transformed several times over the centuries. A park 110 hectares large (approx. 272 acres) surrounds the palatial villa, around which the entire town of Piazzola grew up and expanded.

The more recent history of the complex starts in 1546, when the central body was erected according to the prototype of the Venetian *palazzo*. To the Cinquecento plan, developed around the central salon famous for its balls and receptions, were added, over the course of the 1600s, the vast wings and their plethora of statues and decoration, evidence of a decadent exaggeration of Baroque art.

Also from the seventeenth century are the interior frescoes, which are of considerable interest: those in the *Hall of the Arts and Sciences* are attributed to Dorigny, while those in the *Hall of the Bacchanals* show the strong influence of Giulio Romano's frescoes in the Tea Palace. The *Hall of the Rape of Persephone* is from 1684.

The villa, with its exceptional size, conforms perfectly to the general mood of exaltation and the taste for the spectacular and grandiose typical of the 1600s and inspired by the great courts of Europe.

The happiest moment in the history of the villa at Piazzola came in 1685, on the occasion of the reception in honor of the Duke of Brunswick, when the fish-pools flanking the building were used for mock naval battles, while in the piazzas triumphal chariots paraded by and masked characters amused the guests.

Aerial view of Villa Contarini, and in front, the hemicycle of annexes which describe a large piazza.

The villa's facade and the arches that pass over the fish pond.

On the following pages: The fish pond adorned with statues, once the scene of simulated naval battles.

324

But art continued to flourish at Piazzola even in later centuries: in 1770 Temanza built the family chapel in the neoclassical style, while the palace's interior ws being embellished with new frescoes and a collection of important art. The instrumental and choral concerts also gained notoriety, and the Contarini family's commitment to culture extended even to the point of printing editions of considerable importance. In more recent times the villa has taken on a symbolic value: at the beginning of this century one of its last proprietors, acknowledging the transformations taking place in the socio-economic realm, decided to adapt the palatial complex to productive activities in step with the industrial age. With an enlightened spirit he equipped the place for mechanized farming activities and added lodgings to receive the numerous peasant workers, thus managing to create a self-sufficient farming community which, in addition, was connected to Padua with a special railway line.

VILLA NANI MOCENIGO Canda, Rovigo

NANI
FAMILY

COAT OF ARMS

Never have the vicissitudes of a waterway done so much to alter the physiognomy of a landscape as in the Po delta, where the rivers have undermined the enjoyment of certain villas once mirrored in the water and now smothered by high embankments. Such is the case with the villa Badoera of Fratta Polesine and the villa Nani Mocenigo at Canda.

Rising up on the banks of the Canalbianco, to which it was connected by a stairway, the Mocenigo villa over the centuries has undergone continual tampering, which has radically transformed the simple structures originally conceived by Vincenzo Scamozzi. Indeed, over the course of the 1700s the complex, dramatic facade was realized, which, with the majestic staircases and tall columns of its portico, bears witness to the ambitions of the proprietors. These rather arbitrary and inappropriate interventions did not fit in harmoniously with the pre-existing edifice built by Scamozzi. They failed to create a new unity from the exterior view and overloaded the spacious interiors with baroque decorations. As Semenzato observed, the vast cycle of allegorical frescoes "probably should have helped to resolve the spatial

Sensitive to the importance
of landscpae and an infallible
observer of nature, Vincenzo
Scamozzi showed a
particular talent for scenic
effects in building this villa.
The architecture was later
modified by repeated
structural and decorative
interventions.

Statues from the garden,
attributed to Alvise
Tagliapietra,
eighteenth-century Venetian
sculptor.

continuity," whereas in fact "it ends up
weighing down and further isolating the
different rooms."

Clearly such ill-considered modifications
went against the spirit of the original architect
Scamozzi, who in his work *The Idea of a
Universal Architecture* (1615) said, "In the
well-ordered edifice one takes into
consideration... that which fits: that is, purpose,
form and artifice."

The building was further ruined by the
construction of the attic atop the entrance loggia
and by the careless restorations made after the
fire of 1946. Over the course of the eighteenth
century the park surrounding the villa was
embellished with valuable allegorical statues
that one may still admire today.

VILLA DUODO Monselice, Padua

DUODO
FAMILY
COAT OF ARMS

At Monselice, in the heart of the Euganean hills, there once stood a small fortress of the Carraresi which Venice acquired during its expansion onto the mainland. Its defensive function now obsolete, the castle was given over to three important Venetian families, the most distinguished of which was the Duodo family, "the richest in possessions in Monselice."

Around the end of the sixteenth century Francesco Duodo commissioned Vincenzo Scamozzi to erect, on the site of the old Carrarese stronghold, a villa commensurate with the glory and prestige of his powerful family. The choice of architect was not a casual one; Scamozzi and his patron were on very familiar terms, Duodo having once brought the architect along with him to Poland on an official visit.

As with the Rocca Pisani in Lonigo, Scamozzi used local stone, Euganean trachyte, extracted from the nearby quarries. Trachyte ensured the stability of the villa's supporting structures.

In addition, Scamozzi's customary attention to the importance of the landscape and to environmental circumstances gave him the inspired idea of realizing a "Via Sacra" (Holy Way) – a dramatic route from the center of Monselice leading right up to the villa. Along this road, amid the cypresses, seven chapels were erected, enabling the faithful to enjoy the same indulgences that they enjoyed when visiting the seven Basilicas of Rome. The Duodos gave special attention to the little adjoining church dedicated to Saint George, which they enriched and embellished with numerous relics given them by various Popes and put on display for the people's veneration.

Over the centuries modifications were made with the intention of improving and expanding the original structure of the stately complex; a particularly admirable addition was the staircase built at the back of the villa, following the slope of the hill.

The monumental complex of Villa Duodo, with architectures by Vincenzo Scamozzi and Andrea Tirali, the little church of San Giorgio, and the eighteenth-century staircase that follows the slope of the hill.

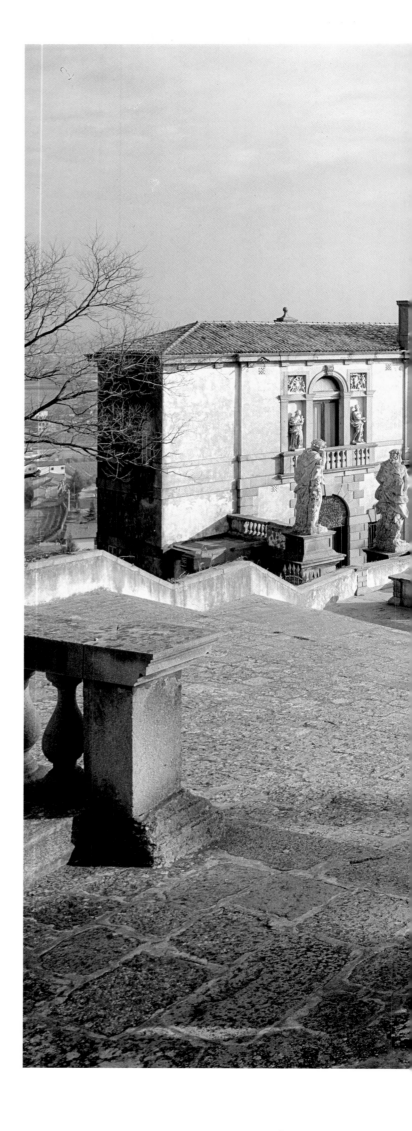

*The end part of the staircase,
which culminates scenically
in a semicircular wall against
the background of the hill.*

*The villa's new wing, which
Nicolò Duodo had built in
1740 from designs by the
Venetian architect Andrea
Tirali.*

In 1740 Andrea Tirali built a new wing also using Euganean trachyte so as not to upset the unity of the construction. In addition, inside the villa there was a wealth of art that included several portraits of illustrious members of the family. The portraits of Pietro and Domenico Duodo, executed by Vittoria, are now kept at the Ca' d'Oro.

LA ROCCA PISANA Lonigo, Vicenza

PISANI
FAMILY

COAT OF ARMS

At the top of a hill, on the site of an ancient medieval fortress, stands the Pisani villa, which still calls to mind the former castle in its simplicity, the neatness of its structures and the restrained use of fretwork.

In 1576, the Pisani family – which already possessed a "villa for income" at Bagnolo and a "palace for reception" at Lonigo – decided, as a reconfirmation of their authority over the territory of Vicenza, to build yet another edifice for pure enjoyment, one that would serve as a safe refuge from the pestilent air of the plague that had broken out that same year in Venice.

"The illustrious segnor Vettor Pisani...," writes Vincenzo Scamozzi, the villa's architect, "despite all the buildings owned by his family in the Bagnoli estates, wanted to build another himself, to have a place near Lonigo for recreation in healthier air. It stands atop a hill called La Rocca, where there are a number of ruins of a fortress. The hill is very lovely to look at, as it is almost perfectly round in form, very pleasant when viewed from other, smaller hills, and detached almost all the way around."

Unlike the Cinquecento farm-villas, in which the needs of both the farmer and prince found their practical reconciliation in the architecture, here the villa dominates the surrounding green plain, as if to express the satisfaction that the Pisani must have felt when gazing out from above onto their vast domain.

It wasn't until the following century that the agricultural annexes were added to the property. They are hidden from sight, however, and located at the entrance of the road that winds around the hill. This circular motif, formerly used by such Quattrocento architects as Francesco di Giorgio Martini, is supposed to allude to the continuity between nature transformed by man, which bears the mark of his rationalizing interventions, and the building itself.

And thus the hill, which provided the building material extracted from a quarry at its base, becomes, together with the villa crowning it, an emblematic example of the fusion between architecture and landscape, fulfilling Scamozzi's ideal of exalting the relationship between house and environment.

Inside, the logic of the architecture, with its nakedness and purity, is not disturbed by

Vincenzo Scamozzi's masterpiece, Villa Pisani, sitting atop a hill "known as the Rock".

*The facade of the Rocca
Pisana, with dome crowning
the central room.*

paintings or decorations, and expresses itself only through the modulated flow of light.

Features of the traditional villa are not lacking, however: the staircase in front of the facade, the columned porch, the geometric crowning of the dome, at the top of which is a circular open window. The light that falls from

this opening heightens the refined outlines of the niches, which are hardly interrupted by the mouldings of the doors and windows. The endless wealth of decoration of Palladio's Rotonda is not, therefore, comparable to the severity and geometric rigor of Scamozzi's delightful building, which overlooks the plain below, almost like a laic sanctuary of the "goddess Health."

In discussing this building in *The Idea of a Universal Architecture,* Scamozzi wrote: "This building is so harmonious that when one stands in the middle of the main room one has the four cross-views of the four large doors, and those of the loggia and the salons where the light enters the room horizontally and from above, while most of the openings of one wall encounter those of the other...; and as it works with the view, so with the purifying of the air as well."

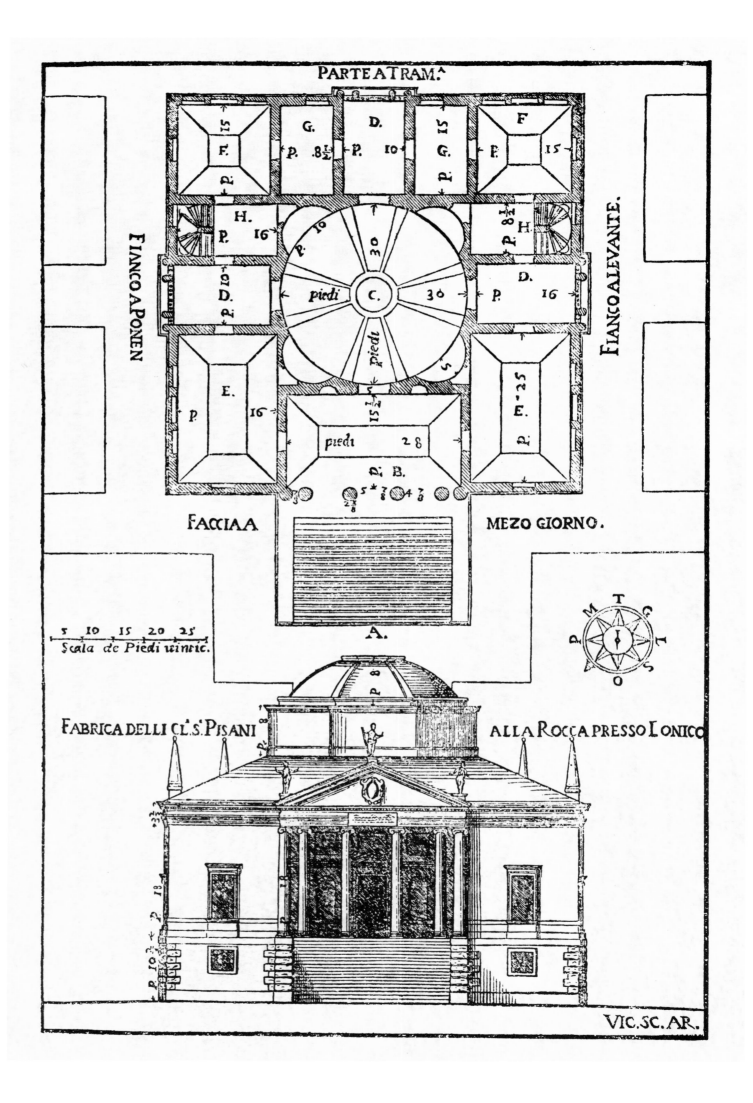

Vincenzo Scamozzi, plan and elevation of the Rocca Pisana (from the Idea of a Universal Architecture, Venice, 1615, part I, book III).

Vincenzo Scamozzi

Architect, hydraulic engineer, essayist, Vincenzo Scamozzi (Vicenza 1552 - Venice 1616) enjoyed widespread fame, not only in the Venetian Domain but in Central Europe as well, where he was frequently called to work. Scamozzi's constant attention to questions of planning and his sensitivity to the lessons taught by Palladio made him one of the most inportant interpreter's of Venetia's "villa culture." In keeping with Palladio's tradition, Scamozzi dedicated a number of pages in his treatise to building materials, and in particular, to the various kinds of stone that can be used for villas. Sensitive to the value of the environment, Scamozzi at times succeeds in realizing a powerful union between edifice and landscape (such as in the Rocca Pisana), using materials available in the quarries at the site. Vicenza, moreover, was famous for the existence of important quarries in its territories, such as the white stone quarry at Costozza and the yellow stone quarry at Nanto. Palladio too preferred to use, over all other stone except that of Istria, the stone of Vicenza, which is porous, sensitive to light reflections and rich in pictorial effects, as he well knew from having worked as a stone cutter in his youth.

On the following pages: Detail of ground floor; detail of central hall of the piano nobile; *the dome which harmoniously encloses the interior space of the hall, with circular aperture at the top shedding light on the whole room.*

340

VILLA MOLIN Mandria, Padua

MOLIN
FAMILY
COAT OF ARMS

At one time, the waters of the Battaglia canal reflected the image of the severe, massive structure of Villa Molin and its majestic, columned pronaos; now the villa stands smothered by the high embankment, which was raised repeatedly over the centuries. Conceived by Vincenzo Scamozzi according to a square plan, Villa Molin has experienced a fate quite different from that of the Rocca Pisana, which still stands intact and triumphant atop its hill near Lonigo. A pupil of Palladio who followed the teachings of that greath architect, Scamozzi also absorbed his mentor's love of landscape, and in his creations he always strove to unite the edifice with the natural environment in a relationship of perfect harmony.

Describing Villa Molin in his book *The Idea of a Universal Architecture,* Scamozzi wrote: "The front of the building looks South-east; in front of it passes the very navigable Bacchiglione river..." Built in 1597 for the Venetian ambassador Nicolò Molin, the villa was later acquired by some of the most illustrious families of Venice and the mainland: the Pisani, the Sagredos, the Capodilistas, and the Dondi dall'Orologio...

The building's central core consists of the majestic, domed hall that gives onto the four vestibules of the independent apartments on the ground floor. Unfortunately, inside one cannot see and appreciate the harmonious proportions that characteristically make Scamozzi's villas so charming. In fact, unlike the Rocca Pisana, the walls are covered with Seicento frescoes which distract one's attention with their exaggerated perspectives and superabundance of decorative elements. The garden must have been very large and impressive, and the fountain, statues and age-old trees in the park suggest what it might have been like.

Now smothered by the high embankment of the canal, Scamozzi's Villa Molin once dominated the landscape in harmony with the natural environment.

Villa Molin in an eighteenth-century fresco at Villa Emo Capodilista at Selvazzano.

Villa Molin, facade reflecting in the waters of the Bacchiglione.

The central salon with seventeenth-century frescoes attributed to Pier Antonio Cerva, which tend illusionistically to amplify the architectural space.

346

VILLA WIDMANN   Bagnoli di Sopra, Padua

WIDMANN
FAMILY
COAT OF ARMS

The Bonazza, a family of sculptors

Around 1742 the noble Widmann family turned to Antonio Bonazza who, together with his brother Francesco and his father Giovanni, belonged to a family of sculptors active in Venetia. The Widmanns commissioned Antonio to execute a vast decorative cycle of statues: 190 life-size statues, as well as a vast profusion of cherubs and little sculptures for the garden of the villa at Bagnoli di Sopra, in Padua province.
An excellent example of Bonazza's creative gifts, these sculptures also bear witness to the new culture of his patrons who, having abandonend the care of the land and "holy agriculture," sought escape and amusement in the "domesticated" nature of gardens.
Significantly, the subjects of the sculptures also change: the Olympian gods, nymphs, deities of the woods and fields which in the Cinquecento – a century inf triumphalistic exaltation – gave to villas and their inhabitants an aura of sacredness.

Built around the mid-seventeenth century, this villa has usually been attributed to Baldassare Longhena, among other reasons because of its vague similarity to the Venetian palace of the Rezzonico family.

A place for pleasure as well as profit – as the vast farming annexes attest – the villa also included a family chapel and a theater that became famous for the many Goldoni plays staged there. In fact, the Venetian dramatist was often a guest of the Widmanns, and he devoted the following laudatory lines to their abode:

... L'anno passà son sta a Bagnoli un mese:
a no lodar bisogneria esser muti
le gran tole, i gran spassi e le gran spese;
ma quel che pi de tuto fa stupor,
del Paron de la casa el gran bon cor.

Last year a stayed a month at Bagnoli:
in order not to praise the great domes,
expanses and expenses, one would have
to stay silent;
but what amazes most of all
is the good, great heart of the master
of the house.

Of particular note is the Italian garden surrounding the villa, filled with statues by the sculptor Antonio Bonazza. The most striking ones break away from the iconographic models of allegories and mythological figures, portraying with charming humor figures from everyday life. Peasants and noblemen, commoners and high-born ladies peer out from the hedges and shrubs, as though from the wings of a stage, suggesting an imaginary parallel with the characters from Goldoni's plays.

348

VILLA EMO CAPODILISTA
Montecchia di Selvazzano, Padua

CAPODILISTA
FAMILY
COAT OF ARMS

The noble Capodilista family possessed vast territories in the Paduan province. Around 1560 they obtained in fee old Monticula, situated between two small elevations at the edge of the Euganean hills. The particular sort of jurisdiction that they exercised over these places found its emblematic expression in the splendid villa erected in 1568 near the old medieval castle.

Dario Varotari, a painter and architect, conceived this highly original edifice, which he decorated himself with a vast cycle of frescoes, creating a complex unique in its homogeneity and unity. With the assistance of Aliense and other painters, Varotari brightened the villa's rooms with grotesques, delicate floral decorations, friezes with mythological scenes and episodes of Roman history. Between great arches one sees the figures of *Sophonisba, Scipio,* and *Antony and Cleopatra;* in other frescoes one recognizes all the villas belonging to the Paduan nobility of the time. The allegories in the eighteenth-century landscape rooms represent *Time, Truth* and *Vice,* while on the ceiling of the ground-floor loggia one finds a new interpretation of the pergola (a common theme in villas that often invokes the richness of wine), with *putti* and animals emerging from the arbor.

The building typology of this edifice is significant, with its square plan and its adherence to a precise symmetry, even in the arrangement of the rooms: four on the ground floor and four on the second floor, with the servant's quarters in the basement. A recurrent inspiration in Cinquecento architecture, the geometry of the square, ad Palladio observed, brought out the excellence of a building more than any other form. Vincenzo Scamozzi, in his 1615 work *The Idea of a Universal Architecture,* wrote that "... the square form comes out much more harmonious and commodious... since it takes up much space with great savings in expenses..."

Dario Voratori designed and decorated this unusual building which dominates the countryside with its four facades.

On the following pages: The charming staircase leading up to the villa; one of the ground floor loggias decorated with landscapes and grotesques by Dario Voratori and his school.

350

Moreover, the centralized-cubic model, one of the most characteristic types of villa since the Roman era – as Ackerman has pointed out – opens up onto the countryside in a manner analogous to Palladio's Rotonda, thanks to the four views embracing the entire horizon. In this way the building becomes the perfect nucleus of harmonious relationship between architecture and environment.

But what mattered most to the villa's proprietors was indeed the charm of the site, the intimate enjoyment of a luxuriant natural setting. What is missing, on the other hand, are the sheds and agricultural annexes, for the utilitarian function common to many villas of Venetia is quite foreign here.

Used as a place for amusement, for hunting parties with other noble landowners, the villa, with the suggestive scenography of its loggias and rooms, lent itself admirably to the staging of dramas, one of the more memorable of these being Luigi Grotto's tragedy, *Il Cieco d'Adria*.

THE HISTORY AND CULTURE OF THE
VENETIAN VILLAS

EIGHTEENTH-CENTURY VILLAS WITH GARDENS AND FRESCOES

VILLA SELVATICO
Sant'Elena di Battaglia, Padua

SELVATICO
FAMILY
COAT OF ARMS

The villa, attributed to Lorenzo Bedogni, is reached by an endless staircase which first passes the tenants' houses and the crosses through the park conceived by Giuseppe Jappelli.

Preceded by a majestic staircase, this original construction stands amid picturesque natural surroundings, crowning a small hill. The brilliant arrangement of the park was the work of Giuseppe Jappelli, who practiced in the area around 1818.

The villa, built in the late 1500s, in an important foreshadowing of the Baroque style. Showing creative brilliance, the unknown architect abandons the classical compactness of the Renaissance and presents a unique encounter of architectural motifs, giving a glimpse onto the strange solutions of the century to follow.

The building is centrally planned, with four facades and a small dome on top; inside it contains an excellent cycle of frescoes representing the story of the *Founding of Padua*, commissioned by the marquis Benedetto Selvatico and Luca Ferrari da Reggio. On the ceiling, a painting by Padovanino depicting the *Glory of the House of Selvatico* celebrates the villa's proprietors, who were hosts to illustrious figures, princes and men of letters.

In the Salon on the first floor of Villa Selvatico, Luca da Reggio painted in 1650 the fresco representing the founding of Padua.

Luca da Reggio, fresco of Antenor's Victory over Valesius.

HIC ODIIS ACTI SVBEVNT BELLA ASPERA PACEM
ANTENOR VALESI SPOLIIS EXVLTAT OPIMIS

VILLA GARZADORI DA SCHIO Costozza di Longare, Vicenza

GARZADORI
FAMILY
COAT OF ARMS

A long staircase climbing obliquely up the hill and flanked rhythmically by statues and broad terraces leads majestically up to the Garzadori-Da Schio architectural complex. Made up of three nuclei – the so-called Ca' Molina, the manor house and the small villa known as Grotto of Marinali – it conforms in its structure to the rocky slope of the hill, and it is overlooked by the old parish church named after San Mauro. The artistic quality of the buildings is itself rather modest; what is most striking and fascinating is instead the sheer sense for natural setting, for picturesque and dramatic arrangement, in the landscape as well as the interiors. Particularly impressive and original is the little villa at the top, part of which is carved

into the rock: inside, one is struck by the harmonious fusion of the natural element and the architectural intervention, so much so that it is difficult to tell where the wall surface ends and the hard rock of the hill begins.

Happily this strange space is lightened by the delicate 18th century paintings of Ludovico Dorigny. With deft illusionism, the artist creates crumbling architectures to counterbalance the solidity of the rock and the lively sculptural style of Orazio Marinali, of which the *Neptune* located in the garden is a magnificent example.

From an iconographical point of view the complex seems inspired by the cycle of the seasons and their eternal rotation. Moreover, the Da Schio villa shows a brilliance of

The picturesque complex follows the contour of the hill amid the trees of the park adorned with statues.

362

The "Grotto of Marinali" takes its name from the sculptor of the statues adorning it; the frescoes painted on the living rock are the work of Ludovico Dorigny.

Villa Garzadori, one of the loggias with Inonic order, and entrance stair adorned with statues.

perspective and design in the structure of its parks, gardens and cedar-groves, which add to its beauty and charm. It is located in a place that in every epoch has been used for life's pleasures and has attracted people's attention for its amenity and luxurious vegetation. In 1580, Luigi Groto, in a letter to Francesco Trento, wrote: "Never will I forget Costozza, which, had I been in the East..., I would have thought myself in earthly Paradise... Never will I forget those cold wines, which quelled at once the thirst and the heat, and made one wonder whether it was Summer or Winter..." It remains one of the most delightful and most elaborately decorated corners of the Berici hills.

VILLA ALLEGRI ARVEDI
Cuzzano di Grezzana, Verona

ALLEGRI
DEGLI HONORI
FAMILY

COAT OF ARMS

Perhaps first built in the 1500s, as a few of the fresco sections attributed to Veronese would seem to indicate, Villa Allegri took on its present aspect over the course of the 1600s.

Stately and grand in appearance, it is particularly striking when observed as a whole, as a single architectural complex. The manor house with its imposing, pretentious facade is in fact of little significance and of modest architectural value. In addition, the villa, flanked by annexes and by two interesting towers, had a strict relationship with the surrounding countryside, being essentially a "landowner's house" that oversaw a farming estate that, by the late seventeenth century, included as many as 314 fields.

The villa, which contains frescoes by Dorigny inside, is surrounded by an Italian garden and complemented by a picturesque chapel.

The farther one goes from Venice, the more one misses the sense of serene harmony that one finds, for example, in the Treviso region, which was particularly attached to the customs of the Serene Republic, and in those territories that had shown themselves willing to embrace the lessons of Andrea Palladio.

In Verona province, on the other hand, the characteristics of the former feudalism remain. Palladio himself, while working on Santa Sofia a Pedemonte, made his art conform to the idea of the power of the region's patrons.

The manor house, at the center of vast farmlands; the villa is said to be the work of Giovanni Battista Bianchi (1656).

On the following page: The interior of the Salon of Villa Allegri, with frescoes by Lodovico Dorigny and perspective wall paintings attributed to Francesco Bibiena.

The little Baroque church of San Carlo, with its lively contours, is decorated inside with frescoes by Dorigny and paintings by Antonio Balestra.

VILLA RINALDI Casella d'Asolo, Treviso

RINALDI
FAMILY
COAT OF ARMS

On a picturesque slope in the heart of the Asolan hills stands Villa Rinaldi, a late-Cinquecento building that was later rebuilt, as one may read on the pediment. The villa is mostly famous for its interior decorations by Pietro Liberi and Andrea Celesti. The architecture, on the other hand, is not particularly special, though it manages to create some pleasant scenic effects: Balconies, loggias, and decorative details together make up a lively, varied whole in harmony with the vast perspectives of the staircases in the gardens. In the facade's tympanum rising above the cornice and surmounted by statues, sits the Rinaldi family coat of arms flanked by two elephants in low relief.

For our history of villas it may be of interest, if not utmost importance, to cite the following reference to the palace and its builders, which we find in an eighteenth-century codex: "The nobleman Francesco Rinaldi..., wanting his descendants to have great memories of him, memories not inferior to those of his forefathers, entrusted his family with the decoration and enlargement of the beautiful palace at Asolo, which is comparable and equal to the splendours of Rome, noteworthy and memorable for its graceful architecture as well as its wealth of marble, its statues carved by the best of sculptors, and its beautiful grotto and fountains, an artistic marvel comparable to those of the Borghese princes of Rome."

*The staircase and rooms of
Villa Rinaldi are embellished
with statues, stuccowork and
frescoes by Andrea Celesti
and his school (1705-1707).*

VILLA CONTI LAMPERTICO also called "La Deliziosa"
Montegaldella, Vicenza

CONTI
FAMILY
COAT OF ARMS

Not far from the Bacchiglione river stands the villa called "La Deliziosa," although not in its original form, which was documented in a seventeenth-century drawing. Over the course of the nineteenth century it was radically renovated and, more importantly, richly embellished with a park that is still admirable today for its state of preservation.

Nevertheless, there are many baroque and rococo elements that survived the nineteenth-century interventions and which arouse the observer's curiosity: the elegant wrought-iron gates, as fancy as fine lace, the statues crowning the villa and those adorning the garden, which include a sculpture group that might have been part of a splendid fountain by Orazio Marinali.

Accessible from the villa and also connected, by a gate, to a public street, the family chapel bears witness to a custom that started in the sixteenth century, that of building next to the manor house a small church which, in accordance with the Church law of the time, had to be open to local inhabitants as well.

Known as "La Deliziosa," this villa is famous for its great park filled with sculptures by Orazio Marinali. To the right, Pantalon converses with the Doctor.

The Sculptures of Orazio Marinali

In the gardens of Villa Conti Montegaldella, Orazio Marinali (Bassano 1643 - Vicenza 1720) gives life to a vast repertory of italian mask-characters scattered amid the box hedges, often portrayed in the act of dialogue, as though acting out a scene.
The 1700s was the century of leisure and the theater, of bourgeois life and the escape into exotic worlds, the century of Goldoni's comedies and Carlo Gozzi's fables. The dwarves of Villa Valmarana, sculptured by Bendazzoli and perhaps designed, as the tradition has it, by Giandomenico Tiepolo, also belong to this theatrical world.

Front view of the villa. The villa was built in 1622 and the upper part renovated in 1868.

VILLA GIOVANELLI Noventa Padovana, Padua

GIOVANELLI
FAMILY
COAT OF ARMS

The history of this villa has been characterized by a sequence of vicissitudes, an alternation of splendid moments and crises. The Austrian authorities actually once put it up for sale as scrap material.

The long sojourn of Imperial troops had in fact damaged it seriously: with the stuccowork partially destroyed, the frescoes ruined, the structures impaired, an eventual renovation must at some point have seemed impossible.

And yet the villa's fame had once been great, as in 1738 when it was host to the King of Poland's daughter, who on an earlier stop had stayed at the Villa Manin in Passariano. It was on this very occasion that, to add to the palace's stateliness and beauty, the Giovanelli brothers, Andrea and Benedetto, embellished the main facade with the solemn pronaos and the statues representing the *Five Senses* dominated by the *Allegory of the Goddess Reason.* The frescoes inside underwent changes when the villa came into the hands of Federico Giovanelli, former bishop of Chioggia and Patriarch of Venice, who took measures to remove several paintings deemed too immodest, and replaced them with ones that were religious in inspiration.

Front view of the villa. Attributed to Antonio Gaspari, the patriarch Giovanni Maria Giovanelli had it built in the 1600s.

The majestic staircase of Villa Giovanelli, constructed in 1738 by Giorgio Massari on the occasion of the visit by the daughter of the King of Poland, Frederick Augustus.

Detail of the staircase adorned with statues representing the Five Senses and the Goddess Reasons; in the foreground, the allegory of Hearing, by Antonio Gai.

VILLA FOSCARINI Stra, Venice

FOSCARINI
FAMILY
COAT OF ARMS

Along the banks of the Brenta there are many buildings that attest to the spread over the centuries of the cult of Palladian architecture. One that stands out is the Villa Foscarini at Stra with its traditional columned portico, which ennobles the customary Venetian residential typology.

Its elegant facade, which reflects in the river's waters, was a favorite subject of eighteenth-century Venetian engravers (such as Costa and Coronelli) who, when depicting the villas of the Brenta, liked to emphasize their relationships with the river, which was always alive with traffic and populated with every imaginable kind of craft.

The series of decorations that grace its interiors are rich and varied. Most of them executed in 1652, on the occasion of the marriage of Giovanni Battista Foscarini, the most highly valued are the work of the baroque painter Pietro Ricchi.

In the eighteenth century these were accompanied by other decorative elements and scenic architectures, while the nineteenth century is documented by Romantic themes done in Pompeian style. The complex enjoyed its best days in the eighteenth century, when Marco Foscarini was a Procurator and then Doge of Venice. Among his many guests he entertained the Duke of Modena at the villa, as is recorded in the writings of Gaspare Gozzi, another illustrious guest of the Foscarini.

The villa's elegant facade, clearly inspired by Palladio, dominates the Brenta waterway, once alive with every imaginable sort of craft. The villa's interiors contain frescoes by Pietro Ricchi and other Seicento painters.

VILLA DI ROVERO
San Zenone degli Ezzelini, Treviso

DI ROVERO
FAMILY

COAT OF ARMS

At San Zenone, in the lush countryside of Treviso, not far from the ancient castle of the Ezzelini, stands the villa that count Cristoforo di Rovero had built around 1610. The edifice has architectural features rather uncommon in the Treviso province. Inspired perhaps by the feudal style, it seems to belong to the castle-villa typology that is widespread in Verona province, where military traditions are deep-rooted.

The builders paid special attention to the conditions of the site: following the motion of the terrain, the building spreads out horizontally with broad side wings inspired by the Maser prototype.

A charming staircase leads up to the main residence and the cedar-groves, at one time the pride of many patrician residences.

In the background, not far from the villa, stands Mount Grappa.

Seicento architecture crowning a small hill; with its turrets, it still evokes the castle-villa typology.

VILLA NEGRI LATTES Istrana, Treviso

NEGRI
FAMILY
COAT OF ARMS

The villa, one of the best preserved in Treviso province, was built in 1715 by the architect Giorgio Massari.

The districts outside cities, once verdant refuges for urban nobles and patricians, have in our century been often subjected to a chaotic growth in building and development that has transformed the countryside. Green spaces have grown smaller and smaller, suffocating building complexes that were originally conceived with the idea of receiving large draughts of air from the surrounding country. Today, Villa Lattes, though a victim of these developments, still welcomes us with its lovely annexes and their curvilinear arcades flanking the body of the main residence.

Giorgio Masari seems to have drawn his inspiration in planning the villa (dated 1715) from a sense of refined and rational harmony of rhythm: its beauty is pure and simple, without decorative excess or neoclassical rigidity. The Palladian influence is undeniable, especially in the arcades enclosing the round courtyard, which are strikingly similar to those of Villa Badoer.

Despite the pitiless assault of the modern building trade, Villa Lattes has retained its charm, remaining a unified and harmonious complex with its orchard, fishpond, its lovely garden, its statues and the family church. Inside, the building – which Massari, significantly, chose as his own residence – contains some curious collections and valuable works of art.

Among other proprietors aside from Massari, we should mention the patron Paolo Tamagnino and the Counts Negri, Massari's heirs and descendants who in the mid-nineteenth century sold it to the Lattes family.

VILLA TRISSINO MARZOTTO Trissino, Vicenza

TRISSINO
FAMILY
COAT OF ARMS

The pilasters of the belvedere in the garden in front of the villa, the work of Francesco Muttoni.

Francesco Muttoni

Palladian teachings, especially those concerning villa architecture, were embraced and re-interpreted with originality by the Lombard Francesco Muttoni, born in Porlezza in 1668 and active in Vicenza province. Muttoni also has the distinction of having published, from 1740 to 1747, a reprint of Palladio's work. In Vicenza he built numerous patrician residences such as the Palazzo Repeta, Palazzo Velo, Palazzo Trento now called Valmarana, and other important buildings more public in nature, such as the seat of the Monte di Pietà. He distinguished himself particularly in the construction of villas; in just two years (1714-1715) he built Villa Da Porto ("La Favorita") at Monticello di Fara; in 1724 he built Villa Valmarana Morosini at Altavilla. Muttoni is also responsible for the two porticoed sheds that flank the Villa Piovene at Lonedo, as well as for the arrangment of the gardens of the upper villa at Trissino. The architect died in 1747.

Girolamo Dal Pozzo. The upper villa and the equestrian courtyard, seen through an arch in the enclosure wall.

The arrival of the Serene Republic of Venice as a political force in the Vicenza province changed local life, sometimes radically, replacing old centers of feudal power and destroying a large number of fortresses and castles.

The house of Trissino, a family of feudal lords of the Agno valley, also adapted to these circumstances, and in the latter half of the

fifteenth century, with the extra incentive of the growing charm of city life, they transformed their castle into a peaceful country residence. This constituted the original nucleus of the current, vast Trissino Marzotto complex, which is composed of several building units arranged along the slopes of the hill and was put together in the eighteenth and nineteenth centuries.

Particularly noteworthy is the park which

connects the various structures and surrounds them with enchanting beauty. Francesco Muttoni deserves most of the credit for the marvelous web of walkways rich in statues and the skilfull arrangement of terraces, fish ponds and hanging gardens distributed at the various levels.

The whole is dominated by a refined, scenic taste, a search for spontaneous dialogue between man and nature, and the aspiration to derive as much enjoyment as possible from a privileged environmental location. The entrance gates by Muttoni and Frigimelica are majestic in appearance, yet characterized here and there by odd solutions. Triumphal columns hold up trophies and enclose exquisite wrought iron gates. Unexpected forms in rococo style, elaborate spires, and strange copings all enliven and increase the attractions of this fanciful architectural complex.

VILLA PEREZ POMPEI Illasi, Verona

POMPEI
FAMILY
COAT OF ARMS

This imposing structure stands at the center of the large fief of Illasi, which was awarded together with the noble title of Count by the Doge Priuli on August 12, 1509, to Girolamo I Pompei, a "man at arms" who distinguished himself in the capture of Mantua and in the defense of Mantua. Since the 1400s the Pompei family had possessed properties in the area that were exempt from taxation, and actually the investiture merely made official a long-standing *de facto* situation.

The present-day villa, which replaced an earlier, late-Quattrocento building, was built at the behest of Giugno III Pompei, after a design by "Gio. Pietro Pozzo, Surveyor, Engineer and Architect of the Court." The central element and right wing were completed in 1737; the left wing, on the other hand, was never built. A construction dating from the 16th century, with a Doric loggia on the top floor, was retained instead.

The villa, which is in an excellent state

of preservation, is characterized by a grandiose central body marked by two stringcourses and animated by large windows that illuminate the vast, sumptuous interiors.

Almost all of the rooms are decorated with eighteenth-century mythological frescoes and furnished with pieces and fabrics of the period.

Also of considerable interest, from an ethnographic point of view, are the kitchen, the cellars, the *lissara,* the *giassara,* the stables and the greenhouses, all of which have been perfectly preserved.

The huge park surrounding the villa dates from the early nineteenth century and is the work of Antonio Pompei. It covers the entire slope of a hill on which stand the ruins of an old medieval castle.

The vastness and richness of the Pompei family's fief – which included many hundreds of tillable fields, vineyards, olive groves and woods, the revenues from which were regularly supplemented by rents, perpetual leases, and tithes – is reflected in the complex of buildings and the park, the magnificence of which indicates the role which the villa came to assume with time, as the economic and cultural nucleus of the entire region.

It was in this context that the Accademia of Lavinia Pompei flourished, counting among its frequenters the likes of Jourden and Pindemonte.

Aside from the church and the many annexes used for work in the fields, a 1788 list of the "Delightful Gardens and Orchards" in the Pompei domain mentions the "garden with vine pergolas, fruit cellars, greenhouses, thickets, playing fountains, avenues, pools of water and other delights."

The villa remained in the Pompei family until 1885, when the last member of the line died, and the estate came into the hands of a cousin, Giovanni Perez Pompei.

VILLA LOSCHI ZILERI DAL VERME Biron di Monteviale, Vicenza

LOSCHI
FAMILY
COAT OF ARMS

Not far from Vicenza, in a valley in the Lessini mountains, stretch the grasslands of Biron, unparalleled in their charm and their subtle and continuous variations of green. At the foot of the Monteviale hill, which closes the valley, stands Villa Zileri with its complex of loggias and annexes, whose architect today remains uncertain.

In 1734 the proprietor, Nicolò Loschi, had the hill leveled and the villa's central part enlarged, incorporating a much older nucleus into the new structures. The architecture does

In 1734 Nicolò Loschi leveled
the hill in order to enlarge the
central body of the villa, the
lateral parts of which are
from an earlier construction.

Eigteenth-century drawing
concerning the Salon.
The drawing is still kept
at the villa.

not have a particularly energetic framework,
being limited to the rhythm of openings
on the outer wall. Divided into three sections,
the facade presents an imposing family coat
of arms.

One of the more significant and felicitous
elements is the dramatic, grand staircase that
leads up to the *piano nobile* and seems to
continue, in parallel fashion, the line of the hill's
ascent.

A curiosity on the ground floor is the
so-called "Grotto of shells," which is connected
to a natural grotto in the hill. The grotto, which
Alfonso Loschi had built in 1665, strikes one as
a fanciful invention – among other reasons for
its strange decoration in shells – that goes hand
in hand with a mentality of jest and surprise.

Inside we find the first cycle of frescoes that
Giambattista Tiepolo realized in the Vicenza
province. The frescoes express a specific
program, moral in tone: we see such themes as
*Time discovering Truth, Activity triumphing
over Idleness,* the *Virtues,* and so on.

A letter written by Giambattista Tiepolo
to Lodovico Faronati on November 17, 1734,
tells of the great painter's work. He worked
in Villa Loschi Zileri Dal Verme at Biron for
three months without stopping.

In these frescoes, Tiepolo definitively breaks
away from the street-scene style and, drawing
on the great Veronese tradition, attains the
classicism characteristic of his mature period.

The park was designed by Muttoni but
realized by Barzaretti later on, in the then
popular romantic, English style, with a balanced
distribution of trees, sometimes valuable, and
broad meadows.

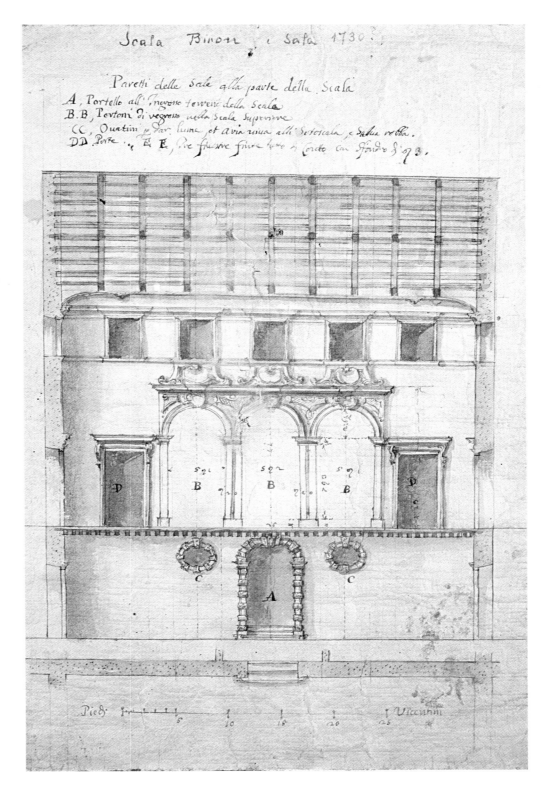

*Villa Loschi Zileri
Dal Verme. The Salon, with
frescoes by Giambattista
Tiepolo.*

Giambattista Tiepolo.
Frescoes in the Salon of Villa
Loschi Zileri Dal Verme:
on opposite page, Honor
being crowned by Virtue, and
on the ceiling, Fame
announcing the triumph of
Glory among the cardinal
virtues.

VILLA PISANI Stra, Venezia

PISANI
FAMILY

COAT OF ARMS

This monumental complex truly deserves the title of "Villa of the Doges." in that it was erected to celebrate Alvise Pisani's accession to the Dogal throne in 1735.

"Few are the foreigners, even those from far away, who do not know the Brenta to be a delightful river, running from the lagoons to the city of Padua, along whose banks stand so many palaces, gardens and pleasant retreats, that one could never ask for anything more magnificent or delectable. Everyone rushes there, at different times, to the amusement of the countryside" (Carlo Goldoni, Il Prodigio, Momoli sulla Brenta, Preface, 1739).

The majestic Pisani that stands on the banks of the Brenta occupies a special and original position in the ranks of Italian villas. It does not in fact constitute the usual combination of eulogistic concern and economic reality, of lordly ambition and agricultural activity. Grandiose in size and perhaps inspired by Versailles and other European royal palaces, Villa Pisani owes its birth to a specific political event: the accession of Alvise Pisani to the Dogal throne from 1735-1741. Through the magnificence of his patrician residence, doge Pisani wanted to display the wealth, prestige and high rank of his family.

After the first design – done in the baroque style by Girolamo Frigimelica and preserved in the form of a rare wooden model at the Museo Correr – was abandoned, the definitive realization of the villa was entrusted to Francesco Maria Preti, who tempered the fanciful inventions of his predecessor with a Palladian sense of restraint. Palladian typologies in fact influenced the large central structure of the rear facade, where the customary Ionic pronaos with tympanum stands triumphant, two stories high and echoed in the rest of the facade. The front facade has a central body with a Corinthian order and to the sides, a lower, combined order. Only the arched porticoes in the wings, with their rusticated ashlar, can be said symbolically to allude, as Ackerman put it, to the "rusticity of the countryside."

The villa is most famous for its park, in which one finds a wealth of architectural caprices such as fountains, gates, portals, and an endless store of inventions, like the celebrated botanical labyrinth. More out of keeping with the whole complex is instead the rectangular water basin that extends from the back of the villa towards the stables; it was built right after the Second world war for experiments in hydraulics.

The villa's interiors are richly decorated with frescoes and paintings by Jacopo Amigoni,

Fabio Canal, Giambattista Crosato, Jacopo Guarana, Francesco Simenoni, Sebastiano Ricci, Giuseppe Zais and Francesco Zuccarelli, while in the central salon Giambattista Tiepolo in 1767 painted a fantastic vision known as the *Glory of the house of Pisani.* In my opinion the main protagonist of this composition is the little boy held in his mother's arms in the lower section; this boy is Almorò Pisani, son of Alvise, and he would become a passionate art lover.

This stately and highly symbolical palace received among its guests the Counts of the North, King Gustave of Sweden, Napoleon, Viceroy Eugenio of Italy, Maria Luisa of Parma, Maximillian of the Habsburgs, and many other illustrious figures.

*Aerial view of the villa of
Stra, the work of architects
Girolamo Frigimelica and
Francesco Maria Preti.*

*Front view of the villa from
the park.*

402

*Villa Pisani at Stra,
the loggia and facade
of the stables.*

The park of Villa Pisani, and a garden structure.

406

409

One of the portals of the enclosure wall of Villa Pisani, seen from inside the park and from the bank of the Brenta.

410

412

413

415

Giambattista Tiepolo Satyrs
and Satyresses on the ceiling
of the Ballroom of Villa
Pisani.

Giuseppe Zais and a collaborator. Two details of the frescoes adorning the corridors of Villa Pisani.

Bartolomeo Nazari. Landscape with venetian villa (Stra, Villa Pisani).

419

*Villa Pisani, the Room of
Bacchus, frescoes by Jacopo
Guarana and quadraturist
collaborators; on the ceiling
the Marriage of Bacchus and
Ariadne.*

VILLA MANIN Passariano, Udine

MANIN
FAMILY

COAT OF ARMS

The founding of Palmanova and the resulting climate of security that came to this border territory in the seventeenth century, favored an increase in land development and the building of canals and roads. The economic rebirth of the Friuli plain also encouraged the Manin family to build their residence in Passariano, and it retains something of the medieval castle, with tower and drawbridge.

Having received a title of nobility in 1651, Ludovico Manin worked out a project aimed at making the villa an emblem of the prestige his family had attained, as well as a vital nucleus of the vast territories acquired. For the realization of this design he apparently turned to Baldassare Longhena, an architect famous for reorganizing the lands on which he executed his projects. The edifice ultimately took more than a century to build, with modifications and reconstructions that compromised its unity and stylistyc harmony. It was above all during the 1700s that the villa was restructured and decorated in a rococo vein to make it conform to the new tastes of the period.

Thus from a utilitarian villa it was transformed into a place of amusement and reception, a monument to the power of the Manin family as well as to the Republic of Venice, being the first stop for voyagers arriving from across the Alps on their way to the capital of the Republic.

The eighteenth-century intervention is attributed to the architect Giovanni Ziborghi, who also saw to the decoration, the layout of the gardens and fountains, and gave more solid and elegant forms to the loggias, porticos and granaries. The changes brought to the villa's physiognomy and the refinement of its structures did not, however, alter its essential function as an agricultural and commercial center. Aided by the local roads and by numerous navigable canals, the Manin residence had in front of it a large, round courtyard used for receiving and sorting out

Built by a family of merchants that acquired nobility through its wealth, this villa served as a stopping point for monarchs from transalpine nations on their way to Venice. In this photograph, the villa is seen from across the canal separating it from the road and from the round piazza in front of it.

the produce of the region, which was then sent on to Venice or to its colonies across the sea.

To better serve their commercial function, the annexes were equipped to lodge and entertain with performances the crowd that periodically converged in the inner square of Villa Manin. Like triumphal arches, the majestic portals leading to the courtyard were always open, allowing passage to and from the public road and giving the villa a sense of collectivity.

Adorned with fish pools and statues and flanked by the comfortable guest-lodgings, the courtyard is surrounded by the curved wings of the annexes, which give a sense of unity to the entire complex.

424

In order to emphasize the public-oriented purpose of the villa the Manins decided that their family chapel should be "for common use." For particular religious holidays the peasants and proprietors participated together in the services, even though the nobles preferred to take their seats in the sacristy connected to the chapel by iron gates.

In order to be able to suggest the most up-to-date ideas to his patrons, the architect Giovanni Ziborghi travelled continuously throughout Italy and abroad. It should therefore come as no surprise that at Passariano he recreated the same atmosphere as in Paris or Vienna. We are, moreover, in a region fairly international in flavor, as attested by its frequent relations with the transalpine feudal nobility and the Friulian custom of using German coins alongside Venetian ones.

Once decorated with a treasure of artworks, today in the rooms and halls of the palatial Manin villa we can still see elegant rococo stuccowork and the strange polychrome decorations of illusory curtains, which seem to reflect a sensibility closer to Austrian rococo than to the Italian style. Still in a state of perfect preservation are the frescoes of Ludovico Dorigny on the ceilings of the ground floor.

Even though some of the wealth and magnificence of the Manin residence has since been lost – like the park constructions, the paintings, tapestries and furniture – the villa still stands today as a testimony of the typically eighteenth-century ambitions and aspirations to theatricality and merriment which made this complex one of the most famous and admired in all of Venetia.

Left: the Judgment of Paris
(c. 1706), by Lodovico
Dorigny, painted in a room
on the ground floor of Villa
Manin.

428

Ceiling with fresco of the allegory of Happiness and Nature.

On the following pages: Front view of the villa seen from the park.

429

Villa Manin. The Montagnola. A path in the park with statues.

432

VILLA CORDELLINA
Montecchio Maggiore, Vicenza

CORDELLINA
FAMILY
COAT OF ARMS

The work of Giorgio Massari, an eighteenth-century interpreter of Palladian principles, this villa, decorated with frescoes by Giambattista Tiepolo and sculptures by the studio of the Bonazza, was an ideal meeting place for highly educated aristocrats and scholars.

Around the mid-1700s, Carlo Cordellina, a Venetian lawyer who handled official assignments for the Republic, decided to have a villa built in the environs of Vicenza, in a place where he would have both the Lessini and Berici mountains in the background. But the spot that Cordellina picked out did not fulfil the essential requirements for the ideal realization of the project, since on that site the villa would have had no available water.

So great was his desire to realize that ancient ideal of a villa, already realized by Palladio at Maser, that Cordellina, envisioning gardens, orchards and fountains as complements to the architecture, tapped the waters of a spring found right there in the side of the hill. Thus he was able to benefit not only his own lands but the entire town of Montecchio, creating a tank into which water flowed for public use.

Cordellina attached his name to the architecture realized by Giorgio Massari between 1735 and 1760, which proved to be one of the most eminent examples of the Palladian revival that characterized much of the villa construction of that century.

The culture of the noble Venetian who chose to realize his humanistic dream in the villa (almost as though it were his own creation) has its counterpart in both the architecture and the decorations. Since he also wanted this to be a meeting-place for the most enlightened gentlemen of the city and the nearby villas, the generous patron had guest-quarters built that were almost on a par in elegance with the master's house.

The Montecchio complex was closely bound up with the benefits offered by the surrounding countryside, and expresses an solid relationship with farming activity: the very statues themselves speak of agriculture, as well as the reliefs of deities, the allegories of the seasons, and the abundance of fruit offered in the vases atop the pilasters of the gates.

The same spirit that inspired the first

authors of the villas in Venetia is here manifest in the frescoes of the Salon, which were commissioned in 1743 from Giambattista Tiepolo. These constitute the second cycle of the series he painted in Vicenza province. On the ceiling of this "temple" dedicated to human intelligence we find a representation of *The light of intelligence putting to flight the shadows of ignorance* (a clear homage to the century of the Enlightenment), while on the walls we find a eulogy of the virtue and ethics of villa life in the representation of the *Mercy of Alexander and Scipio,* a theme also present in such other Palladian constructions as the one at Fanzolo.

The perfect harmony of this complex is further confirmed by the architect's desire, in determining the correct organization ot space, to take acoustical values into account, so that it would be possible and ideal to hold concerts in any of the rooms. In 1801, in his *Memories of the life of Carlo Cordellina,* Giambattista Fontanella wrote of the villa: "I shall always remember Villa Cordellina at Montecchio, where generous hospitality was the custom..., where liberality, life's comforts, the elimination of all labels and fastidious ceremony, and a joyful, noble spirit of merriment made it the delight of all guests."

With the fall of Venice and the resulting spiritual impoverishment and loss of ancient ideals, this need to live "in harmony" also eventually died out, to the point that around the mid-nineteenth century a law was passed that levied specific taxes on luxury buildings, thus encouraging the abandonment or even demolition of many villas that were not sufficiently profitable.

Villa Cordellina, the scene of so much culture, harmony, elegance and aristocratic ideals, was initially abandoned and then revived for industrial and productive ends. The grand salon became crowded with structures necessary for the cultivation of silkworms, damaging the architecture, the stuccowork and the frescoes. Finally in 1954 the philanthropist Vittorio Lombardi provided for its restoration.
Today the villa, under the care of the regional government, is used for cultural events.

436

Giambattista Tiepolo.
The Mercy of Scipio, fresco
on a wall in a Salon of Villa
Cordellina.

438

Giambattista Tiepolo.
The Mercy of Alexander,
fresco on a wall of the Salon
of Villa Cordellina.

440

VILLA MARCELLO Levada di Piombino Dese, Padua

MARCELLO
FAMILY
COAT OF ARMS

Monumental eighteenth-century complex with Italian garden in front and flanked by two porticoed wings.

Surrounded by five hectares (12.35 acres) of park, Villa Marcello at Levada, with its refined furnishings and gardens, constitutes one of the best preserved examples of the 18th century Venetian villa, symbol of the rebirth of Palladian art. Famous for having hosted illustrious members of royal families over the course of its history, today it still belongs to the descendants of the Venetian noble house of Marcello.

Crowned by an elegant tympanum, the central body of the edifice is developed on two levels: the upper one is cadenced by an order of Ionic half-columns, while the lower one is connected with the porticoed wings that enclose the Italian garden.

Stately and majestic, the central salon extends over two stories, and has frescoes of powerful scenes from ancient history, painted by Giambattista Crosato between 1750 and 1755.

*Villa Marcello. Salon with
frescoes by Giambattista
Crosato depicting
Campapses in Apelle's studio
and the Mercy of Alexander.
Opposite page: Giambattista
Crosato, fresco of the
Wedding of Alexander.*

Giambattista Crosato

*Born in Venice in 1685, a
painter and decorator, he had
his earliest experience in art
in his native city, then moved
on to Turin.
After 1742, he comes back to
Venice to work. An esteemed
scene-painter very skilled in
harmonizing painting with
architectonic elements,
Crosato also distingushed
himself as a fresco-painter
for villas: Villa Algarotti
at Mestre, Villa Albrizzi
at Preganziol and Villa
Marcello at Piombino Dese.
He died in Venice in 1758.*

445

VILLA PISANI called "La Barbariga"
Stra, Venice

BARBARIGO
FAMILY
COAT OF ARMS

Near the left bank of the Brenta river, straight and solid, stands the villa that once belonged to Chiara Pisani, who became the wife of Filippo Barbarigo, hence the name "la Barbariga." The noble lady wanted her memory to be associated with the beautifully refined garden which she herself designed in the English style, and in the middle of which stands a clock-tower.

The broad loggias, the side wings and the stables were completed around the end of the eighteenth century.

Inside the main body the rather small rooms are decorated in exquisitely multicolored stuccowork; the tiles of the fireplaces, the ceramics, the mirrors, the frescoes, and the chinoiseries all help to preserve the villa's characteristic atmosphere of 18th century Venetian aristocracy.

The hare hunts here were once famous, and were organized by various different noble Venetian families. The hunt has always been one of the appeals that villa life, the country, the woods and the hills had for nobles, who usually lived in the city and in holiday seasons could rediscover the pleasure of using weapons, something directly connected to their aristocratic origins.

The hunt was an occasion for festive meetings and gatherings that often ended in great banquets and dances on the lawn. Villa Barbariga is still an eloquent document of this custom, with its whole series of sculptures of hunters and loyal dogs which populate the loggias and the garden's walkways.

This villa, with its low, elongated structure, follows the course of the Brenta river. Particularly elegant are the two eighteenth-century wings flanking the seventeenth-century central construction.

On the following pages: Interior of a loggia enlivened by statues of hunters, and a room decorated in delicate stuccowork in the finest Venetian tradition.

VILLA NEGRI PIOVENE
Mussolente, Vicenza

NEGRI
FAMILY

COAT OF ARMS

Like the outline of an imaginary ancient city at the top of a hill, the white facades of Villa Negri stand out in their imposing, majestic mass. Designed by Antonio Gaidon in 1763, the villa reigns over a panoramic landscape that further magnifies its charm. An eminently scenic taste seems to have guided the architect in his creation: the various building units of the main body and guest quarters are articulated according to the horizontal progression of the hill's ridge.

Thus a far cry from the solutions presented in Palladio's Rotonda, which perfectly culminates a small hill, the villa at Mussolente imposes its scenic front and emphasizes its dominion over the countryside, calling up "ghosts of medieval structures."

The taste for exhibition has, in this architectural work, one of its most significant examples. Even the wings, with their series of arches crowned by an array of statues, are almost oblivious of the practical considerations that Palladio had well in mind in designing the facades of almost all of his villas. We are a long way from the contemplation that Petrarch and the humanists sought in the tranquility of hidden vales far from the din and distraction of city life.

Like an apparition at the top of the hill, the white structures of the villa, designed in 1763 by Antonio Gaidon, reflect a strong taste for the spectacular.

VILLA VALMARANA ai Nani Vicenza

VALMARANA
FAMILY
COAT OF ARMS

In the mid-seventeenth century the Venetian jurist Giovanni Maria Bertolo chose the crest of this charming hill as the place to begin a series of constructions that had no direct connection with farming activity. The complex was built exclusively for the purpose of providing leisurely pleasures and fulfilling the cultural ambitions of the nobleman who, in bestowing his collection of books to the city of Vicenza, founded the library that still bears his name today.

The villa, known as "Valmarana ai Nani," was not finished until one century after it was started. At that time Venetian architects, among

This villa (1655-1670) owes its name to the statues adorning the enclosure wall, which are attributed to Giambattista Bendazzoli; in the 1700s the surrounding structures were added. The complex is most famous for the frescoes by Tiepolo.

The Orlando Furioso room, with frescoes by Giambattista Tiepolo and perspective wall paintings by Gerolamo Mengozzi Colonna (1757). The two scenes depict Angelica and Medoro taking leave of the farmers, and Angelica coming to Medoro's aid.

whose names we find those of Massari and Muttoni, built the guest quarters and the stables, thus completing the complex with as much unity as possible.

The famous caricatural statues of dwarves crowning the enclosure wall appear to have been executed by the sculptor Giovanni Battista Bendazzoli, probably from drawings by Giambattista Tiepolo. The *palazzina* and guest quarters of the Valmarana complex contain frescoes painted by Giambattista and Giandomenico Tiepolo, father and son, around the middle part of the century.

Wolfgang Goethe, in his *Voyage to Italy* (1816-1817), wrote the following about Villa Valmarana: "Today I saw Villa Valmarana, which Tiepolo decorated, giving full rein to his talents and shortcomings: He is not as successful in the sublime style as in the natural, but in the latter there are some splendid things. As a wall-painter in general he is full of ingeniousness and resources."

In these works the two different artistic personalities display their distinguishing characteristics. The works by Giambattista, who is still immersed in ancient myths and Renaissance literary themes, are the episodes taken from Ariosto's *Orlando Furioso* and Tasso's *Jerusalem Delivered,* and, in a more spectacular vein, the visions from the *Aeneid* and the *Iliad* in the rooms of the *palazzina*.

The art of Giandomenico, on the other hand, belongs to the bourgeois world. In the frescoes in the guest quarters he shows himself to be an acute observer of everyday life in the country: we see peasants at meal-time and at rest, an old woman selling eggs at the edge of the road, peasant-women going to the city. But these scenes are placed beside others with dances, gypsies and mountebanks, chinoiseries and exotic characters amid picturesque landscapes, rococo decorations and neo-Gothic frames that bear witness to the complexity and crisis of the times.

454

Giambattista Tiepolo. Fresco of Rinado abandoning Armida, in the Room of the Jerusalem Delivered at Villa Valmarana.

Detail of the scene of Eurybates and Talthybios leading Briseis to Agammennon, in the Room of the Iliad.

*Left: Fresco of the
Declaration of Love, in the
room of the Gothic Pavillon;
right: fruit offerings to a lunar
deity, in the Chinese Room.*

461

The Painters Tiepolo

Giambattista Tiepolo and his son, Giandomenico, played a particularly prominent role in the decorations in fresco of Venetian Villas over the course of the eighteenth century. Born in Venice in 1696, Giambattista Tiepolo was one of the most celebrated artists of his time, and was often commissioned for work outside of the Venetian realm. His first works date from around 1716 (the church of the Ospedaletto and San Stae in Venice), though in 1726 we find him in Udine working in the Cathedral and the Archbishop's palace. In the 1730's he is active in Milan (Palazzo Archinti) and Bergamo (Colleoni Chapel), after which he paints the Stories of Cleopatra in fresco in the Palazzo Labia in Venice.

After devoting himself, from 1740 to 1750, to easel painting, he resumes painting fresco cycles on a grand scale: after 1751 he is in Wurzburg at the imperial palace, and in 1754-1755 he decorates the ceiling of the venetian church of the Pietà. From this same period date his paintings in the villas: in 1757, together with his son Giandomenico, he frescoes the rooms of Villa Valmarana near Vicenza, around 1761 he paints the Glories of the House of Pisani in the villa at Stra, and in 1763 he is at Villa Cordellina in Montecchio Maggiore. Having gone to Spain at the request of Charles III, he died in Madrid in 1770.

His son Giandomenico (Venice 1727-1804) often collaborated with his father, and followed him to Spain on his unfortunate voyage. The most memorable of his works are the frescoes in the Guest quarters of Villa Valmarana and the scenes of contemporary life, the celebrations and the clowns with which he decorated his own country house at Zianigo (1791-1793).

Giandomenico Tiepolo. Fresco of the Peasant's family at meal time, in the Room of Rustic Scenes in the Guest house of Villa Valmarana.

On the following page: Peasant at rest, in same room.

462

Giandomenico Tiepolo.
Fresco with detail of Peasant
woman with a basket of eggs,
in the Room of Rustic Scenes.

Giandomenico Tiepolo,
fresco of the Winter
Promenade, in the Room of
the Gothic Pavillon.

Giambattista Tiepolo, fresco of the Charlatan, in the Room of Carnival Scenes in the guest house of Villa Valmarana.

Giandomenico Tiepolo, detail of landscape, in the Room of the Iliad.

Illusionisti painting by Gerolamo Mengozzi Colonna in the Room of Carnival Scenes; the figure of the Negro with a tray has been attributed to Giambattista Tiepolo.

467

VILLA ALBRIZZI San Trovaso di Preganziol, Treviso

ALBRIZZI
FAMILY
COAT OF ARMS

The simple edifice ispired by the prototype of the Venetian house was embellished in the 1600s by Andrea Pagnossin when he added monumental annexes in the Palladian style. In the photographs, the outer view and inside of the portico of one of the annexes.

The original structure of this villa, which is typologically similar to the Venetian house and without any particular stylistic merit, underwent a profound transformation in the 1600s. During that time the architect Andrea Pagnossin built the quasi neoclassical annexes, which are at their elegant best in the middle section enclosed in the Doric colonnade.

The odd conjuction of such widely different styles is striking. The simplicity of the villa's facade, with its elongated windows which take in a lot of light, does not jibe very well with the ambitious ideals visible in the columned annexes. The latter are indeed a far cry from the modest utilitarian buildings that usually flank the master's villa; especially impressive is the magnificent pronaos with tympanum crowned by statues, and the profusion of decorations,

especially in the southern annex where a series of delicate wall-paintings by Giambattista Crosato, with scenes of the chase and athletic competitions, show characteristics of the most elegant rococo.

The villa enjoyed especially happy times in the nineteenth century: a lady of Greek origin, Isabella Teotochi Albrizzi, made it the center of distinguished cultural gatherings, the seat of an academy, and a spot often frequented by artists and poets, among whose number figured the likes of Ippolito Pindemonte, Ugo Foscolo and Antonio Canova.

Like many other villas of Venetia whose noble proprietors, no longer able to afford their maintenance, let them fall in disuse, Villa Albrizzi also was about to encounter the same fate. Fortunately, however, the charm of this

The Terraglio

*This is one of the many villas
that stand along the
Terraglio, the road linking
Venice with the very loyal city
at Treviso. In a certain sense
one might say that the
succession of palaces on the
Grand Canal is continued by
water along the Brenta river,
which links Venice with
Padua, and by land along the
Terraglio, the splendor of
which is recorded by Goldoni.*

ancient abode was enough to convince the government administrators to make it a center of the Department of Architecture of the University of Venice, and as a result one of the finest examples of villa culture was safeguarded and put to good use.

469

Mattia Bortoloni (?),
two decorations in the Room
of the Hunt in Villa Albrizzi.

Opposite page: another
decoration in the Room of the
Hunt (top), and the Chariot
Race (bottom) in the Room
of the Games, also attributed
to Mattia Bortoloni.

VILLA POMPEI CARLOTTI Illasi, Verona

POMPEI
FAMILY
COAT OF ARMS

A stately building in the heart of the region, Villa Carlotti assumed its present appearance in 1737, following the reconstruction undertaken by Alberto and Alessandro Pompei and designed by the latter. Often in the history of the villas of Venetia we have seen how important a role the proprietor, with his personal tastes and ideas, played by intervening directly in the planning, influencing the architect's procedures with suggestions and advice. This tradition was amply documented in Palladio's *Four Books of Architecture,* which had among its protagonists some of the most illustrious political figures active in cultural matters, such as Giangiorgio Trissino and Alvise Cornaro. And there are probably many other villas, thought today to be anonymously designed, that were probably built on the design of the patrician proprietor, with the help of local workmen.

Alessandro Pompei was himself an amateur

*The Salon of Villa Pompei
Carlotti, with a fresco by
Antonio Balestra depicting
Paris and Helen (1738).*

*Nineteenth-century wall
decoration (left) and River
Landscape with ruins, by
Tommaso Porta (1765).*

in architecture, the chosen art of the nobility, and a faithful interpreter of the classical Cinquecento tradition. Particularly attuned to the Palladian tradition, he drew his inspiration, in designing his own residence, from the work of the great architect, as we can see in the pronaos with its Doric columns and the balustrade adorned with mythological sculptures. The villa was then decorated by Antonio Balestra, one of the most famous painters in Verona province at the time.

Yet, alongside the revival of the Classical style, in this villa we also find evidence of the continuance of ancient feudal military tradition, clearly manifest in the two turrets flanking the main facade and emphasizing its image of power.

VILLA TIEPOLO Zianigo di Mirano, Venice

TIEPOLO
FAMILY
COAT OF ARMS

The painters Tiepolo had a villa in Zianigo that was entirely covered by Giandomenico with frescoes now exhibited in Venice at the museum of Ca' Rezzonico. Below, a detail from the fresco of the New World.

Among the simple country residences which, over the eighteenth and nineteenth centuries, began to populate the Venetian hinterland, the villa that the Tiepolos built for themselves is particularly significant and rich in art. Inside, on the frescoed walls painted by Giandomenico between 1759 and 1797, we find a whole series of representations in different styles and with different themes, rich in both biographical content and references to the socio-political situation of the time.

Dating from the earliest period are, for example, the *Triumph of Painting* and the strip of monochromes of episodes from Roman history inspired by the magniloquent and celebratory atmosphere of Giambattista's art.

They are from the moment of greatest fame for the Tiepolos, when they were invited to the royal court of Spain.

Shortly before their departure, Giandomenico painted on the villa's walls, as a kind of mirror of his soul, the melancholy *Rinaldo being forced to leave the garden of Armida,* which seems like an omen of the sad lot in store for the two artists. The voyage to Spain in fact ended with a series of bitter disappointments, and upon the death of his father, Giandomenico retired anew to Zianigo where, in solitude, he painted satyrs and centaurs in a kind of polemical rejection of the gods and sublime heroes that populated the now past world of his father's art.

The ten years from 1780 to 1790 proved to be for Giandomenico rather devoid of significant work, a clear sign of the crisis into which Venetian painting had fallen. Hence the appearance of the three brightly colored, life-size scenes adorning the villa's "portego" seems entirely unexpected. The *Minuet, Promenade* and *New World* appear to bear witness to the new social ideas that were spreading through Venice and characterized a brief but significant moment in Venetian political life.

The festive, overwhelming *Minuet* shows a certain sympathy on the artist's part for the new aristocracy, represented by two young people weaving their dance against a background of green landscape. The grace and vitality of their bearing, the elegance of their clothes, the cheerfulness of the open air scene seem almost like the first canto of some new, extraordinary poem. On the other side, in the *Promenade,* three figures are portrayed from behind, walking towards a remote destination: their clothes and headgear suggest a resemblance to the "citizens" of the French Revolution, and they represent perhaps the new society which, in turning its back on the past, is headed toward a future rich with hope.

Giandomenico Tiepolo.
Country Minuet, fresco
formerly in Villa Tiepolo,
now at the Museum
of Ca' Rezzonico.

The principal and most emblematic scene of the cycle is the *New World* which, in this case, is not a simple description of a common occurence in village fairs: the figure of the charlatan who promises remote, fantastic visions to the mob of nobles and commoners under the sway of his words, is here enriched with significant allusions.

A sense of bitterness, and a satirical attitude toward a society headed toward decadence, can be perceived here. The artist seems to look distrustfully on the mob rushing towards the New World in search of new illusions and a false, artificial life. And this flight from reality, from commitment, involves in equal measure the commoners – here unsparingly portrayed in all their coarseness – and the old, vain and irresponsible aristocracy.

This position on the artist's part seems to arise from the relations he had with such notable figures as Angelo Querini, a noble progressivist who had fought to renovate the tired internal politics of Venice and to save the Republic from falling entirely into decadence. It was, however, to be a short-lived dream.

In the last frescoes painted at Zianigo, dated 1797 and hence contemporaneous with the fall of the Serenissima, all hope has apparently been extinguished and Giandomenico, an enlightened observer, sees his illusions dissolve once and for all. The almost monochromatic group of paintings presenting the adventures of Punchinello shows us a world of imaginary characters mocking life, its customs and its aspirations.

These fatuous beings devoid of identity who we see making fun of heroic deeds and great ideals become symbols of the end of an era in which Venice, its politics and its civilization had been at the center of the world's stage.

THE HISTORY AND CULTURE OF THE
VENETIAN VILLAS

FROM JAPPELLI
TO CARLO SCARPA

VILLA GERA Conegliano, Treviso

GERA
FAMILY
COAT OF ARMS

This monumental neoclassical villa atop the hill of Conegliano was built in 1830 by Giuseppe Jappelli in glorification of the Gera family.
The villa's proximity to the Castle of Conegliano seems to suggest the long process during which villa architecture slowly replaces the castles that once dominated the landscape of Venetia.

Giuseppe Jappelli

An architect and engineer, Giuseppe Jappelli, born in 1783, worked mostly in Padua and the surrounding territory. He collaborated with Selva and in 1836 went to England. A rather eclectic spirit, he realized buildings in the neoclassical style such as Villa Gera in Conegliano and the Caffè Pedrocchi (1816-1831) in Padua, as well as other significant projects in the neogothic style (such as the Pedrocchino). Particularly sensitive to the powers of the landscape, he planned the layout of numerous parks and gardens, such as at Villa Papafava in Bastia, Villa Cittadella in Saonara, or at Villa Wollemburg in Loreggia. He died in 1832.

Around 1830 the wealthy Gera family, perhaps under the influence of the fervid political climate of the time, decided to build, on the hill of Conegliano, a villa proportionate to its own ambitions. For the task they turned to some of the more celebrated artists of the time: the pictorial decoration was entrusted to Giovanni Demin, while Giuseppe Jappelli designed the main house, a majestic neoclassical edifice more academic than Palladian in its inspiration.

Standing next to the medieval towers of an old castle, the villa dominates the landscape with its grandiose pronaos, which is reminiscent of the facade of an ancient temple and uncommonly imposing for a building of Venetia.

It seems strange that Jappelli, usually so sensitive to environmental features, here ignored all relation between the architecture and the landscape, presenting a result that is rather inconsistent and contradictory. Taking advantage of the slope of the hill, he could have emphasized the site's "picturesque" qualities, creating fantastic grottos, fountains and statues (as he had done in Padua province), and inserting a neo-Gothic building that would have been more attuned to the nearby ruins.

Apparently, in realizing the Gera villa the architect had to set aside his own ideals and give way to the pressing requests of his patrons, who wanted to manifest their social and economic predominance with this monumental villa-temple.

*Villa Gera. Interior of the
loggia that looks out onto the
landscape of Conegliano.*

*Giovanni Demin, the
Helvetians being subjugated
by Caesar [2837], fresco in
the villa's Salon.*

VILLA REVEDIN Castelfranco Veneto, Treviso

REVEDIN
FAMILY
COAT OF ARMS

The park with greenhouses. The villa's ballroom, painted by Giacomo Casa (1864-1865). Subsequent pages: the grand staircase, and one of the two horses in the green amphitheate.

From the 1400s to 1600 the place called "Paradiso," at the edge of Castelfranco, contained a residence belonging to the Corner family. In 1607, this was replaced by a villa more adapted to the new economic demands and to the prestige of its proprietors.

Thus Vincenzo Scamozzi built, for Nicolò Cornaro, a huge building complex consisting of two symmetrical edifices, an annex and a garden filled with valuable statues. Yet this architectural work also was short-lived; it was demolished around the mid-nineteenth century,

and in the area of Scamozzi's annexes the grandiose Revedin palace was erected from designs by Giambattista Meduna (1855). The complex includes stable, fish ponds and a picturesque lake. Facing the beautiful, immense park – designed by Antonio Caregaro Negrin – is the main facade of the new villa.

In the middle of the park is an impressive green amphitheater rhythmically adorned by an unbroken sequence of statues by Marinali, and by two monumental horses marking the entrance.

*Villa Revedin Bolasco, the
green amphiteatre, decorated
with statues by Orazio
Marinali, opening onto the
vast park designed by
Antonio Caragero Negrin.*

VILLA OTTOLENGHI Bardolino, Verona

Any discussion of the villas of Venetia would be incomplete if it did not make at least some mention of the endurance of the villa tradition down to our own times.
The distribution of wealth across broad social strata, a phenomenon that was already taking shape in the eighteenth century, has filled the Venetian countryside with many little villas which reflect, at least in some pathetic details, the petit-bourgeois taste for imitating the upper classes.

There are, however, a few noteworthy exceptions that demonstrate a serious approach to the construction of villas. Even the twentieth century, in terms of originality, has added its own chapter to this particular history of architecture and culture.

The most prominent name among such twentieth-century architects is without question Carlo Scarpa (1906-1978) who, starting with his first works in the late 1920s, conceived designs for villas, usually in collaboration with Franco Pizzuto. In these early works Scarpa already demonstates a wide range of ideas, paying particular attention to Middle-European culture. In this sense, though we may speak of a Venetian tradition, such a tradition is not, for Scarpa, merely a provincial taste, but is bound up with the great civilization of Venice as an integral part of the Italian, European and Mediterrenean cultures.

The theme of the villa, which in the twentieth century has been more and more restricted by economic considerations, is a constant in Scarpa's work. In his repeated dealings with this typology, the Venetian architect would span a vast gamut of cultural references and formal suggestions before arriving at the free expression of his late works.

A premonition of Scarpa's mature work is the 1953 project for Villa Zoppas at Conegliano, which constitutes one of the high points of Italian twentieth century architectural research. In the various solutions studied for the villa, Scarpa elaborated a series of inventions which he would persistently come back to and study for later projects.

Though Scarpa, in keeping with Palladio's ancient lesson, is clearly sensitive here to the features of the site, in that the villa has an elongated layout, extended across the terrain according to the natural outlines, he seems in this first work to want to test a composite typological solution, before studying Wrightian forms and Miesian structures. This richness of experimentation would not fail to bear fruit in the work of his mature years: indeed, in Villa Ottolenghi it is not difficult to perceive the compositional procedure of the third project for Villa Zoppas, conceived twenty years earlier.

But the intellectual path linking these two projects is enriched by the realization of Villa Veritti at Udine which, in combining the suggestions of the Venetian environment and the lesson of Frank Lloyd Wright, makes for a remarkably fresh, original result.

The building, with its hollow disposition of masses, its abundance of decoration and its hermetic compositional stratagems, stands entirely apart from the contemporary architectural scene. But Scarpa's originality is even more visible in his work method, and in this sense the work must be analyzed as process, a process of which the construction constitutes the last phase of distillation.

In this respect as well, Scarpa shows himself to be a Venetian architect, one not accustomed to designing in an abstract space, but for whom duration in time, and the investigations made during the practice of one's work are indispensable to the definition of architecture as a living reality. It should therefore come as no surprise that we should find, in analyzing this process, that the various versions of the project for Villa Veritti are always concerned with purifying typically Venetian considerations such as the relation between the construction and the water, the play of light reflections and windows, the arbitrariness of the volumetric juxtapositions.

That the sense of a bond with the site, with Venice and more generally with the Venetian mainland, is a constant in Scarpa's art, is eloquently proved by Villa Ottolenghi in Bardolino, begun in 1974 and ultimately realized through the collaboration of Giuseppe Tommasi and Guido Pietropoli. The edifice lives in a close relationship with the site where it stands, so much so that the facade-less structure seems about to slide into the folds of the hill. But the effect sought by Scarpa is not at all mimetic. Once again, Palladio teaches that a villa is born from the dialectical relationship between nature and the architect's work, which becomes the ordering cornerstone, the discovery as well as creation of a new "landscape." Thus in Villa Ottolenghi, a series of projections emphasized by the presence of massive, elegant columns, protrudes from the geological alignments and opens up the house's rich interior to nature. The sequence of volumes thus defined is, moreover, articulated by a series of paths which insinuate themselves into the body of the construction in the open air and are very narrow in shape. Reminiscent of tight Venetian streets, these paths seem as though they want to transform this villa into a kind of poetic and metaphorical re-invention of the urban environment typical of the city on the lagoon. Unlike the Quattrocento villas, which merely transplanted the typology of the Venetian house onto the mainland, Scarpa's villa is a new reality which, though it takes into account the site for which it is destined, seems to preserve, as though in a dream, the memory of the artist's native city. Thus here once again we seem to encounter the same close relationship between city and country which, as we have seen, is inherent in the very definition of the villa.

This final, refinedly abstract yet emotionally vivid rethinking of the lessons taught by Venice – and their refinement into a fascinating art of seeing – shows us how the villas designed by Scarpa are a reformulation, though not in any vernacular form, of those undying values that architecture may still learn from the unrepeatable experiences that Venice allows us to have.

On this page and the following, various different views of this facade-less construction, which seems to fit into the folds in the terrain, while the interior opens up onto the landscape.

THE HISTORY AND CULTURE OF THE
VENETIAN VILLAS

BIBLIOGRAPHY

1499

[COLONNA F.], *Hypnerotomachia Poliphili*, Venice [ed. G. Pozzi - L. A. Ciapponi, vol. 2, Padua, 1964].

1528

BORDONE B., *Libro ... de tutte l'isole del mondo*, Venice.

1537

SERLIO S., *Regole generali di Architettura..., Libro IV*, Venice.

1550

GALLO A., *Le dieci giornate della vera agricoltura e piaceri della villa*, Brescia.

1556

BARBARO D., *I Dieci Libri dell'Architettura di M. Vitruvio tradutti et commentati da Monsignor Barbaro...*, Venice.

1558

CORNARO A., *Trattato de la Vita Sobria*, Padua.

1566

DONI A. F., *Le ville*, Bologna [ed. U. Bellocchi, Modena, 1969].

1567

CEREDI G., *Tre discorsi sopra il modo di alzar acque da' luoghi bassi*, Parma.

1568

BARBARO D., *La pratica della perspettiva*, Venice.
VASARI G., *Le vite de' più eccellenti Pittori, Scultori ed Architettori* [ed. G. Milanesi, vol. 8, Florence, 1906].

1570

PALLADIO A., *I Quattro Libri dell'Architettura*, Venice.

1574-1575

PALLADIO A., *I Commentari di C. Giulio Cesare...*, Venice.

1581

SANSOVINO F., *Venetia, città nobilissima et singolare descritta in XIII Libri*, Venice.

1583

SCAMOZZI V., *Discorsi sopra le antichità di Roma*, Venice.

1584

SERLIO S., *Tutte le opere d'architettura ... et un indice copiosissimo raccolto da M. Gio. Domenico Scamozzi*, Venice.

1591

MARZARI G., *La Historia di Vicenza*, Vicenza.

1605

PARUTA P., *Historia Vinetiana*, Venice.

1608

BOTERO G., *Relatione della Republica Venetiana*, Venice.

1609

ARETINO P., *Il secondo Libro de le Lettere*, Paris.

1610

FRANCO G., *Habiti d'Huomeni et Donne Venetiane...*, Venice.

1615

SCAMOZZI V., *L'Idea dell'Architettura Universale*, vol. 2, Venice.

1620

PORCACCHI T., *L'Isole più famose del mondo descritte et intagliate da Girolamo Porro*, Padua.

1622

NANI B., *Historia della Republica Veneta*, Venice.

1623

PORTENARI A., *Della felicità di Padova...*, Padua.

1648

RIDOLFI C., *Le Maraviglie dell'Arte...*, Venice.

1660

BOSCHINI M., *La Carta del Navegar pitoresco*, Venice [ed. A. Pallucchini, Venice-Rome, 1966].

1674

BOSCHINI M., *Le Ricche Minere della pittura veneziana*, Venice.

1676

BOSCHINI M., *I Gioieli pittoreschi virtuoso ornamento della Città di Vicenza*, Vicenza.

1678

CONTARINI G., *Della Repubblica e Magistrati di Venetia... con un ragionamento intorno alla medesima di Donato Giannotti Fiorentino...*, Venice.

1691

CORONELLI V. M., *Atlante Veneto*, Venice.

1707

FRESCOT C., *La nobiltà Veneta*, Venice.

1709

CORONELLI V. M., *La Brenta quasi borgo della città di Venezia, luogo di delizie de' Veneti Patrizi*, Venice.

1735

POMPEI A., *Li cinque ordini dell'architettura civile di Michel Sanmicheli*, Verona.

1740-1760

[MUTTONI F.], *Architettura di Andrea Palladio Vicentino... con le osservazioni dell'Architetto N. N.*, vol. 9, Venice.

1750-1762

COSTA G. F., *Delle Delicie del Fiume Brenta espresse ne' Palazzi e casini situati sopra le sue sponde dalla sboccatura nella Laguna di Venezia fino alla città di Padova*, Venice.

1760-1762

BARBARANO P. F., *Historia ecclesiastica della Città, Territorio e Diocese di Vicenza*, vol. IV, V, VI, Vicenza.

1762

TEMANZA T., *Vita di Andrea Palladio Vicentino*, Venice.

1776

BERTOTTI SCAMOZZI O., *Le fabbriche e i disegni di Andrea Palladio*, vol. I, Vicenza.
FACCIOLI G. T., *Musaeum Lapidarium Vicentinum*, vol. I, Vicenza.

1778

TEMANZA T., *Vite dei più celebri Architetti e Scultori veneziani che fiorirono nel secolo XVI*, Venice [ed. L. Grassi, Milan, 1966].

1803-1804

FACCIOLI G. T., *Musaeum Lapidarium Vicentinum*, vol. II, III, Vicenza.

1810

CICOGNARA L., *Elogio di Andrea Palladio*, Venice.

1812-1814

MACCÀ G., *Storia del territorio Vicentino*, vol. 14, Caldogno.

1817

DIEDO A., *Elogio di Daniele Barbaro*, Venice.

1830

SCHRÖDER F., *Repertorio genealogico delle famiglie confermate nobili e dei Titolati nobili esistenti nelle Provincie Venete*, Venice.

1837

CARRER L., *Anello di sette gemme*, Venice.

SCOLARI F., *Commentario della vita e le opere di Vincenzo Scamozzi*, Treviso.

1845

MAGRINI A., *Memorie intorno la vita e le opere di Andrea Palladio*, vol. 2, Padua.

1851

MAGRINI A., *Cenni storico-critici sulla vita e sulle opere di Giovanni Antonio Fasolo pittore vicentino*, Venice.

1861

CABIANCA J. - LAMPERTICO F., *Vicenza e il suo territorio*, Milan.

1866

ZANETTI V., *Guida di Murano*, Venice.

1867

FORMENTON F., *Memorie storiche della città di Vicenza*, Vicenza.

1874

BERTOLDI A., *Michele Sanmicheli al servizio della Repubblica Veneta. Documenti*, Verona.

YRIARTE C., *La vie d'un patricien de Venise au seizième siècle*, vol. 2, Paris.

1876

TRISSINO G. G., *Orazione alla Signoria di Venezia*, Vicenza.

1878

MORSOLIN B., *Giangiorgio Trissino, o monografia di un gentiluomo letterato del secolo XVI*, Vicenza.

1880

PIGAFETTA F., *Descrizione del Territorio e Contado di Vicenza*, Vicenza.

1884

MORELLI J., *Notizia d'opere di disegno*, Bologna.

1886

POMELLO A., *Storia di Lonigo*, Lonigo.

CROLLANZA (di) G. B., *Dizionario storico-blasonico*, Pisa.

1887

TASSINI G., *Curiosità veneziane*, Venice.

1895

BROWN H. F., *Venice. An Historical Sketch of the Republic*, London.

1899

PELLICIER G., *Correspondance politique de G. P. Ambassadeur de France à Venise, 1540-1542. Publiée... par A. Tausserat Radel*, Paris.

RUMOR S., *Il blasone vicentino descritto e illustrato*, Venice.

1905

CIAN V., *La cultura e l'italianità di Venezia nel Rinascimento*, Bologna.

1909

BURGER F., *Die Villen des Andrea Palladio*, Leipzig.

RUMOR S., *Della villa palladiana di Campiglia*, Vicenza.

1910

RUMOR S., *Storia breve degli Emo*, Vicenza.

ZORZI G. G., *La Rotonda di Andrea Palladio*, Vicenza.

1912

SERENA A., *La cultura umanistica a Treviso nel secolo decimoquinto*, Miscellanea di Storia veneta edita per cura della R. Deputazione di Storia patria, s. 3ª, t. III, Venice.

1914

GURLITT C., *Andrea Palladio*, Berlin.

1921

MOZZI U., "L'antico veneto Magistrato dei Beni Inculti", *La Terra*, I, pp. 2-17.

1922

ZORZI G. G., "La vera origine e la giovinezza di Andrea Palladio", *Archivio Veneto-Tridentino*, II, pp. 120-150.

1924

DAMI L., *Il giardino italiano*, Milan.

1925

CAMERINI P., *Piazzola*, Milan.

1926

LOUKOMSKI G. K., *Les Villas des Doges de Venise*, vol. 2, Paris.

ZORZI G. G., *Contributo alla Storia dell'arte vicentina dei secoli XV e XVI*, Venice.

1927

LOUKOMSKI G. K., *Andrea Palladio: sa vie, son oeuvre*, Paris.

1927-1929

MOLMENTI P., *La storia di Venezia nella vita privata dalle origini alla caduta della Repubblica*, vol. 3, Bergamo.

1928

FIOCCO G., *Paolo Veronese*, Bologna.

1928-34

SPRETI V., *Enciclopedia storico-nobiliare italiana*, Milan.

1929

FASOLO V., *Le Ville del Vicentino*, Vicenza.

VENTURI A., *Storia dell'Arte Italiana*, vol. IX, pt. IV, Milan.

1930

ARGAN G. C., "Andrea Palladio e la critica neoclassica", *L'Arte*, XXXIII, pp. 327-346.

BONFANTI S., *La Giudecca nella storia, nell'arte, nella vita*, Venice.

1930-1931

FIOCCO G., "Le architetture di Giovanni Maria Falconetto", *Dedalo*, XI, pp. 1203-1241.

1931

BRUNELLI B. - CALLEGARI A., *Ville del Brenta e degli Euganei*, Milan.

CALLEGARI A., *Il giardino veneto*, in *Mostra del giardino italiano*, Florence, pp. 207-225.

DAMERINI G., *Giardini di Venezia*, Bologna.

1932

ARGAN G., C., "Sebastiano Serlio", *L'Arte*, XXXV, pp. 183-199.

1934

DAZZI M., *Leonardo Giustinian poeta popolare d'amore*, Bari.

1935

GIOVANNONI G., *Palladio*, in *Enciclopedia Italiana*, vol. XXVI, Rome, pp. 117-121.

1935-1956

GOLDONI C., *Tutte le opere*, a cura di G. Ortolani, vol. 14, Milan.

1936

CESSI R., "Alvise Cornaro e la bonifica veneziana nel secolo XVI", *Atti dell'Accademia Nazionale dei Lincei*, CL. di Scienze morali, storiche e filologiche, s. 6a, Rendiconti, XII, pp. 301-323.

1937

ZORZI G. G., *Contributo alla Storia dell'arte vicentina dei secoli XV e XVI. Il preclassicismo e i prepalladiani*, Venice.

1938

FRANCO F., *Classicismo e funzionalità della villa palladiana "città piccola"*, in *Atti del I Congresso Nazionale di Storia dell'Architettura* [1936], Firenze, pp. 249-253.

PRIULI G., *Diarii*, a cura di R. Cessi, *Rerum Italicarum Scri Italicarum Scriptores*, t. XXIV, III, vol. IV, Bologna.

1940

FRANCO F., *Il teatro romano dell'antica Berga e la genesi del Teatro Olimpico*, in *Atti del III Convegno Nazionale di Storia dell'Architettura* [1938], Rome, pp. 171-182.

VENTURI A., *Storia dell'Arte Italiana*, vol. X, pt. III: *L'Architettura del Cinquecento*, Milan.

1941-1942

ARGAN G. C., "Cultura artistica alla fine del Cinquecento", *Le Arti*, XX, pp. 181-184.

1943

DALLA POZZA A. M., *Andrea Palladio*, Vicenza.

1943-1963

DALLA POZZA A. M., *Palladiana*, VIII-IX, "Odeo Olimpico", IV, pp. 99-131.

1945

MORASSI A., *Tiepolo: la Villa Valmarana*, Milan.

PALLUCCHINI R., *Gli affreschi di G. B. e G. D. Tiepolo alla Villa Valmarana*, Bergamo.

1948

PANE R., *Andrea Palladio*, Turin.

REYNOLDS J., *Andrea Palladio*, New York.

1949

ACKERMAN J. S., "Ars sine scientia nihil est", *Art Bulletin*, XXXI, pp. 84-111.

MURARO M., *Mostra del restauro di monumenti e opere d'arte danneggiate dalla guerra nelle Tre Venezie*, Catalogue, Venice.

WITTKOWER R., *Architectural Principles in the Age of Humanism*, London.

1950

GOLZIO V., *Seicento e Settecento*, Turin.

1951

MAGAGNATO L., "The Genesis of the Teatro Olimpico", *Journal of the Warburg and Courtauld Institutes*, XIV, pp. 209-220.

ZORZI G. G., "Alessandro Vittoria a Vicenza e lo scultore Lorenzo Rubini", *Arte Veneta*, V, pp. 141-157.

1952

AA.VV., *Le Ville Venete*, Exhibition catalogue ed. G. Mazzotti, Treviso.

BARBIERI F., *Vincenzo Scamozzi*, Vicenza.

FASOLI G., "Lineamenti di politica e di legislazione feudale veneziana in terraferma", *Rivista di Storia del diritto italiano*, XXV, pp. 61-94.

MAGAGNATO L. - POZZA N., *Prima mostra della Pietra di Vicenza*, Vicenza.

MURARO M., "Tipi e architetture delle ville venete" and "Catalogo delle ville della provincia di Venezia", *Le Ville Venete*, Treviso, pp. 53-92 e 95-165.

1953

BARBIERI F. - CEVESE R. - MAGAGNATO L., *Guida di Vicenza*, Vicenza.

BRAUDEL F., *Civiltà e imperi del Mediterraneo nell'età di Filippo II*, Turin.

COLETTI L., *Pittura veneta del Quattrocento*, Novara.

FIOCCO G., *Alvise Cornaro e i suoi trattati sull'architettura*, Rome.

MURARO M., *Fototeca palladiana*, Florence.

1954

MURARO M., *Les villas de la Vénétie*, Exhibition catalogue, Venice.

PRAGA G., *Storia di Dalmazia*, Padua.

ZORZI G. G., "Progetti giovanili di Andrea Palladio per villini e case di campagna", *Palladio*, IV, pp. 59-76.

ZORZI G. G., "Progetti giovanili di Andrea Palladio per palazzi e case in Venezia e Terraferma", *Palladio*, IV, pp. 105-121.

1955

BELTRAMI D., *Saggio di storia dell'agricoltura nella Repubblica di Venezia durante l'età moderna*, Venice-Rome.

GALLO R., "Andrea Palladio e Venezia", *Rivista di Venezia*, n. s., I, pp. 23-48.

MASSON G., "The Palladian Villas as Rural Centers", *Architectural Review*, CXVIII, pp. 17-20.

1956

ARGAN G. C., "L'importanza del Sammicheli nella formazione del Palladio, in Venezia e l'Europa", *Atti del XVIII Congresso internazionale di Storia dell'Arte* [1955], Venice, pp. 387-389.

CEVESE R., *Ville Vicentine*, Milan.

CHASTEL A., *Le lieu des fêtes*, in *Actes du Colloque sur les Fêtes de la Renaissance* [1955], Paris.

FRANCO F., *Piccola urbanistica della "casa di villa" palladiana*, in *Venezia e l'Europa*, Venice, pp. 395-398.

LORENZETTI G., *Venezia e il suo Estuario*, Rome.

1956-1957

FURLAN G. - MARTIN I., "Villa Emo Capodilista a Fanzolo di A. Palladio" *Architettura*, II, pp. 443-447.

STELLA A., "La crisi economica veneziana della seconda metà del secolo XVI", *Archivio Veneto*, s.5a, LVIII-LIX, pp. 17-69.

1957

DAVIS J. C., *A Venetian Family and its Fortune: 1500-1900*, Philadelphia.

SERPIERI F., *Le bonifiche nella storia e nella dottrina*, Bologna.

1958

BRAUDEL F., "La vita economica di Venezia nel secolo XVI", *La civiltà veneziana del Rinascimento*, Florence, pp. 81-102.

CEVESE R., "La dimora di Angelo Caldogno", *Studi in onore di Federico M. Mistrorigo*, Vicenza, pp. 206-243.

HARTT F., *Giulio Romano*, New Haven.

MANSUELLI G. A., *Le ville del mondo romano*, Milan.

PALLUCCHINI R., "Giulio Romano e Palladio", *Arte Veneta*, XII, pp. 234-235.

PUPPI L., "Sanmicheli a Vicenza", *Vita Veronese*, XI, pp. 449-453.

SEMENZATO C., *Antonio Bonazza (1698-1763)*, Venice.

ZORZI G. G., *I disegni delle antichità di Andrea Palladio*, Venice.

1958-1959

ZORZI G. G., "Vita di Andrea Palladio scritta da Paolo Gualdo", *Saggi e Memorie di Storia dell'Arte*, II, pp. 91-104.

1959

ARGAN G. C., "Tipologia, simbologia, allegorismo delle forme architettoniche", *Bollettino del C.I.S.A.*, I, pp. 13-16.

CAVALCA C. - CANDIDA L., *La casa rurale nella pianura e nella collina veneta*, Florence.

FRANCO F., "Piccola e grande urbanistica palladiana", *Bollettino del C.I.S.A.*, I, pp. 17-20.

PUPPI L., "L'architettura civile di Michele Sanmicheli", *Vita Veronese*, XII, pp. 49-67.

1960

AA.VV., *Palladio, Veronese e Vittoria a Maser*, Milan.

FIOCCO G., "Significato dell'opera di Michele Sanmicheli", *Michele Sanmicheli, Studi raccolti dall'Accademia di Agricoltura Scienze e Lettere di Verona per la celebrazione del IV centenario della morte*, Verona, pp. 1-13.

LAZZARINI V., *Proprietà e feudi in antiche carte veneziane*, Rome.

MAGAGNATO L. - PIOVENE G., *Ville del Brenta nelle vedute di Vincenzo Coronelli e Gianfranco Costa*, Milan.

MURARO M., *Pitture murali nel Veneto e tecnica dell'affresco*, Exhibition catalogue, Venice.

MURARO M., "Giuseppe Zais e un *giovin signore* nelle pitture murali di Stra", *Emporium*, LXVI, pp. 12-16.

ZOCCA M., "Le concezioni urbanistiche di Palladio", *Palladio*, X, pp. 68-83.

ZORZI G. G., "Andrea Palladio architetto della Repubblica di Venezia", *Bollettino del C.I.S.A.*, II, pp. 108-113.

1960-1962

BAROCCHI P., *Trattati d'arte del Cinquecento fra Manierismo e Controriforma*, vol. 3, Bari.

1961

BELTRAMI D., *La penetrazione economica dei Veneziani in terraferma. Forze di lavoro e proprietà fondiaria nelle campagne venete dei secoli XVII e XVIII*, Venice-Rome.

CESSI F., *Alessandro Vittoria architetto e stuccatore*, Trento.

FERRARI G. E., "Schede di bibliografia palladiana dal 1955", *Bollettino del C.I.S.A.*, III, pp. 163-171.

IVANOFF N., "Il sacro e il profano negli affreschi di Maser", *Ateneo Veneto*, CLII, pp. 99-104.

LOTZ W., "L'eredità romana di Jacopo Sansovino architetto veneziano", *Bollettino del C.I.S.A.*, III, pp. 82-85.

LUZZATTO G., "Storia economica di Venezia dal IX al XVI secolo", Venice.

PALLUCCHINI R., "Profilo di Vincenzo Scamozzi", *Bollettino del C.I.S.A*, III, pp. 89-101.

PANE R., *Andrea Palladio*, Turin.

SCHULZ J., "Vasari at Venice", *Burlington Magazine*, CIII, pp. 500-511.

WILINSKI S., "Sebastiano Serlio ai lettori del III e IV libro sull'architettura", *Bollettino del C.I.S.A.*, III, pp. 57-69.

1962

BASSI E., *Architettura del Sei e Settecento a Venezia*, Naples.

BATTISTI E., *L'Antirinascimento*, Milan.

BERENGO M., *L'agricoltura veneta dalla caduta della repubblica all'Unità*, Milan.

CEVESE R., "Il Barocco a Vicenza: Revese, Pizzocaro, Borella", *Bollettino del C.I.S.A.*, IV, pp. 129-146.

CROSATO L., *Gli affreschi nelle ville venete del Cinquecento*, Treviso.

FORSSMAN E., "Palladio e Vitruvio", *Bollettino del C.I.S.A.*, IV, pp. 31-42.

GALLIMBERTI N., *Giuseppe Jappelli*, Padua.

LOTZ W., "La Rotonda: edificio civile con cupola", *Bollettino del C.I.S.A.*, IV, pp. 69-73.

MANTESE G., "La chiesa vicentina. Panorama storico", Vicenza.

MAZZOTTI G., "Le ville venete e l'opera dell'Ente istituito per il loro restauro e conservazione", *Giornale economico della Camera di Commercio, Industria e Agricoltura di Venezia*, n. 7, pp. 817-826.

PUPPI L., "Il Barco di Caterina Cornaro ad Altivole", *Prospettive*, n. 25, pp. 52-64.

ROMANO R., "Tra XVI e XVII secolo. Una crisi economica: 1619-1622", *Rivista storica italiana*. LXXIV, pp. 480-531.

SEMENZATO C., "La Rocca Pisana dello Scamozzi", *Arte Veneta*, XVI, pp. 98-110.

SERENI E., *Storia del paesaggio agrario italiano*, Bari.

TIMOFIEWITSCH W., "La chiesetta della Rotonda", *Bollettino del C.I.S.A.*, IV, pp. 262-268.

WOOLF S. J., "Venice and the Terraferma. Problems of the Change from Commercial to Landed Activities", *Bollettino dell'Istituto di Storia della Società e dello Stato veneziano*, IV pp. 415-441.

ZORZI G. G., "Le statue di Agostino Rubini nel Teatro Olimpico di Vicenza", *Arte Veneta*, XVI, pp. 111-120.

1963

ACKERMAN J. S., *Sources of the Renaissance Villa*, in *The Renaissance and Mannerism. Studies in Western Art*, Acts of the Twentieth International Congress of the History of Art, Princeton, pp. 6-18.

BARBIERI F., "Per la cronologia di Orazio Marinali. L'Annunciazione nell'Arco vicentino delle scalette", *S. Maria di Monte Berico*, pp. 101-109.

FIOCCO G., "La lezione di Alvise Cornaro", *Bollettino del C.I.S.A.*, V, pp. 33-43.

KITZINGER E., "The Hellenistic Heritage in Byzantine Art", *Dumbarton Oaks Papers*, XVII, pp. 95-115.

LOTZ W., "The Roman Legacy in Sansovino's Venetian Buildings", *Journal of the Society of Architectural Historians*, XXII, pp. 3-12.

MAZZARIOL G. - PIGNATTI T., *La pianta prospettica di Venezia del 1500 disegnata da Jacopo de' Barbari*, Venice.

MAZZOTTI G., *Ville Venete*, Rome.

PIOVENE G., "Trissino e Palladio nell'Umanesimo vicentino", *Bollettino del C.I.S.A.*, V, pp. 13-23.

PUPPI L., *Il Teatro Olimpico*, Vicenza.

WITTKOWER R., "L'influenza del Palladio sullo sviluppo dell'architettura religiosa veneziana nel Sei e Settecento", *Bollettino del C.I.S.A.*, V, pp. 61-72.

ZEVI B., *Palladio*, in *Enciclopedia Universale dell'Arte*, vol. X, Venice-Rome, coll. 438-458.

1964

ACKERMAN J. S., "Il Presidente Jefferson e il Palladianesimo americano", *Bollettino del C.I.S.A.*, VI, pp. 39-48.

BARBIERI F., "Palladio e il Manierismo", *Bollettino del C.I.S.A.*, VI, pp. 49-63.

CESSI F., "L'attività di Alessandro Vittoria a Maser", *Studi Trentini di Scienze Storiche*, XLII, pp. 3-18.

CHASTEL A., "Cortile et théâtre", *Le lieu théâtral à la Renaissance*, Paris, pp. 41-47.

GUIOTTO M., "Recenti restauri di edifici palladiani", *Bollettino del C.I.S.A.*, VI, pp. 70-88.

MENEGAZZO E., "Ricerche intorno alla vita e all'ambiente del Ruzante e di Alvise Cornaro", *Italia medioevale e umanistica*, VII, pp. 180-217.

MURARO M., *Civiltà delle ville venete* Venezia, Istituto d'Architettura [Biblioteca Marciana: Misc. A. 3723].

MURARO M. T., *Le lieu des spectacles (publics ou privées) à Venise au XV et XVI siécles*, in *Le lieu théâtral à la Renaissance*, Paris, pp. 318-319.

PANE R., "Palladio e la moderna storiografia dell'architettura", *Bollettino del C.I.S.A.*, VI, pp. 119-130.

RUPPRECHT B., "Ville venete del Quattrocento e del primo Cinquecento: forme e sviluppo", *Bollettino del C.I.S.A.*, VI, pp. 239-250.

VENTURA A., *Nobiltà e popolo nella società veneta del '400 e '500*, Bari.

WITTKOVER R., *Principî architettonici nell'età dell'Umanesimo*, Turin.

1964-1965

DALLA POZZA A. M., "Palladiana, X-XII", *Odeo Olimpico*, V, pp. 203-238.

1965

BARBIERI F., "L'architettura gotica civile a Vicenza", *Bollettino del C.I.S.A.*, VII, pp. 167-184.

FERRARI G. E., "Schede di bibliografia palladiana nel quinquennio 1961-1965", *Bollettino del C.I.S.A.*, VII, pp. 363-391.

FIOCCO G., *Alvise Cornaro: il suo tempo e le sue opere*, Venice.

FORSSMAN E., *Palladios Lehrgebäude*, Stockholm-Göteborg-Uppsala.

WILINSKI S., "Sebastiano Serlio", *Bollettino del C.I.S.A.*, VII, pp. 103-114.

ZORZI G. G., *Le Opere Pubbliche e i Palazzi privati di Andrea Palladio*, Venice.

1965-1966

PUPPI L., "Appunti su Villa Badoer di Fratta Polesine", *Memorie della Accademia Patavina di SS. LL. AA.*, Cl. di Scienze Morali, LXXVIII, pp. 47-72.

1966

ACKERMAN J. S., *Palladio*, Harmondsworth.

BLUNT A., *Le teorie artistiche in Italia dal Rinascimento al Manierismo*, Turin.

FORSSMAN E., "Falconetto e Palladio", *Bollettino del C.I.S.A.*, VIII, pp. 52-67.

FORSSMAN E., "Palladio e Daniele Barbaro", *Bollettino del C.I.S.A.*, VIII, pp. 68-81.

GLOTON J. - J., "La villa italienne à la fin de la Renaissance: conceptions paladiennes - conceptions vignolesques", *Bollettino del C.I.S.A.*, VIII, pp. 101-113.

MENEGAZZO E. - SAMBIN P., "Nuove esplorazioni archivistiche per Angelo Beolco e Alvise Cornaro", *Italia medioevale e umanistica*, IX, pp. 229-385.

MURARO M., "Civiltà delle ville venete", *Arte in Europa. Scritti di Storia dell'Arte in onore di E. Arslan*, Milan, pp. 533-543.

PUPPI L., *Palladio*, Florence.

RUPPRECHT B., *Villa. Zur Geschichte eines Ideals*, in *Probleme der Kunstwissenschaft*, vol. II, Berlin, pp. 120 sgg.

SEMENZATO C., *La scultura veneta del Sei e del Settecento*, Venice.

TAFURI M., *L'architettura del Manierismo nel Cinquecento europeo*, Roma.

ZORZI G. G., *Le chiese e i ponti di Andrea Palladio*, Venice.

1967

ACKERMAN J. S., *Palladio's Villas*, New York.

ACKERMAN J. S., *Palladio's Vicenza: A Bird's-eye Plan of c. 1571*, in *Studies in Renaissance and Baroque Art Presented to A. Blunt*, London, pp. 53-61.

ACKERMAN J. S., *Palladio's Lost Portico Project for San Petronio in Bologna*, in *Essays in the History of Architecture Presented to R. Wittkover*, London, pp. 119-125.

DIONISOTTI C., *Geografia e storia della letteratura italiana*, Turin.

FORSSMAN E., "Palladio e la pittura a fresco", *Arte Veneta*, XXI, pp. 71-76.

FORSSMAN E., "Über Architekturen in der Venezianischen Malerei des Cinquecento", *Wallraff Richartz Jahrbuch*, XXIX, pp. 105-139.

FRANCASTEL P., *La Figure et le Lieu. L'ordre visuel du Quattrocento*, Paris.

ISERMEYER C. A., "Die Villa Rotonda von Palladio", *Zeitschrift für Kunstgeschichte*, pp. 207-221.

IVANOFF N., *Palladio*, Milano.

LOTZ W., "Palladio e Sansovino", *Bollettino del C.I.S.A.*, IX, pp. 13-23.

MANTESE G., "La Rotonda", *Vita Vicentina*, n. 1, pp. 23-24.

MURARO M., "Concretezza e idealità nell'arte del Palladio", *Bollettino del C.I.S.A.*, IX, pp. 108-120.

PUPPI L., "Il Sesto Libro di Sebastiano Serlio", *Arte Veneta*, XXI, pp. 242-243.

ROSCI M., "Sebastiano Serlio e il Manierismo nel Veneto", *Bollettino del C.I.S.A*, IX, pp. 330-336.

TAFURI M., "L'idea di architettura nella letteratura teorica del Manierismo", *Bollettino del C.I.S.A.*, IX, pp. 367-384.

1968

ALPAGO NOVELLO A., *Ville della provincia di Belluno*, Milan.

BARBIERI F., "Il *Corpus palladiano*: la Rotonda", *Arte Veneta*, XXII, pp. 225-227.

BASSO U., *Cronaca di Maser, delle sue chiese e della villa palladiana dei Barbaro*, Montebelluna.

BIEGANSKI P., "La struttura architettonica di alcune ville di Palladio in rapporto alla loro funzione pratica", *Bollettino del C.I.S.A.*, X, pp. 15-30.

MAGAGNATO L., "I collaboratori veronesi di Andrea Palladio", *Bollettino del C.I.S.A.*, X, pp. 170-187.

MARCONI P., "Una chiave per l'interpretazione dell'urbanistica rinascimentale. La cittadella come microcosmo", *Quaderni dell'Istituto di Storia dell'Architettura*, pp. 53-94.

PRECERUTTI GARBERI M., *Affreschi settecenteschi delle ville venete*, Milan.

ROSCI M., "Forme e funzioni delle ville venete prepalladiane", *L'Arte*, n. 2, pp. 27-54.

RUPPRECHT B., "L'iconologia nella villa veneta", *Bollettino del C.I.S.A.*, X, pp. 229-240.

RUSSEL ROOP G., *Villas and Palaces Andrea Palladio*, Milan.

SEMENZATO C., *La Rotonda*, Vicenza.

SCHULZ J., *Venetian Painted Ceilings*, Berkeley-Los Angeles.

SCHULZ J., "Le fonti di Paolo Veronese come decoratore", *Bollettino del C.I.S.A.*, X, pp. 241-254.

SCHWEIKARDT G., "Studien zum Werke des Giovanni Maria Falconetto", *Bollettino del Museo Civico di Padova*, LVII, pp. 17-67.

TIMOFIEWITSCH W., "Die sakrale Architektur Palladios, Münich.

VENTURA A., "Considerazioni sull'agricoltura veneta e sulla accumulazione originaria del capitale nei secoli XV e XVII", *Studi Storici*, IX, pp. 674-722.

WILINSKI S., "La serliana di villa Pojana a Pojana Maggiore", *Bollettino del C.I.S.A.*, X, pp. 79-84.

WOLTERS W., "Andrea Palladio e la decorazione dei suoi edifici", *Bollettino del C.I.S.A.*, X, pp. 255-267.

WOLTERS W., "La decorazione plastica delle volte e dei soffitti a Venezia e nel Veneto nel secolo XVI", *Bollettino del C.I.S.A.*, X, pp. 268-278.

1969

BARBIERI B., "Le ville dello Scamozzi", *Bollettino del C.I.S.A.*, XI, pp. 222-230.

FORSSMAN E., "Del sito da eleggersi per le fabriche di villa. Interpretazione di un testo palladiano". *Bollettino del C.I.S.A.*, XI, pp. 149-162.

FORSSMAN E., "Palladios Erstling. Die Villa Godi Valmarana in Lonedo bei Vicenza by Paul Hofer", *Bollettino del C.I.S.A.*, XI, pp. 469-471.

FROMMEL L., "La Villa Madama e la tipologia della villa romana nel Rinascimento", *Bollettino del C.I.S.A.*, XI, pp. 47-64.

HEYDENREICH L. H., "La villa: genesi e sviluppi fino al Palladio", *Bollettino del C.I.S.A.*, XI, pp. 11-22.

MURARO M., *Palladio et l'urbanisme vénitien*, in *L'urbanisme de Paris et l'Europe: 1600-1680* (ed. P. Francastel), Paris, pp. 211-217.

MURARO M., "Les villas avant la Renaissance", *Bulletin du CIHA*, IV, p. 17.

PUPPI L., "Rassegna degli studi sulle ville venete (1952-1969)", *L'Arte*, n. 7-8, pp. 215-226.

RIGON F., "Torri medioevali come primi nuclei di insediamenti di villa", *Bollettino del C.I.S.A.*, XI, pp. 387-392.

TAFURI M., "Committenza e tipologia nelle ville palladiane", *Bollettino del C.I.S.A.*, XI, pp. 120-136.

TAFURI M., *Jacopo Sansovino e l'architettura del '500 a Venezia*, Padua.

TAFURI M., *L'architettura dell'Umanesimo*, Bari.

VENTURA A., "Aspetti storico-economici della villa veneta", *Bollettino del C.I.S.A.*, XI, pp. 65-77.

WOLTERS W., "Sebastiano Serlio e il suo contributo alla villa veneziana prima del Palladio", *Bollettino del C.I.S.A.*, XI, pp. 83-94.

ZANCAN M. A., "Le ville vicentine del Quattrocento", *Bollettino del C.I.S.A.*, XI, pp. 430-448.

ZORZI G. G., *Le ville e i teatri di Andrea Palladio*, Venice.

ZORZI G. G., "La datazione delle ville palladiane", *Bollettino del C.I.S.A.*, XI, pp. 137-162.

1970

BARBIERI F., "Palladio in villa negli anni Quaranta: da Lonedo a Bagnolo", *Arte Veneta*, XXIV, pp. 63-79.

BARBIERI F. - MENATO G., *Pietra di Vicenza*, Vicenza.

BENTMANN R. - MÜLLER M., *Die Villa als Herrschafsarchitektur*, Frankfurt am Main.

BORDIGNON FAVERO G. P., *La villa Emo di Fanzolo*, Vicenza.

BOSIO L., *Itinerari e strade della Venezia romana*, Padua.

IVANOFF N., "La tematica degli affreschi di Maser", *Arte Veneta*, XXIV, pp. 210-213.

PUPPI L., "Il Trattato del Palladio e la sua fortuna in Italia e all'estero", *Bollettino del C.I.S.A.*, XII, pp. 257-272.

ROSCI M., "Rassegna degli studi palladiani (1959-1969)", *L'Arte*, n. 10, pp. 114-124.

TAFURI M., "La fortuna del Palladio alla fine del Cinquecento e l'architettura di Inigo Jones", *Bollettino del C.I.S.A.»*, XII, pp. 47-62.

1971

CANOVA A., *Ville del Polesine*, Rovigo.

CEVESE R., *Ville della provincia di Vicenza*, vol. 2, Milan.

MASSARI A., *Giorgio Massari architetto veneziano del Settecento*, Venice.

PUPPI L., *Michele Sanmicheli architetto di Verona*, Padua.

PUPPI L., "Un letterato in villa: Giangiorgio Trissino a Cricoli", *Arte Veneta*, XXV, pp. 72-91.

ROMANO R., *Tra due crisi: l'Italia del Rinascimento*, Turin.

1972

BARBIERI F., *Illuministi e Neoclassici a Vicenza*, Vicenza.

COCKE R., "Veronese and Daniele Barbaro: the Decoration of Villa Maser", *Journal of the Warburg and Courtauld Institutes*, XXXV, pp. 226-246.

DA CANAL M., *Les Estoires de Venise (1275)*, ed. A. Limentani, Florence.

MURARO M., "La villa di Passariano e l'architetto Giovanni Ziborghi, *Tagunsbericht. Dreiländer-Fachtagung der Kunsthistoriker in Graz*, Graz, pp. 44-60.

PUPPI L., *La Villa Badoer di Fratta Polesine*, Vicenza.

PUPPI L., "The Villa Garden of the Veneto from the Fifteenth to the Eighteenth Century", *The Italian Garden* (ed. D. Coffin), Washington D. C., pp. 83-114.

1973

AA.VV., *Palladio*, Exhibition catalogue, Venice.

COZZI G., "Ambiente veneziano e ambiente veneto", *L'uomo e il suo ambiente*, Florence, pp. 93-146.

PUPPI L., *Andrea Palladio*, vol. 2, Milan.

1973-1977

AA.VV., *Relazioni dei Rettori Veneti in Terraferma*, ed. A. Tagliaferri, vol. I-IX, Milan.

1974

KUBELIK M., "Gli edifici palladiani nei disegni del Magistrato Veneto dei Beni Inculti", *Bollettino del C.I.S.A.*, XIV, pp. 445-465.

ROMANO R., "La storia economica. Dal secolo XIV al Settecento", *Storia d'Italia, 2: Dalla caduta dell'Impero romano al secolo XVIII*, Turin, t. II, pp. 1813-1931.

WITTKOWER R., *Palladio and Palladianism*, London-New York.

1975

AA.VV., *La villa nel Veronese*, ed. G. F. Viviani, Verona.

BURNS H. - FAIRBAIRN L. - BOUCHER B., *Andrea Palladio 1508-1580. The Portico and the Farmyard*, Exhibition catalogue, London.

SCHIAVO R., *Villa Cordellina Lombardi di Montecchio Maggiore*, Vicenza.

SEMENZATO C., *Le ville del Polesine*, Vicenza.

1976

AA.VV., *Vicenza illustrata*, Vicenza.

GOLLWITZER G., "Interazione tra l'uomo e il paesaggio esemplificata nelle ville venete", *Bollettino del C.I.S.A.*, XVIII, pp. 49-63.

GUIOTTO M., "Vicende storiche e restauro della Villa Tiepolo a Zianigo di Mirano", *Ateneo Veneto*, XIV, pp. 7-26.

SCHULZ J., "New Maps and Landscape Drawings by Cristoforo Sorte", *Mitteilungen des kunsthistorischen Institutes in Florenz*, XX, pp. 107-126.

SPEZZATI G., *Le ville venete della riviera del Brenta*, Dolo.

1977

KOLB LEWIS C., *The Villa Giustinian at Roncade*, New York-London.

KUBELIK M., *Die Villa im Veneto. Zur typologischen Entwicklung im Quattrocento*, vol. 2, Munich.

MURARO M., "Cologna dei Veneziani e le sue ville", *La Mainarda*, I, pp. 147-158.

MURARO M., "Qualche notizia sulla famiglia Adami e sulla loro villa di Pieve di Cadore", *Il Cadore*, XXV, n. 10, p. 3.

1978

AA.VV., *Gli affreschi delle ville venete dal Seicento all'Ottocento*, vol. 2, Venice.

MURARO M., "Feudo e ville venete", *Bollettino del C.I.S.A.*, XX, pp. 203-223.

MURARO M., "Palazzo Chiericati «Villa marittima»", *Arte Veneta*, XXXII, pp. 187-194.

SCHULZ J., "Jacopo de' Barbari's View of Venice: Map Making, City Views, and Moralized Geography Before 1500", *Art Bulletin*, LX, pp. 425-474.

1979

MURARO M., "Giorgione e la Civiltà delle ville venete", *Giorgione*, Atti del Convegno internazionale di studio per il 5° centenario della nascita, Castelfranco Veneto, pp. 171-180.

VOLKAMER J. C., *Ville, Giardini e Paesaggi del Veneto nelle incisioni di Johann Christoph Volkamer...*, ed. E. Concina, Milan.

1980

AA.VV., *Alvise Cornaro e il suo tempo*, Exhibition Catalogue, ed. L. Puppi, Padua.

AA.VV., *Andrea Palladio: il testo, l'immagine, la città*, Exhibition catalogue, ed. L. Puppi, Vicenza.

AA.VV., *Architettura e utopia nella Venezia del Cinquecento*, Exhibition catalogue, ed. L. Puppi, Milan.

AA.VV., *I Benedettini a Padova e nel territorio padovano attraverso i secoli*, Exhibition catalogue, Padua.

AA.VV., *Palladio: la sua eredità nel mondo*, Exhibition catalogue, Venice.

AA.VV., *Palladio e Verona*, Exhibition catalogue, Venice.

AA.VV., *Palladio e la Maniera. I pittori vicentini del Cinquecento e i collaboratori del Palladio, 1530-1630*, Exhibition catalogue, ed. V. Sgarbi, Milan.

ARGAN G. C., *Palladio e palladianesimo*, Vicenza.

BARBIERI F., "Giangiorgio Trissino e Andrea Palladio", *Convegno di studi su Giangiorgio Trissino*, ed. N. Pozza, Vicenza, pp. 191-211.

CEVESE R., *Invito a Palladio*, Milan.

GULLINO G., "I patrizi veneziani di fronte alla proprietà feudale (secoli XVI-XVIII). Materiale per una ricerca", *Quaderni storici*, XLIII, pp. 162-193.

HOWARD D., "Four Centuries of Literature on Palladio", *Journal of the Society of Architectural Historians*, XXXIX, pp. 224-241.

MAGAGNATO L., *Introduzione* a Palladio A., *I Quattro Libri dell'Architettura*, Milan.

MURARO M., "La villa palladiana dei Repeta a Campiglia dei Berici con documenti sulla persistenza del feudalesimo nel Veneto", *Campiglia dei Berici: storia di un paese veneto*, Campiglia, pp. 1-94.

MURARO M., "Civiltà delle ville di Ragusa", *Fiskovićev Zbornik*, Split, vol. I, pp. 321-331

MURARO M., "Il Veneto nel Cinquecento; Fra' Giocondo da Verona e l'arte fiorentina," *Florence and Venice: Comparisons and Relations*, II: *Cinquecento*, Florence, pp. 211-214, 337-339.

PUPPI L., "L'ambiente, il paesaggio e il territorio" *Storia dell'arte italiana*, 4: *Ricerche spaziali e tecnologiche*, Turin, pp. 43-100.

RICATTI B., *Antonio Caregaro Negrin un architetto vicentino tra eclettismo e liberty*, Padua.

RIGON F., *Palladio*, Bologna.

SCARPARI G., *Le ville venete*, Rome.

SCHIAVO R., *Guida al Teatro Olimpico*, Vicenza.

1980-1981

BALDAN A., *Storia della Riviera del Brenta*, vol. 3, Vicenza.

1981

CANOVA A., *L'opera di Andrea Palladio*, Exhibition catalogue, Treviso.

1982

AA.VV., *Brenta: struttura e ambiente, materiali per la conoscenza del territorio*, Exhibition catalogue, Mira.

AA.VV., *Palladio e Venezia*, ed. L. Puppi, Florence.

BAGATTI VALSECCHI P. F. - LANGÈ S., "La villa", *Storia dell'arte italiana*, 11: *Forme e modelli*, Turin, pp. 363-456.

BRUNO G., *La riviera del Brenta. Le stagioni del tempo*, Cittadella di Padova.

MURARO M., "La villa Pesaro dal Carro a Este", *Padova e la sua provincia*, XXVIII, pp. 15-21.

1983

AA.VV., *Laguna, lidi, fiumi. Cinque secoli di gestione delle acque*, Exhibition catalogue, ed. M. F. Tiepolo, Venice.

BARBIERI G., *Andrea Palladio e la cultura veneta del Rinascimento*, Rome.

GUIOTTO M., *Monumentalità della riviera del Brenta. Itinerario storico-artistico dalla laguna di Venezia a Padova*, Padua.

1984

ACKERMAN J. S., "The Faces of Palace Chiericati", *Interpretazioni Veneziane. Studi di Storia dell'arte in onore di M. Muraro*, ed. D. Rosand, Venice, pp. 213-220.

AZZI VISENTINI M., *L'orto botanico di Padova e il giardino del Rinascimento*, Milan.

BOSCHETTI M. G. - COLLA S., "Il tempietto di una villa a Sossano Veneto", *Interpretazioni Veneziane*, Venice, pp. 405-409.

CANOVA A., *Ville Venete*, Exhibition catalogue, Treviso.

COZZI G., "Ambiente veneziano, ambiente veneto, governanti e governati nel Dominio di qua dal Mincio nei secoli XV-XVIII", *Storia della cultura veneta*, 4: *Il Seicento*, Vicenza, t. II, pp. 495-539.

KOLB C. J., "New Evidence for Villa Pisani at Montagnana", *Interpretazioni Veneziane*, Venice pp. 227-239.

MURARO M. - COLLA S. - LOSA L., *La villa Barbarigo a Noventa Vicentina*, Vicenza.

STEFANI MANTOVANELLI M., "Una perizia del Sanmicheli e le vicende artistiche dei Querini Stampalia in Venezia e nella Terraferma", *Interpretazioni Veneziane*, Venice, pp. 221-226.

1985

AA.VV., *Civiltà dei monasteri*, Milan.

AA.VV., *Dueville. Storia e indentificazione di una comunità del passato*, ed. C. Povolo. vol. 2, Vicenza.

CANOVA A., *Le ville del Palladio*, Treviso.

MOMETTO P., "La vita in villa", *Storia della cultura veneta*, 5: *Il Settecento*, Vicenza, t. II, pp. 607-629.

MORANDO DI CUSTOZA E., *Blasonario veneto*, Verona.

TAFURI M., *Venezia e il Rinascimento. Religione, scienza, architettura*, Turin.

504

THE HISTORY AND CULTURE OF THE
VENETIAN VILLAS

INDEX OF NAMES,
PLACES
AND SUBJECTS

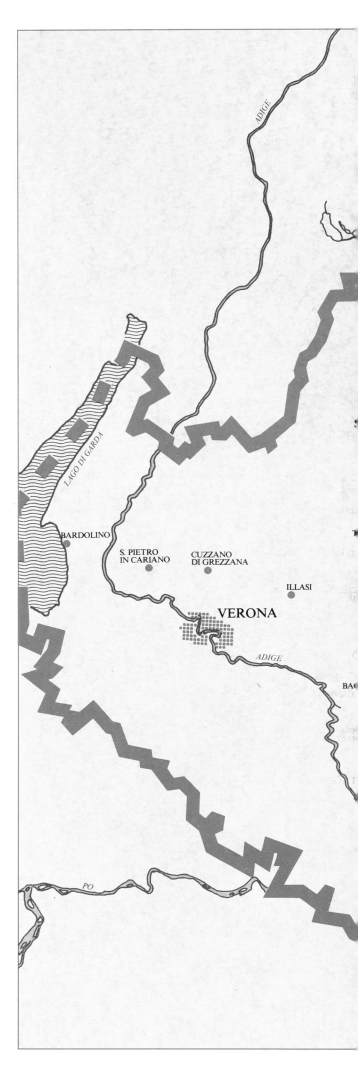

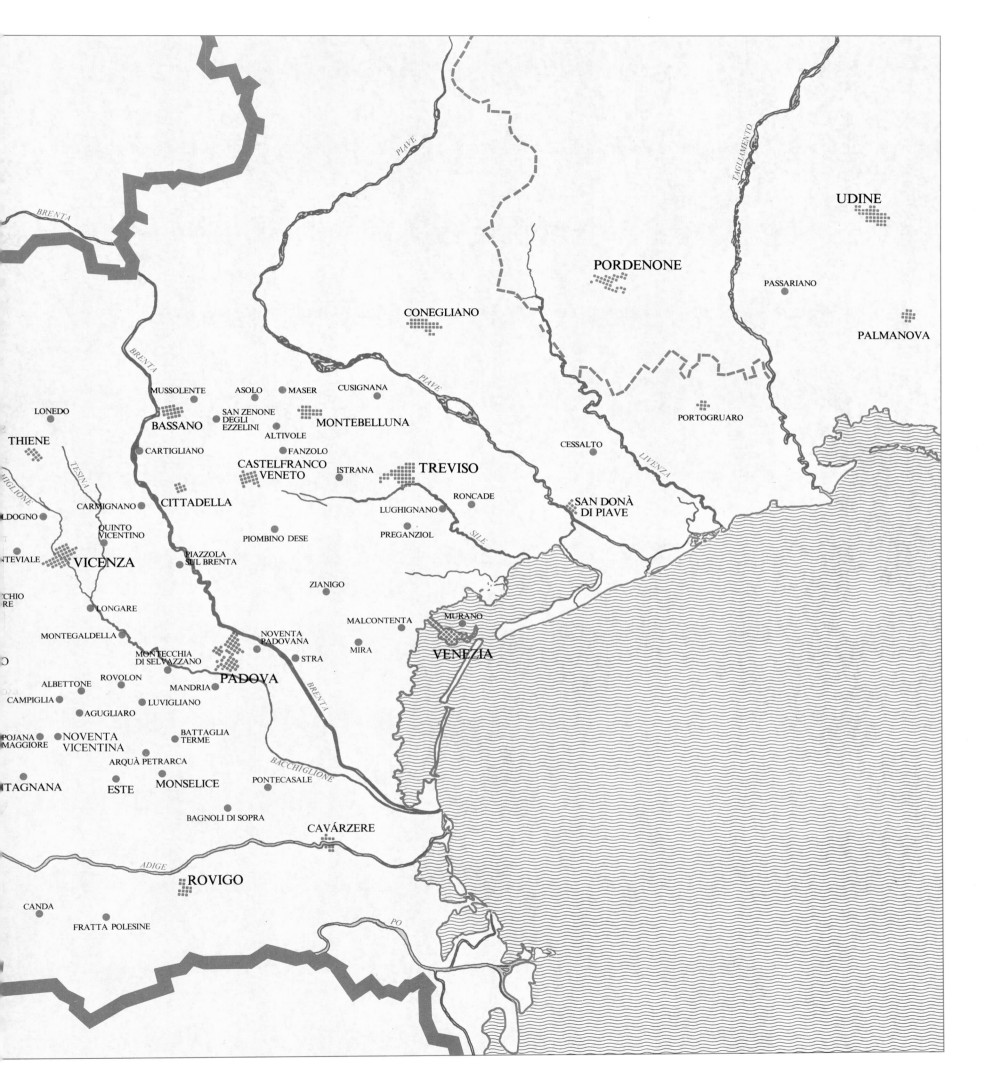

UDINE

PORDENONE

PASSARIANO

CONEGLIANO

PALMANOVA

PORTOGRUARO

MUSSOLENTE   ASOLO   MASER   CUSIGNANA

LONEDO

SAN ZENONE
DEGLI
EZZELINI

BASSANO   ALTIVOLE   MONTEBELLUNA

THIENE

CESSALTO

CARTIGLIANO   FANZOLO

CASTELFRANCO
VENETO   ISTRANA   TREVISO

CARMIGNANO   CITTADELLA   RONCADE

LDOGNO

QUINTO
VICENTINO   LUGHIGNANO   SAN DONÀ
DI PIAVE

PIOMBINO DESE   PREGANZIOL

NTEVIALE   VICENZA   PIAZZOLA
SUL BRENTA

CCHIO
RE

ZIANIGO

LONGARE   MALCONTENTA   MURANO

MONTEGALDELLA   NOVENTA
PADOVANA

MONTECCHIA
DI SELVAZZANO   MIRA   VENEZIA

ALBETTONE   ROVOLON   STRA

MANDRIA

CAMPIGLIA   PADOVA

AGUGLIARO   LUVIGLIANO

POJANA
MAGGIORE   NOVENTA
VICENTINA   BATTAGLIA
TERME

ARQUÀ PETRARCA

TAGNANA   ESTE   MONSELICE   PONTECASALE

BAGNOLI DI SOPRA

CAVÁRZERE

ROVIGO

CANDA

FRATTA POLESINE

PO

BRENTA

PIAVE

TAGLIAMENTO

LIVENZA

SILE

TESINA

BACCHIGLIONE

ADIGE

Printed in Italy
by Grafiche LEMA - Maniago/PN